CALVIN H. REBER, JR.
1715 MANOR PLACE
DAYTON, OHIO 45406

Kimbangu

Marie-Louise Martin

Kimbangu

AN AFRICAN PROPHET AND HIS CHURCH

With a Foreword by Bryan R. Wilson
Translated by D. M. Moore

WILLIAM B. EERDMANS PUBLISHING COMPANY

289.9
K568m
1975

University of Charleston Library
Charleston, WV 25304

© in this translation Basil Blackwell 1975.
All rights reserved.
Printed in the United States of America.
Originally published in German as *Kirche ohne Weisse,* © 1971 by
Friedrich Reinhardt Verlag, Basel.
First American edition published 1976 by special arrangement
with Basil Blackwell; by Wm. B. Eerdmans Publishing Co.,
Grand Rapids, Michigan 49502.

Library of Congress Cataloging in Publication Data
Martin, Marie-Louise.
    Kimbangu: an African prophet and his church.
    Translation of Kirche ohne Weisse.
    Bibliography: p. 185.
    Includes indexes.
    1. Kimbangu, Simon, 1889?-1951. 2. Eglise de Jésus-Christ sur la
terre par le prophète Simon Kimbangu.
BX7435.E44M3713   1975b   289.9 B   75-45371
ISBN 0-8028-3483-3

CONTENTS

FOREWORD TO THE GERMAN EDITION   vii
PREFACE TO THE ENGLISH EDITION   xii
FOREWORD TO THE ENGLISH EDITION   xiii

Part One
HISTORY PRIOR TO THE RISE OF KIMBANGUISM

1 *First Missionary Activity in the Congo
   in the Fifteenth and Sixteenth Centuries*   3
2 *The First Prophetic Movement as a Reaction*   13
3 *The Second Period of Missionary Activity in
   Zaïre in the Nineteenth and Twentieth Centuries*   20

Part Two
THE HISTORY OF SIMON KIMBANGU AND HIS MOVEMENT FROM 1918 TO 1960

4 *The Early History, Call and Initial
   Ministry of the Prophet Simon Kimbangu*   37
5 *Grievances against Simon Kimbangu;
   Interrogation, Flight and Arrest*   52
6 *The History of Simon Kimbangu's
   Movement after the Prophet's Arrest
   (1922–4), and the Rise of Ngunzism*   65
7 *The Radical Suppression
   of the Movement in 1925*   79
8 *The Arrival of the
   Salvation Army; Simon Mpadi*   88

9 *Simon Kimbangu's Movement in the former French Congo (Congo-Brazzaville)* — 94
10 *Towards Toleration and Independence* — 100

Part Three
THE CURRENT POSITION, ACTIVITY AND PROBLEMS OF THE KIMBANGUIST CHURCH

11 *The Attitude of the Kimbanguist Church to Politics* — 117
12 *The Religious and Social Life of the Kimbanguist Church* — 130
13 *Theological Considerations* — 140
14 *Conclusion* — 167

APPENDIX — 178
BIBLIOGRAPHY — 185

GLOSSARY — 191
INDEX OF PLACES — 192
INDEX OF PERSONS — 194
SUBJECT INDEX — 197

FOREWORD

TO THE GERMAN EDITION OF 1971

It was in 1961 in South Africa, as I was working for my doctoral dissertation on 'The Biblical Concept of Messianism and Messianism in the Independent Churches in Southern Africa', that I heard for the first time of the prophet Simon Kimbangu in Zaïre and of the revival movement which he had aroused. At that time my main interest lay in the theological assessment of the independent African churches, sects and movements in Southern Africa, where from 1957 I lectured in divinity—first at the Theological Seminary of Moriah and then at the University of Botswana, Lesotho and Swaziland. What I had read about Kimbanguism kept going through my mind. There was something about it which seemed both stimulating and promising for church and missionary work in the whole of Africa and perhaps even beyond. However, it was difficult to obtain reliable information about the movement. The various descriptions of it contained so much that was legendary and contradictory.

Whilst I was on a short vacation in Switzerland in 1967, Rev. W. Béguin of the Neuchâtel Church sent me the 'Cahiers de la Réconciliation' and 'Essor' which contained reports on the visit in the previous year of Rev. Jean Lasserre and François Choffat (at the time a medical student) to the Kimbanguists. At the same time he arranged for me to meet Mr Lucien Luntadila, the General Secretary of the 'Church of Jesus Christ on Earth through the Prophet Simon Kimbangu', as the Kimbanguist Movement has been called since 1956. The picture which I now gained differed from that which I had formed from my reading of K. Schlosser, E. Andersson, G. Balandier, and even V. Lanternari, though Lanternari did view the future of the movement more optimistically than the others.

Along with Rev. Béguin, I was commissioned by the Moravian

Church in Switzerland to go to Zaïre in 1968 for three months in order to produce for it, and more especially for the World Ecumenical Council of Churches, a report on the Kimbanguist Church, seeing that this church had meanwhile applied for membership of the Ecumenical Council. Our mission was primarily intended to answer a number of questions. Was the Kimbanguist Church a truly Christian church and not simply one of many syncretistic and nationalistic sects which have sprung up in Africa, reviving in Christian dress the traditional African religion and Weltanschauung? Was the Kimbanguist Church 'messianic', as we then thought and as I had portrayed it to some extent in my book on messianism published in 1964? In other words, was Jesus Christ overshadowed or even replaced by Simon Kimbangu? How was the role of the Holy Spirit regarded? These are some of the important theological questions which movements and groups in Africa raise for missiologists.

These questions had to be answered with regard to the church which had arisen in Zaïre through Simon Kimbangu. In circles closely associated with our mission, it was assumed that our report would be critical. During the period of our studies in Zaïre we were not, as often happens in similar cases, to look at the church as it were from outside, But the Kimbanguist leaders had made it a condition that we should live completely within the church of Simon Kimbangu, sharing in all its functions, in its joy and problems, in its worship and social occasions. In this way we were to remain in constant contact with church members, both educated and simple folk, men and women, young and old. 'Vous venez vivre le Kimbanguisme'—'You're coming to live Kimbanguism' is the way His Eminence Mr Joseph Diangienda, the head of the church and the youngest son of Simon Kimbangu, put it to me in a letter. And when I look back on the three months which we spent in Zaïre in 1968 and assess them in the light of the time I have now lived in Zaïre, I am sure that this is the only right way of really coming to a proper understanding of a church which is so historically and culturally different from the churches in the West. Thus I wonder whether we (and I expressly include myself) have not sometimes come to wrong conclusions in South Africa since the law no longer allows whites to be fully integrated into a non-white community for any length of time.

We had the great privilege of living in the home of Mr Charles Kisolokele, the eldest son of Simon Kimbangu, and being welcomed completely into the family. Mr. Kisolokele has witnessed the movement from its very beginnings when, as a seven-year-old boy, he never left his father's side, not even when the prophet was staying in Mbanza Nsanda after his flight. From earliest youth right up to the present he has kept a journal and he often reads it, though as yet he has not shown it to anybody. However, he has given us very important information and answered our questions on the basis of his notes. Mr Joseph Diangienda, his youngest brother—who, as we have already said, is the leader of the church—took us with him on his travels, first to the west (to what is known as Lower Zaïre) to Nsona Bata, Inkisi, Mbanza-Ngungu, Nzundu, N'Kamba, Matadi, and Boma, and then to Shaba (formerly Katanga) in the south, to Kivu Province in the north-east and to Kisangani, where for a week we shared in joys and sufferings, the humble living conditions and the rich spiritual life of the Kimbanguists with its times of communal prayer.

In the course of these journeys we got to know urban and rural groups of the population and we were able to talk to them directly or, where necessary, by means of interpreters. In this way we were able to form a picture of what draws so many people to the Kimbanguist Church and what it is that particularly appeals to them in it. I was able to make tape-recordings of sermons, addresses and prayers, as well as of the many hymns in which the faith of the church finds its expression. We witnessed rites of healing and blessing and of the varied use of the sacramental N'Kamba water. Of particular importance to us were the spontaneous conversations at table with Mr Joseph Diangienda, which provided us with many historical, theological and practical details about the church. We tried to take careful note of everything.

To begin with our positive reports were received by some in Europe with a measure of distrust; but they were corroborated by leading churchmen who had also had contact with the Kimbanguists.

My special task was principally of a theological nature: I had to try to interpret the creed of the church, which by and large has not yet been formulated, and to compare it with similar movements in Africa. In November 1968 I published through the 'Christian Institute of Southern Africa' in Johannesburg a preliminary booklet under the title 'Prophetic Christianity in the Congo'. It provides a provisional picture, and a few historically unimportant details need correction, as I discovered during my second stay in Zaïre.

After my first stay in the country I resolved to pentrate more deeply into the material. I was able to look at secret documents of the early period, which are of great importance both for the history of Kimbanguism as well as for the theological and particularly the missiological aspect of the church. Most of these documents have not yet been edited, so they are quoted in this book simply with the date. They have been compared with the reports of those witnesses of the early period who are still alive, and this has brought new facts to light. There is a great deal more material as yet unavailable for study.

The present work provides first and foremost a history of the Kimbanguist Movement with special emphasis on its early phase, which is essential if we are to come to theologically and missiologically sound conclusions; and it ends with a description of the present state of the church.

Considerations relating to the theology of missions are to be found principally in the last two chapters. I myself was amazed to see how extensively ancient patterns of thought and ancient religious lore were transformed on the basis of the Gospel and vested with new content without succumbing to the danger of syncretism. For instance, the ancient Kongolese fetish priest (witch-doctor) surrounded himself with singers in order to discover evil and drive it out. For Kimbangu and the leaders who have succeeded him in the church this custom became a means by which the company of believers intercedes for the sufferer and thus takes an active part in his healing. Prayers are still sung today or are improvised by the humming of tunes.

Above all I owe the three sons of Simon Kimbangu—Mr Charles Kisolokele our host), Mr Joseph Diangienda (the head of the church), and Mr Solomon Kiangani Dialungana (the Custodian of the Holy Place, N'Kamba-Jerusalem)—my gratitude for their understanding and co-operation and for allowing me to see documents from the earliest period, which were handed over to the Kimbanguist Church after the new State of Zaïre gained its independence. The British Baptist Missionary Society (BMS) made available to me the material in their archives in London, and Simon Kimbangu's fellow-workers as well as missionaries who knew the Kimbanguist Movement gladly gave me information. I would like to take this opportunity to thank them for their help. I am also grateful to the interpreters who accompanied us on our extensive travels and constantly translated for us from the various African languages sermons, addresses, hymns, conversations and also prayers.

My thanks also go to the University of Botswana, Lesotho and Swaziland in Roma (Lesotho) which gave me leave of absence in 1968 to study the church of Kimbangu; to the Swiss branch of the Moravian Church, which financed our travel; and to the German Missiological Society (*Die Deutsche Gesellschaft für Missionswissenschaft*) which enabled me to procure the necessary material for tape-recordings and photographs. I am particularly grateful to Rev. Paul

Theile of the Moravian Missionary Society (*Brüdermission*) for his careful checking of the manuscript and for his suggestions.

It is my wish and intention that this study should help remove misunderstandings concerning the Kimbanguist Church and especially that it should assist in distinguishing—on the basis of documents and the testimony of Kimbangu's fellow-workers and opponents—between the pseudo-Kimbanguist and Ngunzist movements and the true heritage of Kimbangu. Moreover, I was concerned to show how a church came into being which is not based on a mere adoption of European thought and Western ways of formulation but which is an African expression and presentation of the Gospel of Jesus Christ, rooted in African tradition and using African cultural forms.

If you live with the Kimbanguists you find yourself transferred, despite all the shortcomings which are to be found in any Christian communion, to the time of the earliest New Testament witnesses, and yet not in an archaic form, but rather adapted to the rapidly advancing social transformation in Africa, which began with colonization and which since the middle of the 1950s has made unexpected strides forward. Admittedly, this is not accompanied by a demythologization in the Western sense nor by an exclusive reliance on the world of science and technology. The African lives in a sphere which binds closely together this world and the next. God is for him neither dead nor merely a cipher. *Nzambi pungu*, the Lord Almighty, is a reality to him. Perhaps the African way of expressing the Christian faith can be an inspiration to those who have reached a spiritual deadlock. Certainly, in one way or another, it can show possibilities of new development for the churches of the West.

Kinshasa (Zaïre) and Lucerne (Switzerland), August 1971

PREFACE

TO THE ENGLISH EDITION

I am very glad that this study has been translated, since visitors and missiologists to Zaïre often ask for detailed information on the Kimbanguist movement and Church, but are unable to read the German edition. I wish to thank Dr David Moore (whose work of translation presupposed a great deal of intuition) and Mrs Cecilia Irvine, both at Aberdeen, for their encouragement.

Since the book has appeared in German, many new developments have taken place; and I have tried by means of small alterations and footnotes to introduce the reader to recent developments, as far as this was possible within the framework of the translation.

Since October 1972 the ex-Belgian Congo has been renamed Zaïre, and this applies also to the River. This development has been taken account of in this translation, and the name Zaïre has been used even where it may appear anachronistic. Only in a few cases has the name Congo been retained; the name Kongo refers to the former Kingdom. The people of Zaïre have changed their (European) Christian names to Zaïrian ones, often the names of ancestors. Thus, the Kimbanguists' spiritual head is now called Diangienda Kuntima, and his elder brother Kisolokele Lukelo (the general secretary of the church) is known as Luntaeila Musiangani. In order to facilitate comparison between this translation and the 1971 German edition, the former (European) names have been retained, but for regions, towns and rivers we have adopted the following new names: Katanga has become Shaba, the Central Congo is Lower Zaïre, and Thysville is called Mbanza-Ngungu or simply Ngungu.

It is my hope that this account of Kimbangu and his movement may stimulate new thinking and perspectives particularly in Africa where so many independent African Churches exist, and where both, the Black theology from southern Africa and from the USA and the theology of Liberation at present plays such an important part.

Lucerne (Switzerland) July 1974   M.-L. M.

FOREWORD

Sociologists and historians of Africa must reconcile themselves to the vexing fact that they are never likely to have information even approaching accuracy about the incidence of prophets in sub-Saharan Africa before the incursion into that continent of the culture-bearers of Christianity and Islam. Even the evidence about this matter from the early centuries after the penetration of men from literate cultures into the illiterate sub-continent is—and is likely to remain—very limited. Only from the mid nineteenth century onwards do the records begin to make plain the frequency with which, in many different parts of Africa, prophets were arising. Whatever may have been the incidence of prophets before, with the arrival of these two vigorous proselytizing religions, each with its own powerful prophetic tradition, the native prophet became a significant social phenomenon in diverse areas of black Africa.

At one time, administrators and even historians were disposed to regard prophets as little more than an indication of the abundance of psychopathic personalities in particular cultures or periods, and of the gullibility of illiterate populations. But in recent years, in the study of European history as well as in African studies, there has been growing recognition of the social importance of a range of phenomena associated with prophetism: messianism; witchcraft; outbursts of fanatical faith in the supernatural intervention in human affairs; and the sudden enthusiasm for purification rites, witch-cleansing, holiness cults, and pietistic exercises.[1] The role of such phenomena in social development—long ignored—has become

[1] There are, of course, important differences between the ethically-orientated revivals of personal holiness, pietism, moral re-armament, and spiritual living, in the West, and the witch-cleansing and fetish-eradication cults in Africa, which in themselves have often involved profound

increasingly accepted.² Some of these movements have come into being without being prompted by a particular prophet. In other cases, there has been a succession of prophetic figures, and what I have elsewhere called *charismatic demand*. It must also be apparent that prophets emerge, as such, only when there are populations receptive to prophecy and responsive to a prophet's claims to inspiration and leadership. It remains profoundly true that publics make prophets. Yet the fact of the prophet, and the style of the prophet, cannot be ignored. Men may respond to a message, sometimes they show that they also want a man. They may, if they believe sufficiently in the man, allow him to change his message, suddenly, capriciously, and frequently, without losing faith.³

In less-developed societies, the prophet who calls into being a movement is a figure about whom crystallizes complex and powerful emotions. He becomes not only the symbol, nor merely the expression, but the very instrument, of hope and certainty in conditions of despair. The prophet embodies the collective will to overcome present distress. Distress may, of course, be heightened by the conflicts that sometimes ensue when men acclaim someone a prophet. Excitements, collective behaviour, outbursts of ecstasy, have often brought forth repression and persecution from ruling classes. Persecution, at least for a time and as long as it falls short of the extermination of significant segments of the affected populations, increases distress, and stimulates the demand for a prophet. Something of this pattern can be discerned in the story of Simon Kimbangu, who, brief as was his active career, may, in respect of so much that was subsequently done in his name, be regarded as one of the great prophets of the twentieth century.

In our own and recent times, the prophets who have had greatest social and cultural significance have arisen in less-developed societies.

belief in magical procedures. Yet there is a striking point of similarity that appears to transcend cultural differences and differences in levels of social development in the periodic waves of enthusiasm, whatever their specific cultural expression, which have the aim of eliminating evil of all kinds.

² The growing interest of historians in phenomena of this kind is now apparent, and most evident in recent works such as Keith Thomas, *Religion and the Decline of Magic*, London: Weidenfeld & Nicolson, 1971; Hugh Trevor-Roper, *The European Witch-Craze of the 16th and 17th Centuries*, Harmondsworth, Pelican 1969; Michael Barkun, *Disaster and the Millennium*, New Haven: Yale University Press, 1974.

³ This point is taken up at greater length in Bryan R. Wilson *The Noble Savages*, Berkeley: University of California Press, forthcoming.

Prophetism does still occur in advanced countries, of course, but the influence of these prophets is usually limited, often to a self-selected minority, whilst the vast majority regard prophets, and the very conception of prophecy, with utter contempt. Often their influence is further diminished by their dependence on religious traditions in which the book has replaced the man as the vehicle of possible prophetic utterance. The general public, more aware of the principles of natural causation, is disposed to be sceptical, and indeed, in order to live in a society in which mass-media and mass-advertising dominate men's daily lives, they have acquired a protective cynicism towards even modest promises of future benefit. In such societies, men expect untoward circumstances and social distress to be overcome by a conscious process of analysis and diagnosis through research techniques, by deliberative decisions about social goals and calculated programmes for their attainment which may even include policies for planned social reorganization. The publics of these societies are unlikely to see the solutions for their problems embodied in the acts or the saving grace of a deity, much less of a prophet. It is only in less-developed societies that the prophet is likely to receive widespread acclaim. When men experience concrete situations without the benefit of abstract, generalized, and comparative analysis, they are more likely to look for a supernatural agent to effect desired social change. How, for such peoples, will distress and tragedy for which their traditional nostrums are inadequate, be overcome? They have no solutions except to hope for a man of exceptional power. Hence the importance of the prophet in societies such as those of the medieval European past and of the more nearly contemporary third world.

The prophets of late nineteenth- and early twentieth-century Africa of whom we have the best records were men living in societies undergoing extraordinary processes of social change, not only in the regulation of economic, social, and political life, but also in the variety of spiritual resources that were available. It should be in no sense surprising that most of these prophets pronounced a message that was a synthesis of indigenous elements and items drawn from the new faiths that they had encountered. In some cases, this syncretism includes practices drawn from Islam as well as beliefs and practices learned from Christianity, but most of the prophets who have gained a wide and persisting following have been men who harmonized indigenous concerns with Christian prescriptions, often decking out Christian practices with embellishments drawn from the traditional native culture. Each individual prophet has produced his own unique combination of ancient and modern items, and although, for purposes of sociological analysis, these new religious leaders may be regarded as a distinctive type, in practice the balance of the Christian and the indigenous is struck in different ways in different cases, and this may be of more importance to the ethnographer and the theologian. Some retain techniques that can be described only as magical, and some use Christianity as a repertoire of magical devices. Some pick up themes from the Scriptures that bear parallel to their own contemporary circumstances, and re-work them as legitimations for their own society, and thus it is that Old Testament provisions—for polygyny, fasting, dietetic taboos, and dream interpretation, for instance—are common in African prophetic movements. It remains a plausible generalization, however—for reasons that cannot be explored here—that those prophets whose prescriptions have been closest to Christian orthodoxy have tended to be most successful, and to have gained widest acclaim.[4]

It is not therefore surprising that so many of the prominent third world prophets of the early decades of this century should have begun their careers as mission boys or even as catechists in one or another Christian mission. It was Christianity which provided the inspiration, the basic language of spirituality, and perhaps even the model of prophetship, which were so often to be wedded in the prophet's message with persisting indigenous preoccupations. But, if mission stations were often the socializing agencies for indigenous prophets in the third world, they were also the prison-houses for the aspirations and ambitions of the growing mission boy. Christianity is a religion of promise, but it operates in a time-dimension that is far more historically informed than that of third-world peoples. The unstinting promise of Christian hope is offered in the western world within the context of a long accumulated sense of patience, and an awareness of the paramount need for persistence, dedication, and the life-time of devoted service. In the third world, the contrasts of the benefits enjoyed by white men, identified with Christianity, and those known to black men, were perhaps too great for the message of patience to be so welcome. Prophets are men in a hurry. They have a sense of urgency, and this urgency they seek to communicate to men and to the whole social process. Part of the promise of Christianity may always have been personal, of course. Many Africans saw in Christianity a means of upward social mobility in a world in which the old fixed statuses had suddenly been destroyed. New religious movements often serve as agencies of mobility for their

[4] For a general discussion on this and related themes, see Bryan R. Wilson, *Magic and the Millennium*, London: Heinemann, and New York, Harper and Row, 1973.

functionaries, and it is usually the case that training as a religious specialist in a new religion is less onerous, less time-taking, and promises quicker rewards than in older, traditional religious systems. No one surveying the history of prophets in the third world can avoid being struck by the frequency with which the new prophet is the frustrated catechist, unable to progress further in the hierarchy of the newly introduced, but yet thoroughly traditional, system of Christian ministry. Prophetism was an alternative source of legitimation of a claim to high religious status. The prophet could cut away the demand for patience and perseverance in devotion, and could offer a more expansive vision.

To make these points is not to raise doubts about the validity of the spiritual inspiration of those who became prophets, but merely to make apparent another side of prophetism which the sociologist in particular cannot afford to ignore, much less to conceal. Prophets are men, and they, too, like other men, have their motivations. There have been prophets whose claims have been a vehicle for political aspirations, and those—although they are more readily dismissed as pretenders—who have used the prophetic style as a means of enriching themselves at the expense of their clientele. Economic and political motives we readily recognize as extraneous to the nature of religious inspiration, but the claim to superhuman knowledge or power is intimately involved with a claim to a special social status, to a high measure of social honour. A prophet may, of course, not long enjoy the social esteem that his followers regard as his due entitlement. He is, after all, a challenge to all existing social, political, and religious status-holders, and, except in highly tolerant and pluralist societies, the claims he makes (or has made on his behalf) are likely to lead to conflict with the establishment. If his following persists, the strongest claims for his high status may indeed be made when he is no longer in a condition—whether through death or imprisonment—to enjoy them.

Among the African prophets who had considerable experience of Christian missions, were Simon Kimbangu in what was then the Belgian Congo, and Josaiah Olunowo Ositelu, in the western region of Nigeria. Their careers, and that of the dramatic prophet from Liberia, William Wadé Harris, whose brief itinerary through the Ivory Coast and Ghana has left its diverse results in several movements, would bear thorough comparison.[5] Together, these three may

[5] On William Wadé Harris, see Gordon MacKay Haliburton, *The Prophét Harris*, London: Longmans, 1971: on Ositelu and the Church of the Lord, Aladura, see H. W. Turner, *African Independent Church*, 2 vols., Oxford: Clarendon Press, 1967.

certainly claim to be the most important prophets of recent African history, unrivalled in the permanent effects of their activity even by Alice Lenshina in Zambia, or Reuben Spartas in East Africa, or by the somewhat obscure leaders of the Maria Legio schism from the Roman Catholic Church among the Luo in Kenya.[6] About each of the three, and about the movements that have arisen in their names, there has now appeared a considerable literature, of which that on Simon Kimbangu and those who have emerged claiming to follow him is the most copious. To this literature, Dr Marie-Louise Martin has now made, in the pages that follow, an important contribution, drawing on previously unavailable sources, both from the Belgian administration, and from the authorities of the Church which now bears Kimbangu's name.

The literature on Simon Kimbangu is extensive and controversial. By far the greater part of it is concerned with his early prophetic career, and with the movements initiated by men who arose later, claiming to be his successors, both in the then Belgian and French Congo. Understandably, anthropologists and sociologists have been most interested in the effects of cultural contact, in the syncretism of the various movements that called themselves Kimbanguist, and by the way in which a variety of indigenous concerns were worked out in the tensions of the colonial situation and in response to a mission Christianity that was not always sympathetic to such well-rooted local practices and beliefs as polygyny, the power of witches and of fetishes, and the magical use of 'holy' water. In the following pages, Dr Martin provides the first discussion and appraisal, from a strictly theological point of view, of the life of the prophet and the growth of the Church over which his sons are now the custodians. Although her perspective is theological and her purpose close to that of Christian apologetics, her study, as the first full-length account of the development of *L'Église de Jesus-Christ sur la terre par le prophète Simon Kimbangu* (EJCSK), will command the interest of sociologists on several counts. It provides not merely new

---

[6] For accounts of Alice Lenshina, see John V. Taylor and Dorothea A. Lehmann, *Christians of the Copperbelt*, London: SCM Press, 1961, and R. I. Rotberg, 'The Lenshina Movement of Northern Rhodesia', *Rhodes-Livingstone Journal*, XXIX, June, 1961, pp. 63–78. On Reuben Spartas, see F. B. Welbourn, *East African Rebels*, London: SCM Press, 1961. My information on the Maria Legio movement is drawn primarily from Peter J. Dirven M.H.M., *The Maria Legio: The Dynamics of a Breakaway Church among the Luo in East Africa*, Unpubd. Doctoral Thesis, Pontifica Universitas Gregoriana, Rome, 1970. (The movement is also sometimes referred to as the Legio Maria.)

light on Kimbangu himself as a charismatic leader, but provides some preliminary indications of the way in which the movement is being institutionalized, is acquiring systematic and routine procedures, is becoming concerned with the regulation of the training of a ministry, and is devising methods of socializing a stable clientele. Inevitably, the story as she tells it from a contemporary perspective, lacks the dramatic elements of the usual account of charismatic or messianic movements: it is rather the history of the establishment of a new Christian denomination, differing in its own cultural expression from those of the western world, but emphasizing—and emphasizing increasingly—elements that are part of the broad Christian tradition. An important aspect of her study, is her attempt to explain the source of those items in which the Kimbanguist Church differs from conventional western Christianity and, most at issue, from the Christianity of the free churches which, in the Baptist missions and the work of Salvation Army, most directly influenced the new Zaïrian Church.

The development of the Kimbanguist movement through the fifty-five years since Kimbangu first emerged as a prophet, has been affected not only by his arrest and imprisonment, but also by the changing political, social, and educational milieu of modern Africa. It is not possible now to know just how Kimbangu himself may have envisaged the future of the movement that began round him, nor do prophets normally have very much idea of the course of regular social change. Their projections are apocalyptic at the social level, soteriological at the individual level, and generally obscure and ambiguous with respect to specific future events and developments. In the main, prophets are men with little time-perspective and little sense of history: they live in the moment, even if it be a moment with an apocalyptic prospect. Their message is essentially for their own time rather than for the future—however it may subsequently be interpreted. Least of all are they planners prescribing ordered steps towards the institutionalization of a new movement. They are not even in control of their own message. Since prophets are made by their followers, it is the terms of acceptance rather than the terms of pronouncement which are the essential clue in the explanation of prophetic movements. At the beginning, a following accepts a message because it meets their present needs—for explanations, for hope, for ecstasy, for promise of better times. Only later are they likely to adjust their lives in conformity to the requirements of the message and the form in which it has become institutionalized.

Neither Kimbangu nor William Wadé Harris were ever really fully in control of their message nor of those who received it.⁷ As Dr Martin makes clear in the case of Kimbangu, and as is well documented in the case of Harris, different men were very differently inspired by what they took to be the message of their prophet. Just as there arose movements much more preoccupied with healing, witchcraft eradication, and revelations in the wake of Harris—the Déima cult in the Ivory Coast, and the Church of the Twelve Apostles in western Ghana—as well as a more orthodox Christian movement, so too, Kimbangu's inspiration fed several very diverse streams of religious enthusiasm.⁸ For many, Simon Kimbangu symbolized something very different from what he eventually came to symbolize to his sons and the leaders of EJCSK. Although some of these other interpreters of the message have continued to the present time, the increasing rationalization of the religious life of members of the EJCSK has provided it with the authority to make the most sustained and impressive claim to be the true inheritance of the prophet. The appeal of the name of Kimbangu was much more closely associated with indigenous religious concerns in the 1930s than it is in the 1970s. Kimbangu's own partial re-enactment and dramatization of events from the life of Christ, which may then have been seen as a black counter-claim of messiahship, is now differently re-interpreted. The claims made for Kimbangu as the inspiration of an autonomous Christian church in Africa, are not those of popular folk mythology in which the prophet has been regarded as a mes-

⁷ The reputation of each man spread far beyond his immediate area of operations. The prophetic career of each was very brief, and many of those who were influenced had no direct knowledge of the men or their message. Each, too, uttered a number of statements that were capable of diverse interpretations. Each used equipment which may readily have been seen as of intrinsic importance or, as Christians have preferred to interpret it, as of merely local symbolic significance. Each acquired a reputation for healings or exorcisms, although reliable verification of the 'miracles' attributed to them is lacking.

⁸ Efraim Andersson, *Messianic Popular Movements in the Lower Congo*, Stockholm: Almqvist and Wiksell, 1958, is perhaps the classic work on early Kimbanguism. He traces in some considerable detail the prophets who arose in succession to Kimbangu. See also Georges Balandier, *Sociologie actuelle de l'Afrique noire*, Paris: Presses universitaires, 1955. For some of the movements arising from the prophetic ministry of Harris, see C. G. Baëta, *Prophetism in Ghana*, London: SCM Press, 1962; J. F. Köbben, 'Prophetic Movements as an Expression of Social Protest', *International Archives of Ethnography*, XLIX, Pt 1, 1960, pp. 117–64; B. Holas, *Le Separatisme religieux en Afrique noire*, Paris: Presses Universitaires, 1965.

sianic saviour of his people. Dr Martin, whilst recognizing the wide currency of some of these ideas, discounts them in presenting the understanding now current in the EJCSK.

The denominational formulation of the original message, and the increasing accommodation of particular Christian precepts into the life of the EJCSK have been influenced by the wider educational experience of Africans since those early days, by the changing character of relationships between Africans and Europeans, and, perhaps most especially, by the new relations between and within Christian churches in Africa. The interpretation of a prophet's message to provide the basis for stable and sustained church life is in itself not easy. In Kimbangu's case, the development owed much to the initial persecution of the prophet and his immediate followers; to the entangled social, political, and religious aspirations of some of his followers; to the gradual change of attitude, and the growing tolerance, of westerners towards indigenous African customs and concerns; and to the slowly evolving willingness of missionary bodies (impelled in part, perhaps, by the steeply mounting costs of mission work) to recognize local initiatives of which in earlier years they would have been suspicious. On the other side, it was also the case that the social climate was conducive to the general infusion into the Kimbanguist message of a more vigorously-expressed Christian orthodoxy. Dr Martin emphasizes that theological formulations have both a limited appeal and, as yet, an unsophisticated character in African churches, but we cannot doubt the direction of change that existing theological perceptions will undergo as they are steadily extended and incorporated into the life and practice of the EJCSK.

Where such a process of theological and organizational reform occurs, a church that can trace its roots to an African leader is today likely to be more acceptable than conventional mission Christianity in contemporary Africa. From the very beginnings of Kimbangu's career, there is evidence of the incompletely articulated desire to localize, africanize, and acculturate the central Christian myth. In some respects, it may be regarded as remarkable that the de-colonization of Africa has occurred, in very large part, without the de-structuring of the various Christian denominations planted in Africa. Local autonomy has been acquired, of course, but—given the demand for complete political independence—the extent to which absolutely new beginnings were effectively demanded in religion has been surprisingly small. Any demand for complete cultural autonomy in religious matters has been limited by a variety of circumstances, the most important of which is the absence of an indigenous religious tradition which contemporary Africans regard as respectable. There have been some attempts to rehabilitate essentially African religion—for example in Ghana under Kwame Nkrumah attention was paid to the surviving divination shrines; more perfunctorily, and with less official backing, there was a nationalist religious cult that focussed on Dr Azikewe in Nigeria. In some areas, Islam provides an alternative to the general Christian tradition, and it is sometimes asserted that some of its appeal has been derived from the fact that it is clearly not the religion of the white man. But in general, western Christianity in one or another of its forms, has successfully survived the disturbances occasioned by the struggle for political independence. The vast majority of the many new independent churches continue to claim to be Christian.[9] The association of Christianity and education has been a significant bulwark for the churches, and even in countries now committed to an africanized version of socialism, or to brutal forms of totalitarianism, the general commitment to Christianity persists. The rooting of Christianity in Africa has indeed produced more vigorous new growth there than occurs in the countries from which the effort at transplantation was made.

That the demand to throw off western tutelage has not been more radical in religious matters, even among the independent churches, also relates to the continuing dependence of African religion on financial aid from the west. Help—in cash; in trained personnel; in courses of training; and the maintenance of a variety of ancillary activities—continues to flow, and not only to the local branches of denominations established in the west, but also to some of the newly-founded independent churches. Despite the successful transmission of Christianity to Africa, in general it has proved to be a religion too expensive for local people to maintain. In some respects, independent churches may reflect an issue in religious economics: indigenous religion, or africanized Christianity, may be a cheaper form of religion. Yet the independent churches also draw their inspiration in part from the west, and the models that are increasingly influential with the leadership of these churches are the models of western Christian denominations. The need for economic assistance is thus not unassociated with the theological reformulations that are to be expected, and that are already occurring in African independent churches. The independent African church that throws off western leadership and asserts principles in contradiction of those of the parent missions—the Maria Legio movement in Kenya is one example—does so at the cost of foreign financial support. The hope

[9] For a survey, see David Barrett, *Schism and Renewal in Africa*, Nairobi: Oxford University Press, 1968.

that the independent churches have of acquiring better education for their ministers, of being able to train their own personnel, of establishing and maintaining welfare institutions, is dependent on their Christian orthodoxy. It is thus likely that the process of theological reformulation will continue in those churches, such as the Church of the Lord, Aladura, in West Africa, the African Brotherhood Church in Kenya, and the EJCSK in Zaïre, that have established relationships with western churches and with their agency, the World Council of Churches.

The pressure to conform to some generalized Christian standards as understood in the west has been moderated both by the growing ecumenical tolerance within Christendom, and by the increasing uncertainty about the contours of orthodoxy within the western churches. There are fundamentalist churches in the west that are as literal in their approach as are many Africans, even if the focus of their concern is different. Dr Martin compares the conditions of the Congo in Kimbangu's period of mission with those of Old Testament times, and some of the preoccupations of Kimbanguists, with dreams and healings, for example, and with the exorcism of demons, may be even further from modernist Christian orthodoxy than the literal interpretations of Scripture of some contemporary American and European fundamentalists. Dr Martin is able to make a case for the vibrancy of African Christianity, and to compare its vigour with the often Laodicean character of churches in the west. But it is also clear that the diplomacy of Christian ecumenism, given its attitude to some denominations in the west, is faced with a variety of difficulties in relation to some aspects of African Christianity. Not all Christians will wish to accept even Dr Martin's guarded interpretation of Kimbangu's prophetic claims, since they know that there are others, even in contemporary Europe, whose claims might stand the same test but who have been thus far utterly ignored by the leaders of the churches. Elements of EJCSK practice will remind some Christians of the more magically conceived Christianity of the past, and not everyone will wish to see those conceptions of the faith reinvigorated.

What will become clear to the attentive reader of Dr Martin's investigation of the Kimbanguist Church, is the complexity of spiritual evolution. That Christianity, even when transplanted with care, cannot function in identical ways in different cultures is a sociological truth that missionaries should long ago have recognized. That its local viability is dependent on a variety of particular conditions (and we have mentioned the economic cost as one) must also be apparent. That it must accommodate the particular cultural demands of its local clientele is also evident. That it will find its vigour by re-enactment in the specific folklore of a people (as indeed happened in other parts of the world) must also be expected. The orthodox have not always accepted—indeed have usually anathematized—these variants, when they might, with patience, have guided them into whatever were eventually to be regarded as acceptable modes. Dr Martin is both historian and theologian, and advocacy is evidently part of her concern. The reader will be impressed by her candour and her sympathy in examining the events and developments of what, in the German version of this book, she called 'the church without whites'.

All Souls College,   *Bryan R. Wilson*
Oxford.

Part One

HISTORY PRIOR TO THE RISE OF KIMBANGUISM

CHAPTER 1

FIRST MISSIONARY ACTIVITY IN THE CONGO IN THE FIFTEENTH AND SIXTEENTH CENTURIES

Zaïre has had one of the most stirring histories of missionary activity, which still continues today. What we now have before us is the result of the interplay of numerous forces—evangelization, resistance and attacks on the part of the ancient African religion, slave-trading, the struggle of European powers for the possession of the country, the partition of the former territory of the Kingdom of the Kongo among three European powers (namely Portugal, Belgium, and France), and the rise of prophetic and nationalist forces within the African population. We shall focus our main attention on missionary activity and the rise of prophetic movements, particularly on the greatest of these (not only in modern Zaïre but on the African continent in general) namely *Kimbanguism*, which is by and large united today in the 'Eglise de Jésus-Christ sur la Terre par le Prophète Simon Kimbangu', 'The Church of Jesus Christ on Earth through the Prophet Simon Kimbangu.' We can understand this phenomenon properly only when we see it in its wider context of the early missionary activities of the Portuguese, and the reaction to colonization, to slave-trading and to later Protestant and Catholic missionary work.

1. THE BEGINNINGS

King John II of Portugal, who reigned 1481–95, sent out a number of ships in search of a route to India. In 1482 Diogo Cão landed at the estuary of the Kongo, called at that time Nzadi but named *Zaïre* by the Portuguese. Diogo Cão heard that a great king had his residence a few days' march away, so he sent a delegation with many gifts to assure the unknown monarch of his good intentions and to tell him that the whites would be glad to trade with him. Having sailed a little further south, Cão returned to the Zaïre estuary only to find that the men he had sent to the king had not returned. He was in a hurry to return to Portugal and took four African 'hostages' with him in exchange for his emissaries, promising to return to the Zaïre estuary within the next fifteen months. After a time, Cão did in fact return to the Kingdom of the Kongo with his four hostages, who had been very well treated in Portugal, to collect his emissaries.

This was the beginning of the trade and missionary relations between Portugal and the Kingdom of the Kongo which, according to the ancient descriptions, probably extended as far as present-day Lake Malebo (Stanley Pool) near Kinshasa (formerly Léopoldville) and included areas to the south and the north of the River Zaïre. The realm of the Manikongo (or King of the Kongo) was a federation of six provinces; each province had its chieftain. A large part of it— Cabinda to the north of the Zaïre estuary and in particular large territories to the south, including what was then the royal city of Mbanza Kongo (the residence of the King of Kongo), renamed after Christianization São Salvador—is still Portuguese today. The central portion, to the north of the lowest course of Zaïre and to the south of what is known as 'Lower Zaïre' as far as Kinshasa, became Belgian. Bordering on this area to the north is the ex-French territory of the People's Republic of Congo-Brazzaville. However, the people who live in all these regions of the former kingdom of Kongo belong to the same ethnic group of Bakongo and speak Kikongo.

After a relatively short voyage from the mouth of the Zaïre taking him further south, Cão returned to Zaïre and journeyed to the royal city to see the Manikongo and bring him the presents of the Portuguese ruler. At this meeting he exhorted the Manikongo to foresake the gods of his ancestors, to believe in Jesus Christ, and thus to save his soul. The establishment of trade relations and the spread of the Christian Gospel thus went hand in hand.

The Manikongo showed interest in the Christian Gospel and presented costly gifts for the King of Portugal. He also sent a few of the high-ranking men from his court to Portugal—either with Diogo Cão or later—so that they could receive instruction in the Christian faith and be baptized. He asked the King of Portugal to send him priests as missionaries, as well as farmers and oxen to promote agriculture and Portuguese women to teach the Kongolese women how to run a home. All this sounds very modern.

According to an ancient Portuguese account,[1] Cão left some Por-

[1] F. Pigafetta/D. Lopes (1591): 'Description du Royaume du Congo et des contrées environnantes', ed. W. Bal, ch. II, Louvain, Editions E. Nauwelaerts.

tuguese behind in the Kongo including a priest, who had a successful beginning to his missionary work by converting the Governor of Sonyo, the aged uncle of the Manikongo. He prepared the ground for the missionaries who were awaited from Portugal, learnt Kikongo and was able to act as interpreter for the missionaries when they arrived.

In 1491 the missionaries arrived, probably Franciscans and Knights of St John bearing opulent gifts from Portugal. They were laden with altars, vestments,[2] images, Christian symbols—in a word, with all they needed for Catholic worship. To begin with they had to baptize the Governor of Sonyo. As a sign of his acceptance of the Christian faith, he immediately destroyed all idols—most probably the *minkisi* or 'fetishes', objects possessing special power intended to combat evil, from the Destroyer (*kindoki* or 'witchcraft'). This can be seen as a significant step, for even today many church-going Christians find it difficult to make a break with these protective objects. However, this can also be regarded, as G. Balandier[3] suggests, as the more powerful *nkisi* (in this instance the symbol of the cross) banishing the weaker *nkisi*, and if one takes this view then the belief in fetishes cannot be said to have been really overcome.

After the baptismal ceremony in Sonyo the missionaries went in triumph to Mbanza Kongo to the Manikongo. In accordance with West African custom, the roads (for a distance of over 70 km.) were cleared of filth and weeds. After marching for three days they reached Mbanza Kongo, where they were met by emissaries of the king (a very special favour) and welcomed with music. The solemnity and joy of the African ceremonial on such occasions, especially in the Kongo, cannot be adequately imagined. The king was waiting for them in his palace, seated upon his throne, in complete accordance with African custom. The gifts from Portugal for the furnishing of churches were presented, and the king commanded that church-building should begin at once. Whilst the building was in progress the king and his court were instructed in the Christian faith.

The king did not want to wait for baptism until the church was ready but wanted to be baptized right away. The ancient account of F. Pigafetta and D. Lopes (dating from 1591) relates that disturbances had broken out in the kingdom to the north of the river rapids and that the king therefore wanted to travel to that region—but not before being baptized. On 3 May 1491, he was baptized João

[2] C. P. Groves: 'The Planting of Christianity in Africa', London, 1948, Vol. I, pp. 127 ff.

[3] G. Balandier: 'La vie quotidienne au Royaume du Congo du XVIe au XVIIIe siècles' Paris, 1965, p. 259.

(John) and his wife was baptized Eleonora a little later, thus taking the names of the King and Queen of Portugal at that time. Six of the most influential chieftains were baptized along with the king and it is said that about 100,000 people took part in the festivity.

The king returned victorious from his campaign in the interior of the country and was present at the baptism of his son Afonso (Alphonse) in June. Several important chieftains were baptized at the same time and, after this had been done, their subjects also followed their example.

Thus the first missionary outreach began with great success. But it became evident that this success was only superficial, with the possible exception of Afonso's conversion.

King João, as the Manikongo was now called, soon returned to the faith of his fathers. He had new *minkisi* made and, after having switched over to monogamy in accordance with the teaching of the missionaries, he now took several wives again.

After his death a conflict arose. The forces of ancient African tradition mobilized themselves against the far too radical reform. Could it have been otherwise? The belief in the presence and power of ancestors and their customs is so strong that a break with them, as was evident from the disposal of the *minkisi*, could only end in catastrophe. Should the people not fear the revenge of their ancestors? Would not the power of evil (of *kindoki*) gain ascendancy? Could Jesus Christ and could the saints of the church give protection against this mysterious power? That was the big question.

2. INITIAL CONFLICT

The conflict was epitomized in Afonso and Mpanzu (also known as Pango), the two sons of the Manikongo João—two rivals struggling for the throne. At the same time this was a conflict between the ancient and the new religion. The christian historians of the time describe the conflict as a struggle between God and the Devil.

Whereas Afonso, the *Mbemba a Nzinga* (that is 'the son and heir of the old king'), had become a Christian, the younger son, the *Mpanzu a Nzinga*, resisted all attempts to convert him. He became the leader of the reaction to the Christian faith and tried to usurp the throne. Armed conflict broke out. The polygamous wives (and probably their families) who had been deserted by their Christian husbands gave their support to the Mpanzu. Many of those who had been baptized, having such cursory instruction in the faith, relapsed and also followed the Mpanzu. Prince Manuel, the uncle of the deceased king, the Governor of Sonyo and the first royal Christian, is said to have intervened and exhorted the waverers to 'trust in Jesus Christ'. King Afonso prayed in the church and made a vow: 'I promise Thee, O God, to honour Thee all my life and to proclaim faith in Thee and Thy holy name and Thy saving doctrine.'[4] As a sign of his faith a cross was erected in front of the church.

During the struggle, Afonso had a vision not unlike that of Constantine the Great: he saw a shining light and two swords in the form of a cross.[5]

He gained confidence and triumphed over his brother, who was slain in the battle. The cause of the church seemed triumphant.

3. THE REIGN OF KING AFONSO

Afonso seems to have taken Christianity and his vow—if this is not just a legend—seriously, though the accounts of contemporaries are certainly biased towards the church (as G. Balandier[6] has suggested). He sent emissaries to the Portuguese king, among them the nobleman Dom Rodrigo, so that they could learn Portuguese and gain a deeper insight into the Christian Gospel. At the same time, Afonso introduced measures to impose Christianity throughout the kingdom of the Kongo. *Minkisi*, other talismans and the masks used in ancestral worship all had to be destroyed and the new religion embraced. Compulsory Christianization appears today as a contradiction in terms. But were not these the very methods which were being used in Europe? During the Reformation and even later, the principle of *cuius regio eius religio* prevailed. In other words, the ruler claimed the right to prescribe the religion or the denominational allegiance of his subjects. Freedom of religion in Europe has only existed since the eighteenth century.

That this religious compulsion produced a merely formal Christianity among the masses goes without saying. King Afonso's measures were determined largely by political considerations and the close link with Portugal. He was very probably supported by the Portuguese in the struggle against his brother. We also know that in the interests of trade relations he sent Kongolese slaves to Portugal. Did not this give him prosperity which, to the African

---

[4] F. Pigafetta/D. Lopes: op. cit., p. 92.
[5] G. Balandier: op. cit., pp. 37 ff.; here the vision of the cross is ascribed not to Afonso but to his enemies, who fled in terror.
[6] G. Balandier: op. cit., pp. 39 ff.

mind, expresses the very life-force?[7] Could it have been that this whole attempt to Christianize the Kongolese Kingdom was partly determined by this striving for a vitality that the Portuguese seemed to have, and to be able to supply?

The same striving also encouraged the spread of Christianity and the European way of life elsewhere. But in place of the prosperity and 'blessings' which were expected to result, it was the hardship of the Cross which emerged. So, while Christianity was not completely abandoned, there was a return to ancestral cults: the old gods and the traditional rites were now resurrected in modern guise.

For the time being Afonso's ideal was to train a Kongolese Christian élite which was to promote Christian influence little by little throughout the kingdom and in this way to consolidate his rule. Afonso asked Portugal to send new bands of missionaries; and it sounds modern when we hear that he sent his own son Henrique (Henry) to Portugal in order to study theology. He was thinking of an indigenous clergy.

The opposition which had nearly cost him his throne taught him that Christian education was a cardinal requirement of missionary work. At the beginning of the sixteenth century that was certainly an important realization comparable with that of the Reformers. Luther urged that schools should be built so that children should receive instruction in the Scriptures and the catechism and should learn to sing hymns. Afonso began in the Kongo with a boarding-school in which 400 sons of chieftains, many of them relatives of the king, were to receive a Christian education. The priests who came from Portugal were entrusted with the task of giving a proper schooling to these young people, not only in the Christian religion but also in other subjects usually taught in Europe at the time. This boarding-school was to be the cradle of a Christian civilization for the Kingdom of the Kongo.

However, Afonso had not simply the sons of chieftains in view. Since Christianity had become the state religion many were keen to be baptized, and Afonso was conscious that these masses also stood in need of instruction. Thus he asked the King of Portugal for aid in the form of more priests. But these requests remained unanswered.

So he decided to train an indigenous clergy. The Kongolese he had sent to Portugal generally did not come up to his expectations and he decided to build a seminary for priests on the nearby island of São Tomé. But Portugal did not want this. Thus, Afonso had no

---

[7] P. Tempels: 'Philosophie Bantou, Présence Africaine' (French 1949, English 1959), Paris, in both edns., pp. 30 ff.

other choice but to develop the school system in the country itself. The boarding-school was extended in order to cater for 1,000 pupils. Schools were built in other parts of the kingdom and some of the teachers were Kongolese catechists. Even schools for girls were founded. The king wanted *all* his subjects to receive a school education—an ideal which even today has hardly been realized in any African state.

In 1521, Afonso's son Henrique returned from Portugal to the Kongo with the title of bishop, accompanied by three or four Portuguese advisors. He was the first African bishop. The episcopal see, however, was not São Salvador (as the royal city was now called) but in São Tomé. Unfortunately, Bishop Henrique had only a short life; and he was succeeded by a Portuguese bishop.

Again King Afonso appealed to Portugal to provide him with new missionaries. But because of her commitments in India Portugal had insufficient priests available.

4. DECLINE

Despite all the efforts of King Afonso, decline was inevitable. The slave-trade was booming and it seems that Afonso had a bad conscience about this.[8] The lives of the Portuguese traders who had come to the Kongo were not morally beyond reproach and did not set the Africans a good example. Tensions arose between the priests and the bishop. Certain secular priests lived more like pagans than Christians. Cuvelier and Jadin (Quoted in Baladier's book) have it that 'where there should have been missionaries there were often only mercenaries bereft of virtue'.[9] They participated in slave-trading. More and more Portugal was interested first and foremost in material gain and not so much in missionizing. King Afonso was given to understand that the Christian mission to his country cost so much that Portugal should be compensated for this: ships bringing missionaries had to be laden with copper, ivory and slaves for the voyage back to Portugal.

'The lack of missionaries, the greed and scandalous immoral practices of the secular priests and missionaries, and most of all the slave-trade, which was robbing the Kongo of its people, made it impossible to have real success.' Afonso was disappointed in the Portuguese and no longer trusted their methods of colonization.

[8] E. Andersson: 'Messianic Popular Movements in the Lower Congo', Uppsala, 1958, p. 34.
[9] Cuvelier/Jadin: quoted by G. Balandier, op. cit., p. 49.

Nevertheless, he was loyal to the Christian Gospel until his death in 1543.

A Jesuit commission of inquiry, which drew up a report in 1548 on the state of the mission, clearly pointed out how bad the state of affairs had become.[10]

Jesuit missionaries had come in 1547 to the Kongo, but their practices were no better. In mass baptisms they baptized thousands within a short time. Nevertheless, they recognized the importance of Christian education and the schools, which Afonso had begun and which had in the meantime been neglected, were given new life. Despite these efforts on the part of the Jesuits there was hardly any noticeable improvement. King Diogo, the grandson of Afonso, was merely a nominal Christian. He loved luxury, was always in need of money and acquired it through slave-trading. Despite the warning of the Jesuits, he took several wives, and disloyal secular priests did not hesitate to administer Communion to him and his wives although this was not in accordance with church practice. In 1555 the Jesuits had to leave the Kongo; Franciscans were sent to replace them. After Diogo's death there was a revival of traditional religion, and ancient customs were restored.

In 1569 the Yaga invaded the country (we still do not know for sure who the Yaga were or where they came from). Portuguese troops were able to thrust them back. Jesuits were sent once more in 1623 and it was they who printed the first catechism in the Kikongo language. Despite opposition from the secular priests, they worked in the Kongo until 1669.

In 1645 the first Capuchins arrived and began important missionary activities in the Kongo.[11] They had the greatest difficulties in gaining access to the Kongo because the order was made up of Italians and Spaniards and the Portuguese insisted that all priests and members of orders should be Portuguese. Even at that time Portugal was pursuing in its African colonies the same policy as today, requiring that the Africans accept the Portuguese culture and way of life; the Catholic faith, part and parcel of that way of life, must also have a Portuguese colouring.

The Capuchins went on journeys throughout the kingdom and set up mission stations in virtually every province. They were courageous men, not afraid of uncovering abuses or of struggling against the immorality of the secular priests and Portuguese traders, against

[10] E. Andersson: op. cit., p. 34, note 1.

[11] J.-F. de Rome: O.F.M. Cap. 'La Fondation de la mission des Capucins au Royaume du Congo', 1648, ed. F. Bontinck, Louvain, Nauwelaerts, pp. xvi, 39 ff.

polygamy among Kongolese Christians and against the use of *minkisi*. They openly declared themselves against slave-trading, and their courage brought them the hostility of the Kongolese chieftains, the secular priests and of the other religious orders.

The decline could no longer be stemmed. In 1665 the Kongolese troops suffered in Ambouila such a defeat at the hands of the Portuguese and their Yaga allies that they never recovered; King Antonio I was beheaded.[12] Massamba-Débat speaks in this connection of a double defeat—that of Christianization and that of 'modernism' (by which he means Western civilization).[13] Civil war broke out. Three kings arose as rivals in 1667 and now struggled to secure the throne. The decline brought great misery with it. In this situation, as we shall see in the next chapter, the first prophetic movement in the Kongo was born.

By 1684 there was no longer a missionary to be found in São Salvador. Andersson[14] describes the years from 1707 to 1866 as the period of the complete decline of the old Catholic mission to Zaïre. In 1717 the Capuchins had to withdraw to what is today known as Angola after two Capuchins in the province of Sonyo (the home of the first Kongolese Christian) had as early as 1673 been taken captive, flogged, robbed, then put on the other side of the River Kongo and there left to their fate.

When the first Protestant missionaries came to what used to be the ancient Kongo in 1879 they found there a brand of 'paganism' with Christian trimmings. Holman Bentley reports: 'The king and his people were given to fetish worship... A few ruined walls from the old cathedrals were still to be seen... the sad remains of a false venture.'[15] A large crucifix and a few images of saints were in the possession of the chieftain and were borne through the city in solemn procession at times of drought. Crosses were used as charms when hunting; they were supposed to possess magic power as long as the hunters did not transgress any of the abstention taboos which were in force during the hunting season. Memories of the Christian services which had once been held in São Salvador were still alive, because reports concerning them had been passed down from one generation to the next by word of mouth. Thus ended after about 200 years a missionary enterprise which began with such high hopes. But was this really the end? It was from the ruins of the old

[12] G. Balandier: op. cit., p. 256.
[13] A. Massamba-Débat: 'De la révolution messianique à la révolution politique', Brazzavile, 1968, p. 22.
[14] E. Andersson: op. cit., p. 37.
[15] C. P. Groves: op. cit., Vol. I, p. 131.

that the new arose: we cannot understand the new without knowing the old.

This first missionary enterprise in the Kingdom of the Kongo is also of interest to the theological historian from another point of view. We find in southern Africa a whole number of concepts and legends in the world of African religion which are to my mind indirect witness to the fact that as long as 500 years ago Christian thinking had penetrated central Africa and, despite the revival of the ancient beliefs, was absorbed into the African religions. This should not be overlooked in any study of the history of African religion.

One such example is the legend of the boy Senkatana in Lesotho who vanquished the dragon *Kholumolumo* at great risk to life and limb and thus liberated the victims from inside its body. These, however, proved ungrateful for their deliverance and forsook Senkatana's dominion.[16] A further example is the legend of *Ngoma Lungundu* among the Bavenda of the north Transvaal, which has a large number of parallels with the biblical story of the Exodus and the role of the ark of the covenant.[17] Yet again, there is the Central African form of the legend of the serpent which seduced the first human beings in Paradise.[18]

[16] M.-L. Martin: 'The Biblical Concept of Messianism and Messianism in Southern Africa', Morijah, 1964, p. 162.

[17] H. von Sicard: 'Ngoma Lungundu', Studia Ethnographica Upsaliensia, Uppsala, 1952.

[18] E. Andersson: 'La notion de Dieu chez quelques tribus congo-camerounaises', Journal of Religion in Africa, Leiden, 1969.

CHAPTER 2

THE FIRST PROPHETIC MOVEMENT AS A REACTION

During the course of history, missionary activity and colonization have repeatedly called forth resistance and reaction. Ancient customs and ancient religious thought patterns are of course deeply rooted, and cannot be easily replaced by new values. Moreover, the missionary activity in the ancient Kongolese Kingdom had made the country dependent upon a European power which was seeking material gain more than anything else. The ships which brought the missionaries had to return to Portugal with cargoes of ivory, copper, and slaves; and this had a drastic effect on the ancient traditional way of life in the Kongo.

We have already described one early reaction: the Mpanzu, Afonso's brother, tried to usurp the throne in order to restore the ancient religion and way of life of his people, but he had no success.

A second noteworthy reaction occurred at the beginning of the eighteenth century after a good two hundred years of missionary work and colonization on the part of the Portuguese. After a short heyday under the rule of King Afonso, a steady decline began which could not be halted despite all the efforts of the Jesuits and Capuchins. The reaction was crystallized in the figures of two prophetesses. The first of these, of whom we know very little, was Fumaria, who was described as mentally ill. She claimed to have been given revelations through the Virgin Mary that God would punish the people for their sins. This message contained, then, a call to conversion.[1]

---

[1] E. Andersson: op. cit., p. 244.

1. DONNA BÉATRICE AND HER PREACHING

The other prophetess, the Kongolese girl Kimpa Vita who was given the name Béatrice at her baptism, is better known.[2] Of aristocratic stock and in her early twenties, she experienced in dreams and visions her death and resurrection, like so many African prophets after her. A contemporary informant, Father Bernardo de Gallo,[3] tells us that Donna Béatrice had been dangerously ill, when a Capuchin monk appeared to her and revealed himself to her as St Anthony, one of the saints particularly venerated in São Salvador, Béatrice 'died' and in place of her soul St Anthony came to dwell in her. If this report of B. de Gallo is reliable, we have here again an ancient African form of expression and of belief. Just as the ancestral spirit takes possession of the non-christian prophetess and healer, so the spirit of St Anthony took possession of Donna Béatrice and revealed himself through her. This was, in fact, the only way she could express her spiritual experience. We must surely be careful when trying to explain the reality behind these events, since this may be a genuine instance of syncretism, or just a form of expression.

Through St Anthony, Béatrice was given a new life: She was 'resurrected', and now had the task of preaching and teaching. Before she embarked on her mission, the respected young noblewoman—as Francis of Assisi—gave away all her possessions. She then began to proclaim the coming judgement of God. Her preaching was a massive protest against the Catholic church. She forebade her followers to observe the set periods of fasting and other church ceremonies as well as to sing the 'Ave Maria' and the 'Salve Regina'. Andersson comments that she was probably protesting against the thoughtless, mechanical repetition of empty words. She wanted to see crosses, crucifixes and images of the crucified Christ destroyed because, as we have already seen, the cross had become for many a new, more powerful fetish (*nkisi*). She taught that Christ was born as an African in São Salvador and that His apostles were blacks. The aim of her preaching was fixed on the restoration of the ancient Kingdom of the Kongo, which would bring the Kongolese great prosperity and splendour—a sort of Paradise on earth.

Donna Béatrice tried to found a church with a hierarchy of its own. In so doing she came into conflict with the foreign priests. This African Christian movement spread rapidly as a reaction to the weaknesses of the first missioning of the Kongo and as a protest

[2] E. Andersson: op. cit., ibid.; A. Massamba-Débat: op. cit, pp. 22 ff.; G. Balandier: op. cit., pp. 267 ff.   [3] G. Balandier: op. cit., p. 262.

against the national decline which had followed Portuguese colonization. Her efforts turned despair and resignation into hope.

There are three important aspects of Donna Béatrice's preaching. The first is her reaction against the cross. Was this simply a healthy reaction against a magical interpretation and use of the cross and the crucifix? Or did the reaction go deeper than that? Was it, in fact, also a repudiation of the biblical preaching of the cross, which promises liberation from sin and new life through the very death of the one Messiah, Jesus Christ? This question cannot be answered conclusively because we do not know how the Gospel was preached in the Kongo in this period of decline. Béatrice replaced absolution, the forgiveness of sin through the cross by the ancient ceremony of exposing oneself to rain.

In the second place, we encounter here for the first time the idea of the black Christ. Behind this lies a tremendously deep and important desire to have a Christ who identifies himself with the African. We shall find this desire taking a very special form among the Kimbanguists. The pictures of Christ known so far were pictures imported from Portugal and other European countries, showing Christ with white, European features. How could this Christ, the Christ of the exploiting European, help the suffering Africans who were longing for liberation? Béatrice's apostles were black, too. Nor must we forget that, in the tradition of the Catholic church, the apostles are saints who can intercede for people. Why should it be whites who intercede with God and Christ on behalf of the blacks? Behind all this there is the manifold problem of the role of deceased ancestors in African religion.

Whether consciously or subconsciously, Donna Béatrice strove for an 'Africanization' of the Christian message. In a prophetic way she sensed problems with which missiology has been concerned only since the middle of the twentieth century.

In the third place, the prophecy of Béatrice was keyed to the prosperity which was coming, to a kind of paradise on earth and to the restoration of the ancient Kingdom of the Kongo. Have we here a manifestation of the cyclical thinking which is the basis of the ancient African view of the world, or is this an eschatology through which the cycle is broken and something new emerges? In order to answer this question we would need to know more about Donna Béatrice. Perhaps we are mistaken, but it seems that her vision remained fixed in the context of essentially cyclical thinking. Professor Mbiti[4] observes that in traditional African thinking time moves

[4] J. Mbiti: 'Eschatologie und Jenseitsglaube', in 'Theologie und Kirche in Afrika', ed. H. Bürkle, Stuttgart, 1968, p. 211.

backwards rather than forwards, from the present back into the past. This seems to have been the case with Donna Béatrice, although we can show from our vantage point in time that she saw problems which only came to be recognized as such more than a hundred years later.

By pointing to a further time of prosperity and the restoration of the ancient order (viewed in an ideal light), Béatrice took up a theme which belongs to African tradition, namely that prosperity is a sign of the blessing of God (or of the gods and ancestors). Prosperity is the outward sign of the vital force.[5] Where prosperity is lacking the community rests under a curse which must be removed.

2. BÉATRICE AS A NATIONAL HEROINE AND MARTYR

Béatrice, who claimed that she enjoyed uninterrupted communion with God, became a national heroine. She kindled new hope at a time of Kongolese decline and despondency. Her preaching according to Massamba-Débat,[6] led to an aggressive nationalism. The movement which she kindled was called Antonianism or the Antonian sect and it spread rapidly. Almost all the kingdom was dissatisfied and turned to the Antonian sect, Andersson reports.[7] From far afield people came to see and hear Béatrice, and they venerated her as a saint. Her closest followers were called 'angels'; emissaries, or apostles, whom she sent throughout the kingdom, proclaimed her message. Then she took practical measures, calling the chiefs to gather in São Salvador to restore the ancient kindom under a new monarch. That was sedition and heresy! The fact that she gave birth to a baby boy made her position even more critical. She claimed that she had followed in the footsteps of the Virgin Mary and had conceived a child by the Holy Spirit—a phenomenon which also crops up occasionally in later prophetic movements.[8] Under pressure from the Capuchins, King Pedro IV had Donna Béatrice arrested (in 1706). He hoped to make people believe that he was handing her over to the Bishop of Angola, whose see was in Luanda, but then to free her on her way there. However, the Capuchins, filled 'with zeal for the glory of God', influenced the royal council into sentencing Donna Béatrice to death at the stake along with her little son and, according to other reports, along with the apostle who was the father of the child. As Joan of Arc is sup-

[5] P. Tempels: op. cit., pp. 30 ff. in both the English and French versions.
[6] A. Massamba-Débat: op. cit., p. 23.
[7] E. Andersson: op. cit., p. 245.   [8] M.-L. Martin. op. cit., p. 121.

posed to have done, Béatrice died with the name of Jesus on her lips. A. Massamba-Débat comments: 'She was burnt alive because she had believed in the restoration of her country.' After her death her supporters had to be suppressed by force.

3. BÉATRICE—A UNIQUE PHENOMENON IN AFRICA?

As we shall see, prophecy in Africa is a widespread phenomenon which arises particularly in times of crisis. We should distinguish between different kinds of prophet, but they have this in common, that they all claimed to be called through dreams or visions, either by God or one of the gods or deceased ancestors, and then stand in uninterrupted communion with the source of their call. They have messages to bring to the people of their nation and age. The element of predictive prophecy is prominent in the case of many of them. In 1793 (forty years before the arrival of the first missionaries) 'Mantsopa Makheta was born to a 'prophetic family' in Lesotho. As a prophetess she lived at the court of King Moshoeshoe, predicted all kinds of important events and also gave religious and moral instructions. She believed in the old *modimo* (god) and proclaimed a *new* god who interceded with the old god on behalf of people. Is Christian influence to be detected in this? According to ancient Sotho tradition *modimo* also means 'ancestor'. The ancestor who has recently died is the new god who brings the old *modimo* the requests of the surviving members of the family on earth. 'Mantsopa could make it rain, which was a tremendous boon to a country suffering from periodic drought and starvation. At the end of her life (she lived for more than a hundred years) she became a Christian. 'Mantsopa, like Béatrice, was concerned with a message from the beyond and with the welfare of the people. But the political situation in Béatrice's time was very different from that in 'Mantsopa's day. The latter became a national heroine who was not an opponent of the king but his collaborator. The missionaries arrived when she was already famous, and, although they were suspicious of her, it did not lead to conflict.

Another prophetess who made her mark in the history of South Africa is Nongqause of the Xhosa people in the eastern Cape Province. She appeared in connection with a whole series of prophets—the first notable prophetic movement of South Africa.[9] Nongqause

[9] O. Raum: 'Von Stammespropheten zu Sektenführern', in 'Messianische Kirchen, Sekten und Bewegungen im heutigen Afrika', ed. E. Benz, Leiden, 1965, pp. 49–70.

was 'visited' by her dead ancestors and was able to describe their appearances in detail. Like many African prophets, she took up the struggle against black magic or witchcraft. At a time when the white settlers were pentrating more and more deeply into the territory of the Xhosa, friction between settlers and Africans on the one hand and missionaries and tribal leaders on the other was the order of the day. There now arose an intense longing for peace and prosperity. In this instance it was hardly possible to return to the old order and so prophecy was concerned with what seems to Westerners the fantastic promise that the ancestors and all their cattle would rise from the dead, drive out the British and thus cause the good things of the whites to fall into the possession of the Xhosa. There was, however, a condition of fulfilment: all cattle had to be slaughtered, the corn destroyed and no fields were to be cultivated. The day of the great resurrection (a concept which is not part of African tradition but was borrowed from Christian preaching and modified in terms of human utopias) was expected on 18th February, 1857, but never dawned. The consequences of this prophecy were devastating, for thousands of people starved to death.

Nongqause and her predecessors had things in common with Béatrice and 'Mantsopa and yet they were very different in other ways. This time it was the ancestors who spoke to the prophetess. The only aspect of her teaching with a Christian colouring was the resurrection.

In our own century a new type of prophet arises and we shall meet it with Simon Kimbangu. This is the genuinely Christian prophet who calls to conversion, repentance and renewal of life, the prophet through whom Christ performs His works of healing and sanctification, the prophet who recapitulates the story of Christ's sufferings and death but also (as the Ngunza Movement will show) runs the risk of mixing Christian and pagan elements and confusing the Holy Spirit with the ancestral spirit. In certain cases he is worshipped by his followers as the new Christ.[10] We shall see, however, that in the case of Simon Kimbangu and of others, whom we shall mention for the sake of comparison, Christian prophecy in the New Testament sense has arisen spontaneously in a situation which missions have often scarcely recognized. Thus, in a society caught up in great change, people were bound together in brotherhood on the basis of Scripture through the preaching, healing and new initiatives of the prophets. They look to Jesus Christ and are filled with the Holy Spirit. Even this Christian type of prophet may occasionally

---

[10] B. Sundkler: 'Bantu Prophets in South Africa', London, 1961, p. 114.

engage in predictive prophecy. Chiefly in former colonial territories and in countries which are still today under white domination, he can also be a figure who stimulates the national consciousness of the African without encouraging blind nationalism. Whereas one prophet may do this by identifying himself entirely and exclusively with his black community, another may be eager to cultivate contact with Christians of different nationalities and skin colour.

As examples of earlier prophecy we have mentioned womenfolk, namely Donna Béatrice, 'Mantsopa, and Nongqause. Donna Béatrice, the woman of the Kongo, came from a matriarchal social order where the women occupy a not insignificant position in the family and in the religious life of the community. 'Mantsopa and Nongqause came from patriarchal social orders. But even there women played a more important role in both the religious life of the community as mediums of the ancestors as well as in sacrificial rites and other ceremonies than was assumed in missionary literature, which was often inclined to make facile generalizations. Rather, it was the Christian churches of the West, on the basis of legalistic interpretation of some Pauline passages, that had restricted the role of women in Christian fellowship. The fact that in Africa prophetesses have arisen, and the role which churches like the Kimbanguist communion accord to women might influence the development of Christianity at a time when the whole question of clergy—laity is being examined afresh. Many feel that, on the one hand, women should be allowed to participate more fully in the Church's ministries, and on the other that spiritual gifts such as prophecy, faith-healing, exorcism, and even speaking in tongues ought to be given their rightful place.[11]

[11] For comparison see the chapter on Alice Lenshina in the study by D. Lehmann/V. Taylor: 'Christians in the Copperbelt', London, 1961, pp. 248–67.

CHAPTER 3

THE SECOND PERIOD OF MISSIONARY ACTIVITY IN ZAÏRE IN THE NINETEENTH AND TWENTIETH CENTURIES

1. THE COLLAPSE OF THE ANCIENT KINGDOM OF THE KONGO

The eighteenth century brought struggles for royal power and, in consequence, anarchy. Rivals fought to secure the throne in São Salvador. In the nineteenth century the kingdom, which formerly consisted of six provinces, shrank to a miniature realm surrounding the capital São Salvador. The rivalries of the various claimants to the throne were not solely to blame for this decline; other factors were the decimation of the population through Portuguese slave-trading and the exploitation of the people of the Kongo by the Yaga,[1] whose invasion in 1569 we have already mentioned. The Yaga were used by the Portuguese as plunderers. When George Grenfell, the Baptist missionary, sailed up the River Kongo (Zaïre) in 1884 he saw many smoking ruins of native villages. Many of the people had been murdered by Arabs and by Arab half-castes, and many had fallen a prey to the slave-trade.[2]

In São Salvador itself the ruins of churches and monasteries could still be seen. The struggle between the European powers for ascendancy in the Kongo (and in other African territories) had now begun, but the shrunken Kingdom of São Salvador remained in the hands of the Portuguese as part of Angola, whilst the British and the King of Belgium contended for possession of the Congo.

[1] See Chapter 1, pp. 10–11.
[2] 'Africa in the 19th and 20th Centuries', ed. J. C. Anene/G. Brown, Univ. of Ibadan, 1966, pp. 284 ff.

2. THE STRUGGLE BETWEEN THE EUROPEAN POWERS FOR POSSESSION OF THE CONGO

In 1877, the Congolese hinterland was opened up through Stanley's great expedition.[3] Until this point Britain had been showing an increasing interest in the Congo. In the same year the British Baptist missionaries began their work in the Congo after Robert Arthington, a wealthy industrialist from Leeds, had encouraged an initial missionary expedition to the country as early as 1874.

However, in 1876 Leopold II, King of the Belgians, stepped in. Motivated by personal ambition cloaked by a show of philanthropy towards the natives, he wanted to create for himself a kingdom in the Congo. He sent exploratory expeditions to the Congo, the most important being under the leadership of the Welshman H. M. Stanley, who had entered the service of King Leopold in 1879.

France, too, entered the arena. De Brazza made treaties for the French with native chieftains on the north bank of the river near Stanley Pool (today Lac Malebo), a lake-like widening of the Zaïre situated between the present-day capitals Kinshasa—formerly Léopoldville—and Brazzaville. Stanley, for his part, made similar treaties on behalf of King Leopold. Britain opposed the designs of King Leopold, and France wanted to assert the ancient Portuguese claims on the Congo. In the Anglo-Portuguese treaty of February 1884, Britain recognized the Portuguese claim to the Congo estuary and Portugal guaranteed free access to British traders and missionaries. But neither France nor Leopold of Belgium was inclined to recognize this agreement between Britain and Portugal.

Germany under Bismarck also took an interest in events, and in November 1884 the West-African Conference gathered in Berlin to discuss the way in which international control might be exercised over the Congo. The conference was aimed against Britain. King Leopold, in order to win their favour, shrewdly convinced the American delegates that he was planning a crusade against slave-trading. France gave way when Leopold gave an assurance that he would hand over the Congo to France if he found himself unable to govern the country. The Berlin conference finally agreed to recognize Leopold's 'Congo Free State'. The Belgian parliament gave its approval to this agreement, but at the same time made it clear that there was no connection between Belgium and the king in this matter (and thus no further obligations on the part of Belgium)

[3] K. B. Westman/H. von Sicard: 'Geschichte der Christlichen Mission', Chr. Kaiser, Munich, 1962, p. 150.

except where the monarch specifically so desired.[4] Leopold assumed the role of a liberal, only to show himself later all the more of an exploiter. Rubber was deemed of more value than human life. In the years 1890–8 Leopold had the famous—or infamous—railway built from the port of Matadi in the west across the hills to Kinshasa. Stretching 388 km., it cost thousands of human lives.

The scandal of the exploitation under Leopold was so great and at certain times the financial difficulties, which after all fell on Belgium, were so immense that already around the turn of the century British and American voices were raised against Leopold. The Belgian parliament drew attention to the scandal and enquired how it was that Belgian Catholic missionaries remained silent about the state of affairs.[5] The question was raised whether the Belgian government should take over responsibility for the Congo. The Belgian Socialists were in principle against any form of colonialism and any kind of intervention at first, and Leopold resisted any change of régime in the Congo. Eventually pressure from outside grew so great that by 1906 there was a majority in Belgium in favour of taking over responsibility. The debate on this issue began in the Belgian Chamber and Senate in 1908. The Socialists wanted the Congo to be an international protectorate, but the majority of Representatives voted for the annexation of the country by Belgium despite the opposition of the king. On 16 November it was officially announced in Boma, on the Congo estuary, that Belgium had assumed authority over all territories which until then had belonged to King Leopold's so-called independent Congo State.

3. THE PROTESTANT MISSIONARY ACTIVITY IN THE COUNTRY

The first missioning in the Congo had proved in the long run a failure. It is true that the Portuguese had pretended to recognize the Africans as equals and had given a Congolese élite a good education in Portugal. They had ordained African priests and even a Congolese bishop, but Christianity remained a foreign affair for all that. It had appeared in Western, Portuguese dress, and thus it remained. Moreover, the Portuguese had made themselves unpopular through slave-trading and Portuguese secular priests had set a bad example. It is pertinent at this point to wonder whether the second phase of missionary activity in the country will be as unsuccessful, or whether

[4] R. Slade: 'King Leopold's Congo', Oxford, 1962, p. 43.
[5] R. Slade: op. cit., p. 200.

Second Period of Missionary Activity

it will manage to avoid the mistakes of the first missionaries and learn from the prophecies of Donna Béatrice?[6]

The second missionary movement in the nineteenth century began with the advantage of being partly prompted by the protest against slave-trading. The evangelical revival in England had the tremendous effect of awakening social conscience on the one hand and missionary interest on the other, and the mission to the Congo was actively supported by evangelical circles in Britain and America. But for the second time the Gospel was to appear in Western dress, this time mixed with Western technological culture, with the feeling that superior knowledge was being brought to the poor backward natives. The Congolese were looked upon as children (as a number of early letters sent by missionaries to England show). True the missionaries knew that the day would come when the children would have matured into adults and responsible people; but this day still seemed far away and there was no thought of handing over to the Congolese at an early stage a full share in the responsibility for the mission and its leadership and strategy.

Moreover, Christian missionary endeavour was now split into rival Catholic and Protestant missions.

(a) First Beginnings

Robert Arthington, the Leeds industrialist, was the first to see the significance of the newly discovered Congo route into the African interior. His aim in life was to hasten the Second Coming of Christ by foreign missions in accordance with the words of Jesus in Matthew 24:14. He offered the London Missionary Society £5,000 (a considerable sum at that time) on condition that it advance from East Africa, where the mission was already working, to the region of the eastern Zaïre. In 1877 the London Missionary Society sent its first expedition to Ujiji, the place where Livingstone and Stanley had met. In the same year Arthington offered the British Baptist Missionary Society £1,000 on condition that it begin missionary work in the Congo, operating from the west coast. Its missionaries were to advance as fast as possible along the River Congo and then to meet the missionaries of the LMS coming from the east. These plans were warmly supported by the Baptist missionary and explorer, George Grenfell. The idea of a chain of missionary stations stretching from the west to the east of Africa found enthusiastic approval.

Apart from the London Missionary Society and the British

[6] R. Slade: op. cit., pp. 141 ff.

Baptists, other Protestant missions came to the Congo with the same wish to advance as rapidly as possible into the interior of the country, among them Albert Simpson of New York, formerly a Presbyterian who had then joined the Baptists of the 'Gospel Tabernacle'.

Progress, however, was neither as rapid nor as free from obstacles as had perhaps been hoped in the first flush of enthusiasm. After the Baptists had accepted the offer of Arthington, two expeditions tried to advance into the interior from the west. The expedition of Thomas Comber went to São Salvador and tried to make progress from there, only to meet with great resistance on the part of hostile tribes.[7] A second Baptist expedition, under H. Crudgington and Holman Bentley (who had by now made a name for himself as a Bible translator), took a different route and reached Stanley Pool, now known as Lake Malebo, above present-day Kinshasa, in July 1881. Further advance into the interior of the country was accomplished by using a steamboat with which the Baptists were able to sail upstream for a stretch of about 1,500 km. from Stanley Pool to Kisangani (formerly Stanleyville), which is situated a fair distance below the Stanley Falls. Even today the Zaïre steamer is the only good link between Kinshasa and Kisangani, apart from the modern aeroplane, which can cover this distance in two-and-a-half hours (instead of five to ten days). Mission stations were set up at wide intervals along the river and this part of Zaïre is still today by and large the preserve of the Baptist church, except that Catholic missionaries are also at work having followed on the heels of the Baptists.[8]

(b) Further Missionary Societies

In 1874 H. and F. Grattan Guiness had been responsible for the formation of the Livingstone Inland Mission with the aim of evangelizing Central Africa by way of the Congo. The mission reached Boma on the Congo estuary in 1878 and built a mission station in the port of Matadi. In 1885 the American Baptists and the Swedish Missionary Society each took over part of the work of the Livingstone Inland Mission. Some of the missionaries of the Livingstone Inland Mission, however, disapproved of this decision and in 1888 founded the Congo Balolo Mission.

American (Southern) Presbyterians went to Kasai Province and the first missionaries Lapsley and Sheppard (who was an American

[7] R. Anstey: 'Britain and the Congo in the 19th Century', Oxford, 1962, pp. 34 ff.; R. Slade: op. cit., pp. 29 ff.

[8] S. Neill: 'A History of Christian Missions', Penguin, Harmondsworth, 1964, pp. 380 ff.; R. Anstey: op. cit., pp. 34 ff.

negro), arrived in Luebo in 1891, where they concentrated at first on the Baluba working from Luebo.

(c) The Plymouth Brethren

The Plymouth Brethren, who have no ordained ministry, developed in Shaba (then known as Katanga) through what was called the *Garenganze Evangelical Mission* a significant work with missionary methods which strike us as modern. In 1886 the Scottish pioneer F. S. Arnot, who had come from Barotseland in presentday Zambia, had been welcomed there by the great and feared chief Msiri in his capital Bunkeya to counter the influence of the Arabs.[9] It was a unique enterprise: Msiri had created his Katangan realm as a tyrant; now he was allowing white missionaries to settle in his country as his agents. That gave them the advantage of being able to become fully conversant with the customs and thought patterns of the Katangans, but, on the other hand, it prevented their involvement in really vigorous missionary expansion. They were not free. In 1890 Dan Crawford arrived in Bunkeya along with other Plymouth Brethren, and he stayed there for twenty-two years. They adapted themselves completely to the way of life of the Africans, and Dan Crawford learnt to 'think black'. In this way he was able to win the trust of the Katangans, and one wonders whether this was not basically of greater value than rapid missionary expansion would have been. After the assassination of Msiri, the people flocked to Crawford and showed that at least they were open to the Christian Gospel. He was called 'Konga Vantu', which means 'the man who gathers the people'. He founded a new, Christian city—Luanza on the northern bank of Lake Mweru.[10] The people did not come to the Plymouth Brethren and to Dan Crawford just for the sake of material advantage, as so often happened in missionary work, but with the wish that he should help them after the collapse of the old order to find their way to a new one. This was the time when the copper mines in Shaba were being discovered and a great social upheaval loomed on the horizon. The missionaries saw themselves therefore compelled to accept social responsibility. Dan Crawford was a remarkable man: he lived in poverty and counted solely on God to help him.

By the beginning of the twentieth century Protestant missions of the most varied shades had begun missionary work all over Zaïre— not to compete with one another but spurred by the zeal to save souls. However, they soon found a variety of other work to do in all

[9] J. C. Anene/G. Brown: op. cit., p. 287.
[10] S. Neill: op. cit., p. 381.

departments of life and, although it was a source of worry to many that they were unable to apply themselves completely and utterly to the task of pure evangelism, they took on these new commitments.

4. ROMAN CATHOLIC MISSIONARY WORK IN THE COUNTRY

Michel Merlier[11] claims that Leopold II could not turn the evangelization of 'savage' tribes sufficiently to his own advantage to disguise his own plans for trade and exploitation; to this end he sought in particular to use the Protestant missions to the country, which were financed by wealthy British philanthropists.

The Catholic Belgians opposed this policy. The king himself had turned as far back as 1879 (even before the Berlin Conference) to the Belgian Jesuits, as well as to the Scheut Fathers, asking them to send missionaries to Zaïre, but neither order had shown any interest.[12] However, the French 'Pères du Saint-Esprit' (Fathers of the Holy Spirit) and the White Fathers of Cardinal Lavigerie did take up missionary work in Zaïre, and Leopold feared that this might enhance the influence of France and he accordingly asked the cardinal to recruit the Belgian missionary candidates to his order. In 1885 Leopold secured the assurance of the Pope that 'his Congo' should be reserved for Belgian Catholic missionary work, and this despite the fact that the Berlin West-African Conference had insisted on freedom of missionary activity.[13] From the very beginning the Catholic missionaries defended the aims of the colonial administration and were by and large its tools.

At the beginning of 1886, Pope Leo XIII granted King Leopold's request, and so similar aspirations to those of the first missionary endeavour in the Kongo were now pursued: Catholic missionary activity was bound up in the closest possible way with a particular Western culture and cultural power. Only now the Catholic mission had to work in 'competition' alongside the Protestant missionary societies, which were much freer. The Pope suggested that Leopold should found a seminary in Louvain to train priests for African missionary work, and a year later the Scheut Fathers declared themselves ready to co-operate as missionaries in Zaïre. An apostolic vicariate for Zaïre was created and the Scheut Fathers were entrusted with its direction. In May 1888 Mr van Eetvelde, the

[11] M. Merlier: 'Le Congo de la colonisation belge à l'indépendance', Paris, 1962, pp. 215 ff.
[12] R. Slade: op. cit., pp. 164 ff.
[13] M. Merlier: op. cit., pp. 215 ff.

Second Period of Missionary Activity

Governor-General of the former Congo Free State, could write to the Belgian minister, de Pittens, who was accredited at the Vatican: 'Now Catholic mission work in the Congo is founded on a permanent basis. No more of the Portuguese patronage, no more interference from foreign missionaries; the new state (Congo) is becoming Belgian from the religious point of view as it already is on the political side, and I hope we shall soon have an army of missionaries going to help found a new greater Belgium in that far-off land.'[14] Protestantism was at that time so small and insignificant in Belgium that it was of no consequence, and there was as yet no thought of sending out Protestant Belgian missionaries. This move to set up a new Catholic Belgium in Zaïre is one of the factors which later will have played a part in the rise and particularly the persecution of Simon Kimbangu and his movement. The fact that so many prophetic groups (Ngunzists) of all shades, some with anti-white slogans, were later to spring up in Zaïre must be understood as a reaction against the 'new Catholic Belgium in the Congo' and against the consequences of the social upheaval caused by colonization.

In 1891 the Jesuits re-established themselves in Zaïre followed in 1895 by the Trappists, and other orders between 1897–9.

The Protestants had begun the second evangelization of Zaïre, but soon the Catholic missionaries set up their stations all over the country. The Protestant 'heretics' were to be superseded and their efforts destroyed. The age of ecumenism was not yet arrived.[15] The Scheut Fathers, for instance, took the same route as the British Baptists and set up their stations along the Zaïre river. Admittedly there were also unevangelized regions to which the Catholic missionaries turned; other regions remained the preserve of the Protestants, like the district in present-day Lower Zaïre around Ngombe-Lutete and N'Kamba, where Simon Kimbangu began his work. But not far away the important Catholic station of Ngombe-Matadi was set up with its church, school, and hospital.

5. MISSIONARY AIMS AND METHODS

Ruth Slade[16] has said what is probably true of most missionary areas (except for a few modern exceptions): 'The Western missions came with their dynamic new ideas and their totally different way of living to exert their influence on the static tribal life. This could only

[14] R. Slade: op. cit., p. 147.
[15] S. Neill: op. cit., p. 438.
[16] R. Slade: op. cit., p. 148.

lead to cultural conflict.' By and large the Western missionaries of the nineteenth century were convinced that the African way of life was depraved and must give way to that of the Western-minded missionaries. The idea of freeing the Christian Gospel from its Western shell and of putting it in African terms, using African forms of expression, culture, and symbolism, was still not in sight. Thus the Western Missionaries were not only working to make men new (in accordance with the teaching of the Gospel) but also to establish a foreign culture and way of life. This will be one of the factors behind the reaction which found its expression in the prophetic movements.

But is it possible for the Christian message to appear in the idiom of African culture and way of life? Can one, for instance, take the African way of life and make a clear-cut distinction between the 'good' and the 'bad', accepting the one and leaving aside the other, as is so often suggested (and that by Africans)? Does not African culture with its ways of thinking, living and acting, form a unity which cannot readily be broken down into 'good' and 'bad' elements and used or repudiated at will? This is an enormous problem which the African Kimbanguist Church is trying to resolve. Nor is this whole area of difficulty eased by the mixing of cultures and ways of thinking and expression in the age of mass media when many Africans travel to the West. However, this much can be said: in the Christian message it is always a matter of an affirmation and a negation, of continuity and discontinuity. The old does not simply disappear—for it belongs essentially to people of an era, a certain tradition, culture and mode of expression; but through the Gospel a transformation takes place. It is the African, with the way he feels life, with his aims and his means of expression, who is gripped by the Gospel and as an African becomes a new creation. This African does not have to be first a European, to dress in a European way, to express himself like a European, and to accept a European way of life, in order to be a Christian. For Europeanism is not Christianity. That has surely become clear to us in the last decades. Apart from a few exceptions, these problems were of course not yet recognized by the missionaries of the nineteenth century and even of the first half of the twentieth century. But it is precisely due to the fact that Christianity was presented as European that we have today in Africa at least seven to nine million Christians who belong to the African independent churches (often misleadingly called sects). They want as Africans to be Christians without going through the process of westernization.

Because this problem was not seen—perhaps indeed was unseeable—there was to begin with a blending of the white way of life and Christianity.

The pattern which developed was the mission station with its settlement of Christians—a little realm in its own right. That was indeed inevitable, for round the missionary there gathered children of slaves, who had bought their freedom, and people who had lost their tribal identity, as well as refugees and young folk who were anxious to learn from the missionaries and thus improve their prospects.

The white missionary was the ruler, the chief, even if he did not want such a role. He had to act as judge in palavers and bore full responsibility for the freed slaves, mostly children, whether he had bought their freedom or whether they were assigned to him by the government, which in Zaïre occurred only with Catholic missions.

Protestant missionaries, with their ideal of converting individuals, were not at first so happy about this 'mission colony' or mission station plus Christian village. The Catholic missionaries, who preferred group conversion and wanted to construct a Christian community within the old non-Christian unit, were favourably disposed towards the development of such new communities consisting of freed slaves, refugees, and young folk eager to learn. The liberated slaves formed the nucleus of what was called a *chrétienté* (Christendom). In order to construct many such Christian colonies the Catholic missions acquired land and became owners of vast estates. The *chrétienté* was to support itself by means of agriculture.

The Plymouth Brethren had, as we have already seen, a different approach. They lived within the old village community, and in their new city (after the death of Msiri) they made no attempts 'to whitewash the African'.[17] The city of the Plymouth Brethren was a 'semi-pagan' city.

Order and discipline were necessary in the Catholic *chrétienté* as well as on the Protestant missionary station with its Christian settlement. Rules were drawn up because they were indispensable, so one cannot reproach the missionaries with authoritarianism from the very beginning. Sometimes the whip was used and complaints about ill-treatment were vociferous and possibly inflated. In both Catholic and Protestant settlements the nuclear family was preferred to the customary African extended family. Extended families, made up of whole networks of relatives, did not usually go over in their entirety to the mission. It was rather individuals who came, who later married and founded their own nuclear families. In this new

---

[17] Tilsley: 'Dan Crawford', p. 494, quoted by R. Slade: op. cit., p. 152.

social order of the mission colony, polygamy lost its significance and part of its function (distribution of labour). But despite all the criticism levelled today against this missionary approach, the people who settled at the mission found security; they no longer had to fear the slave-catcher, who was up to his mischief until the turn of the century. They were able to learn what was of vital importance, such as how to engage in agriculture or work at a trade, and this helped them on in life. These mission colonies and villages were distinguished for their prosperity; they were self-supporting, receiving little aid from overseas. The extent of cultivation in Zaïre today and the fact that the State President Mobutu Sese Seko attaches great importance to agriculture is a compliment to the work of these early missionaries.

The drawback of these colonies and villages was, however, that they stood like ghettos in the midst of the ancient tribal units, isolated from the life of the majority of Africans and therefore without real missionary outreach. The missionaries were aware of this and opened schools for African catechists or evangelists. Although the trainees were also cut off from the tribal community, at least during the period of their training, and although some of them lost all contact with it, many of them did later do good work out in the bush, where they were visited regularly by their missionaries. The American Presbyterians seem to have been the most successful with this kind of 'indirect' evangelism in the province of Kasai.[18]

The African evangelist, who was at the same time a teacher, was an important bridge in the transitional period from traditional tribal life, which was surrounded by a firm framework of rules, customs, taboos and rites, to the new pattern of life imposed upon the Africans by the colonial power.

As we have seen, the missionaries (particularly the Protestants) made use of individual evangelists to influence the tribal community whereas the Catholics formed groups for this purpose. The Jesuit van Hencxthoven was a pioneer in this. He was the founder of what was called the *ferme-chappelle* system (farm-chapel).[19] A team of native Christians was sent out by the central mission in order to settle near an African tribal group. In this little community there were catechists who also acted as teachers and agricultural pioneers. Surplus produce was sold to the near-by tribal community, thus establishing a relationship with it, and human contacts between Christians and non-Christians developed. As a result a Christian village grew up alongside a non-Christian village. One wonders

[18] R. Slade: op. cit., p. 157.
[19] R. Slade: op. cit., p. 159.

whether this form of evangelism is not more in keeping with African communal thinking. The African as a rule does not act as an individual but within a firmly united group.

Christians soon came into conflict with the powerful *nganza*, the witch-doctor, whose function is central in the traditional African tribal order. In all cases of sickness, sterility, fear, danger, and death it is to him that men turn to discover the cause and to obtain the necessary curative and preventive remedies. He protects the community from the curse of sorcery (*kindoki*). Illness is not simply a matter of the body, but also of the soul. The religious component must not be left out of consideration; it may be due to witchcraft, neglect of the family, or the ancestors. Moreover, illness and misfortune concern not only the individual but also the whole community. The missionaries, in providing medical aid, sought to replace the witch-doctor, but the African conception of sickness made (and makes) such aid incomplete. This insufficiency of Western missionary work with regard to healing was one of the reasons for the overwhelming success of the preaching and faith-healing of Simon Kimbangu. Even today, African Christians—both Protestant and Catholic —go to the prophets and healers of the independent African churches when they run into trouble or feel ill (usually without the knowledge of the missionary). This fact is one which I have often observed over the years in various parts of Africa, and the tendency to do so is increasing rather than decreasing.

6. PERSONAL AND ECUMENICAL CONTACTS

In the relationship between black and white, or between missionary from the West and African church member, the Portuguese in the fifteenth and sixteenth centuries allowed the Africans to be treated as equals, but (what a contradiction!) despite this engaged in slave-trading—an affront to all human dignity. The missionaries of the nineteenth and the beginning of the twentieth centuries opposed the slave-trade but were not as quick to accept the Africans as their equals and partners. The Protestants for their part reiterated the formula that the African church—to begin with, the various congregations—should be self-supporting, self-propagating (through evangelism) and self-governing. But this ideal was set for the future— presumably the distant future. They made the same mistake as the Belgian administration, which spoke of Congolese self-government becoming a reality in the distant future, only to be suddenly startled from such dreams by the events at the end of the 1950s.

The Catholics did not think in terms of self-supporting, self-propagating and self-governing congregations because each congregation belonged primarily and principally to the universal Catholic church with its hierarchy. And yet the Catholics founded in Kimuanza as early as 1896 a seminary for the training of priests. It appears, however, to have been a premature enterprise, and in 1919 a fresh start was made. Nor did the Protestants for their part hurry to train Zaïrians as ministers. This was in fact difficult because the Belgian colonial government directed all its attention to elementary schooling and made only a few belated attempts to establish secondary schools. Finally, it can be said that in Zaïre, as elsewhere, the paternalistic streak in Christian missionary work was very strong. Ecumenical relationships (particularly between Catholics and Protestants) left much to be desired, mainly because the Catholic church co-operated from the start in the closest possible way with the Belgian Catholic colonial power, seeking to turn the Zaïrians into Catholic Belgians.

Catholic missionaries were given preference from the start and enjoyed privileges which the Protestants did not have. The Catholics had about 367,500 acres of land at their disposal for their *chrétientés* and *ferme-chapelle* colonies whereas the Protestants had about 21,500 acres. Merlier claims that the system of collecting orphans (in the first instance, children of slaves) was abused by the Catholic missionaries until 1911. Moreover, the Catholic schools were subsidized by the Belgian administration, whereas Protestant schools were not given state aid until as late as 1946.[20]

The story of Simon Kimbangu will show what tensions existed between Catholics and Protestants and how these tensions were partly responsible for the inability of the protestants to stand up more vigorously for the prophet. The blame for all so-called 'sectarianism' was laid at the door of the Protestants. The Catholics forgot that there had been an Antonian sect long before there had been any Protestant missionaries in Zaïre. Nor was it just Protestants, but also Catholics as well as non-Christians, who joined the Kimbanguists or the Ngunzists.

In the second period of missionary activity in Zaïre in the nineteenth century, and more particularly in the twentieth, more and more Protestant missions entered the country, many of them sponsored by conservative, fundamentalist circles, with the result that there were eventually no less than forty-six different societies

[20] Slade–Reardon: 'Catholics and Protestants in the Congo', in 'Christianity in Tropical Africa', ed. C. G. Baëta, Oxford, 1968, pp. 83 ff.

and churches working in Zaïre, which amalgamated in 1970 to form the 'Church of Christ in Zaïre', Only a few of these belong to the World Council of Churches.

Nevertheless, as far back as 1902 a certain Protestant ecumenical trend became apparent. Joint missionary conferences were held, which led in 1924 to the foundation of the 'Conseil Protestant du Congo', whose member churches united in 1970 as the 'Church of Christ in Zaïre', since when have been added various communities notably Pentecostalists and ex-Kimbanguists.

Until recently, however, relations with the Catholics remained strained, though now since the Second Vatican Council a relaxation of tension has been evident and gives cause for hope.

Part Two

THE HISTORY OF SIMON KIMBANGU AND HIS MOVEMENT FROM 1918 TO 1960

CHAPTER 4

THE EARLY HISTORY, CALL AND INITIAL MINISTRY OF THE PROPHET SIMON KIMBANGU

1. SECRET SOCIETIES

Both the first and second periods of colonization and evangelization of the Zaïre produced consequences and reaction—such was the prophetic movement and the foundation of the 'Antonian Church' of Donna Béatrice. Reactions took the form of non-Christian, as well as Christian, movements, but we shall concern ourselves only briefly with the non-Christian reaction in Zaïre. There are secret societies of *féticheurs*—sorcerers, who discover new 'medicine' in order to neutralize the irresistible power of the whites. Such secret societies are able to summon up active resistance. People have refused to buy imported goods and to do compulsory labour; all agricultural activity has been abandoned at times in the expectation of a fantastic event which would restore the old balance of forces or bring a paradise on earth, comparable to the 'primordial state'. In South Africa it was the prophets Mhlakaza and his niece Nongqause who, as mentioned in Chapter 2, appealed to the people to kill all their livestock and to burn all their provisions in the expectation of a glorious resurrection of their ancestors, who would drive the whites into the sea. In Zaïre, the witch-doctor Epikilipikili discovered in the region of Sankuru in Kasai Province a means whereby he promised to reduce the power of the Belgians. A rising resulted.[1] A recent similar rising occurred in 1920 for which the witch-doctors were reputed to have made their followers immune to the bullets of the whites—a motif which can be traced throughout Africa. The bullets would dissolve into water, the people were assured,

[1] M. Merlier: 'Le Congo de la colonisation belge à l'indépendance', Paris, 1962, pp. 232 ff.

usually with terrible consequences. This same promise was made a few years ago when, in Zambia, there arose an armed conflict between the Lumpa Church of the prophetess Alice Lenshina and the government troops of Dr K. Kaunda.

We could cite further examples of this reaction in Zaïre: for instance, the doctrine of Kitawala (the African version of the Jehovah's Witnesses, originating in South Africa and Malawi), which claims that, in the battle of Armageddon, the whites will be vanquished. All the examples have in common a form of reaction essentially distinct from the Christian prophetic reaction. But the latter was also a reaction against a force which destroys traditional values, disturbs the balance of power and, by intellectual, spiritual, and above all economic means, forces people into an alien way of life.

2. EARLY HISTORY OF SIMON KIMBANGU

(a) Source Material

Missiologists who have already read accounts of Simon Kimbangu will be surprised to see that our account differs on various points. The fact is that until recently there were hardly any accessible documents concerning the beginnings of the movement and its founder. I have discussed elsewhere[2] the accounts of the early period and would now need to extend the list of history books which give incorrect details. The account which now follows is based on documents dating from the earliest period, which were made accessible to me. They consist of a report which was made by Simon Kimbangu's two secretaries Nfinangani (his cousin) and Nzungu, which was confiscated by the Belgian authorities on 17 June 1921 and which was translated. Although this document had gaps when it came into the possession of the Belgians, it gives a good insight into events. We have an original report by the Belgian territorial administrator L. Morel, which from his own point of view, relates the same events and which agrees in essentials with the account of Nfinangani and Nzungu. A number of letters and reports from British Baptist missionaries are available in the London archives of this missionary society (BMS), giving detailed information concerning the events of 1921.

Moreover, I had the opportunity to have a look at other documents which were written by the sons of Simon Kimbangu; these

[2] M.-L. Martin: 'Prophetic Christianity in the Congo', Johannesburg, 1968, pp. 32 ff.

The Early History of Simon Kimbangu

were still children when the main events occurred, but they learned the details from their mother. I was also able to question eye-witnesses of what occurred in the first period, particularly Mikala Mandombe and Pierre Ndangi, who belonged to the first assistants (*bansadisi*) which Simon Kimbangu chose and who are still active today in the church; I also had the opportunity to have a short talk with the Rev. Hillard, now retired in England and one who witnessed the first episode in the train of events as a young missionary in Ngombe-Lutete (then called Wathen mission). My colleague W. Béguin, who was a fellow member of the first Study Commission, gathered additional material from Rev. Kina Paul, one of the early workers in the Kimbanguist Church, now ministering in Nsona-Bata. I received valuable details concerning the period from 1936 to 1960 from Rev. Alexandre Kimu and Mr Lucien Luntadila, the General Secretary of the Kimbanguist Church. My account of the movement in the former French Congo is based on the testimony of Samuel Matuba, who knew Simon Kimbangu, and of other eye-witnesses.

Incorrect accounts, particularly of the call and short ministry of Simon Kimbangu, have their basis in the legends which formed early round the person of the arrested prophet. In these legends the numinosum, the extraordinary, is given prominence to the point of confession. Thus, for instance, the following is what such legends tell of the call of the prophet: Simon Kimbangu was accompanying his parents (they were in fact his foster-parents) to a neighbouring village because a friend had died there. Suddenly he fainted and fell into a hole, and when he regained consciousness he found his mother in the same hole. An undefined being, neither black nor white, appeared to him with a Bible in his hand and said to him, 'This is a good book. You must read it and proclaim its contents.'[3] Others[4] tell how Simon Kimbangu was ill when he was not obedient to God's call and how as a consequence a strange being encountered him in a vision, neither white nor black, with a Bible in his hand. This being told him to go to a certain village to heal a child. Another legend reports how the young Simon, in a game with friends, turned a rotten coconut into a good one.

[3] E. Andersson: 'Messianic Popular Movements in the Lower Congo', Uppsala, pp. 50–1.

[4] K. Schlosser: 'Propheten in Afrika', Brunswick, 1948, p. 300; J. E. Bertsche: 'Kimbanguism a Challenge to Missionary Statesmanship', Practical Anthropology, Vol. 13, No. 1, 1966, p. 14; H. W. Fehderau: 'Prophetic Christianity', Practical Anthropology, Vol. 9, No. 4, 1962.

These legends came from Ngunzists and also from Kimbanguists, who claim to have received them from contemporaries of Simon Kimbangu. It is, however, noteworthy that in Kimbangu's family these legends are neither told nor have any importance. I do not think I am mistaken to assume that, during the period of persecution in secret meetings at night here and there in the bush, such tales were told and embroidered. The same is indeed also true to some extent of a few of the Old Testament prophetic figures, such as Elisha.

One of these legends very clearly has a historical basis, and that is the one which tells how the young Kimbangu visited a neighbouring village and fell into a hole, where he suddenly found his mother. This is an embroidered version of the true report which is to be found in the diary of Nfinangani and Nzungu,[5] according to which his foster-mother one day followed the little Kimbangu to a neighbouring village where he had come sick with dysentery. She set out for the village at night, found neighbours gathered round a fire, asked for a burning piece of wood to use as a lantern, and then went off. Then it seemed to her that someone was calling her back, which was not so. She went into a hut, found little Kimbangu, lifted him onto her back and wanted to carry him home. On the way he had to go aside from her because of his illness and he got lost, because he fell into a hole in the ground and probably lost consciousness. Finally he was found, and Kinzembo thanked God for helping her. On the way back to N'Kamba a man met her and assured her that the child would get better—at that time by no means a matter of course. At this Kimbangu asked for something to eat, for *kinsukulu*, a bitter fruit, which he was given by a girl called Marie Mwilu. She was later to become his wife. He ate the fruit and also other food and recovered from his illness.

The legendary elaboration, telling of the strange being (neither white nor black nor mulatto), which represents the three races which Kimbangu knew, has presumably a deep symbolic meaning: it represents Christ, who is neither black, nor white, nor mulatto but the universal Lord, who is the Saviour of people of all races and is calling Simon Kimbangu to a mission which, according to what Kimbangu himself said, was to have world-wide significance.

Some of these legends were published in a little booklet entitled *Nkanda Bisamu bia Tata Simon Kimbangu* with the French subtitle *Office du Prophète Simon Kimbangu*,[6] which is supposed to have

[5] Document secret, Annexe 3, 'Histoire de l'apparition du prophète Simon Kimbangu', Suite 1.

[6] The booklet is no longer available.

been edited in 1961 by Kimbanguist ministers with the approval of the head of the church. It is a kind of prayer-book, containing psalms, and prayers and hymns published for the first time, and illustrated with photographs. There is also mention in this booklet of what the Scheut Fathers recounted[7] concerning Romain Nkaya, one of their evangelists, who, in disguise, is supposed to have betrayed the prophet during his flight to Kinshasa and Kinkole—a tale which even Chomé[8] has accepted as historical. But in this little prayer-book all crucial historical facts are missing. I have been able to ascertain conclusively that this booklet is counterfeit. When I showed it to Charles Kisolokele without comment, he read the so-called historical part and said spontaneously, 'Much of this is not true.' Joseph Diangienda confirmed this and, independently of him, so did a number of well-educated Kimbanguists. The booklet (apart from the fact that the Kimbanguists do not use prayer-books) is counterfeit and stems from the pen of a former Catholic seminary student. It should not in any way be used as source material.

J. van Wing has it that Simon's father used to be a witch-doctor (*féticheur*),[9] and Andersson maintains that his mother cured the sick by means of herbs and leaves.

Bazola claims that Kimbangu's aunt, who brought him up, was a 'healer'.[10] All these are attempts to place Kimbangu among the many traditional African witch-doctors or healers. However, we must take account of the historical facts and see how these have been transformed. Finally, K. Schlosser reports, on the basis of an account by Thwaite,[11] that Kimbangu preached in a long silk robe and blessed his followers in a theatrical fashion. This could be true of the Ngunzists, about whom we shall have more to say later, and I myself have seen Simon Mpadi, who separated himself completely from the Kimbanguists, in such dress. But it is certainly not true of Simon Kimbangu and is as inaccurate as the report that he fastened a piece of red fabric to his prophet's staff.[12] Simon Kimbangu's prophet's staff is still preserved today, without any red flag

[7] Revue des Missions, Pères de Scheut, 1951.
[8] J. Chomé: 'La Passion de Simon Kimbangu, Présence Africaine', Paris, 1959; out of print.
[9] J. van Wing: 'Le kimbanguisme vu par un témoin', Zaïre No. 12, 1958, Louvain.
[10] E. Bazola: 'Le Kimbanguisme', Cahiers des religions africaines, Lovanium-Kinshasa, January 1968.
[11] K. Schlosser: op. cit., p. 305.
[12] E. Andersson: op. cit., p. 53.

attached to it. His closest fellow-workers who are still alive confirm that he carried only the staff, and that without decoration. According to all the testimonies which I was able to gather, he was, and remained, an extremely modest man, just like his sons, who are following the example of their father. Despite his charisma he was extremely sober, just like his youngest son Joseph Diangienda who has entered into his father's heritage. This clearly emerges from the original documents and testimonies.

It is not easy to gain access to the documents, simply because the authorities of the Kimbanguist Church are still (doubtless with good reason) somewhat distrustful; so we cannot reproach most of those who have written about Simon Kimbangu until now. Without access to the sources, they had to base what they wrote partly on unreliable reports which ascribe various traits and occurrences to Simon Kimbangu instead of to one of the many *bangunza*, whom we shall discuss later.

(b) Simon Kimbangu's Early Youth

The name Kimbangu has, as is true of most African names, deep significance. We were told that the word 'kimbangu' was shouted out at the birth of a child when the newborn infant would not breathe. The family of Kimbangu has subsequently translated the name as *celui qui révèle ce qui est caché*, 'the one who reveals what is hidden'. Kimbangu is said to have been given the name because he was one of these still-born babies who was called to life through shouting this name. The expectation of great things was attached to this miracle. H. J. Casebow in England, who spent more than thirty years as a missionary in Zaïre and is very conversant with the Kikongo language, believes that we have here a case of later interpretation since 'kimbangu' means, from what he knows of the language, 'skill' (this theory of Casebow's is, however, contested). Simon is his Christian name.

Soon after his birth in 1889 he was blessed by a Baptist missionary. His mother Lwezi had died shortly after his birth, and his father Kuyela also died when Simon was still a child. He was brought up by his aunt Kinzembo, the youngest sister of his mother.

Simon Kimbangu's secretaries tell[13] how one day a white man (Mr Comber, the missionary mentioned in the last chapter) appeared in N'Kamba; N'Kamba is situated in the district of Thysville (today Mbanza-Ngungu). Everyone fled, except Kinzembo, to whom the missionary Mr Comber is supposed to have said, 'Peace be with you.

[13] Document secret, Annexe 3, 'Histoire de l'apparition du prophète Simon Kimbangu'.

Those who fled will not have peace.' Comber's successor, the missionary Cameron Nzangamane (the second name was given him by the Zaïrians and means 'the tall' or 'the giant') also came one day to N'Kamba. The inhabitants of the place did not want to give him any water. He went to Kinzembo and asked to see her child (so Simon Kimbangu's secretary tells us), but because the father was not there she could not show him the boy. Cameron came a second time to her. His third visit almost cost him his life. He was followed and shot at. He fled to Kinzembo, who gave him something to eat and drink. Then he prayed with her, and finally he said, 'God's blessing be with you and your children. Your faith has helped you.' R. H. C. Graham, a missionary of the British Baptist mission in São Salvador, wrote in a report on the 'Prophetic Movement'[14] the following about this very episode: 'Kimbangu is the son of a woman who in the beginning of our work in that district, when practically everybody was bitterly antagonistic to it, gave Mr Cameron a drink of water and showed sympathy although nobody else would have anything to do with him. The "prophet" was then a baby in his mother's arms' (as we have seen, it was his aunt). According to Kinzembo, 'Mr Cameron prayed for a blessing on her child (Simon Kimbangu) as he thanked her for the drink she had given him. The man (Kimbangu) thinks that probably on account of this (blessing) he has since had a dream or vision and been appointed by Christ as a prophet of these people, with power to heal the sick.' In African as in Hebrew thought, words of blessing and cursing are indeed words of power. This incident took place in 1889 or 1890. The simple version of Graham seems to be the more authentic.

According to another tradition, Cameron's visit took place as early as 1885; he blessed Kinzembo with the promise that her daughter would bear a child who was destined for great things. This seems to be legendary, also because Kinzembo would then have been Kimbangu's grandmother when she was in fact his aunt.

3. HIS CONVERSION

Kimbangu became a Christian as a young man. He received instruction and was baptized, along with his wife Mivilu Marie and his later fellow-worker Mikala Mandombe and others, in the river Tombe, which flows past Ngombe-Lutete. That was in July 1915. His marriage, which had been contracted according to customary

---

[14] Baptist Herald, BMS, October 1921, Vol. 103.

law was now solemnized in church.[15] For a short time he was a teacher at the mission school in Ngombe-Lutete.[16] His missionary describes him as of above average intelligence, a strong personality and a man with a good knowledge of the Bible.[17] For a time, he was also an evangelist in the village of N'Kamba, some 20 km. away. The missionaries described him as a good and thoughtful man who read his Bible and performed his tasks conscientiously.[17]

4. KIMBANGU'S CALL TO BE A PREACHER AND HEALER

One night in 1918, whilst the 'flu epidemic was raging in Zaïre, as in so many other parts of the world, when thousands were dying without medical relief and the doctor, who had been promised by the mission, did not arrive in Ngombe-Lutete, Simon Kimbangu heard a voice saying to him, 'I am Christ, My servants are unfaithful. I have chosen you to bear witness before your brethren and to convert them. Tend My flock.' Simon replied, 'I am not trained and there are ministers and deacons who are able to serve in this way.'[18a] But night after night Simon Kimbangu heard the same voice calling him, and his wife heard him answer.

Again and again he declined to follow this call. At length he tried to run away from the call of Christ by going to the city of Kinshasa (at that time Léopoldville), which was 225 km. away, and he became a labourer. He worked in various places, including an oil-refinery. However, even in Kinshasa the voice of Christ reached him. Despite his faithfulness and honest work, he had no success and was ultimately compelled to return to N'Kamba and cultivate his fields again as he had done before. Today the banana trees he planted and his manioc fields can be seen at the foot of the hill on which N'Kamba is situated. Was the failure in Kinshasa a sign that God would no longer let him go?

---

[15] There is some uncertainty about the date of the Church-marriage; it may have taken place before adult-baptism.

[16] Letter from the missionary Thomas to missionary HQ in England, 30 June 1921.

[17] Letter from the missionary Thomas to missionary HQ in England, 7 October 1921.

[18] C.R.I.S.P. (Centre de Recherche et d'Information Socio-Politique), Brussels, No. 47, 8 January 1960, 'Le Kimbanguisme', p. 5.

[18a] From a private letter from Joseph Diangienda.

5. THE FIRST MIRACLE: THE HEALING OF NKIANTONDO

On the morning of 6 April 1921 (which is regarded today as the date of the foundation of the church) Simon went to market and passed through Ngombe-Kinsuka, the neighbouring village on the hill opposite N'Kamba. As if against his will he entered the house of a woman called Nkiantondo, who was critically ill in bed. He laid his hands on her and healed her in the Name of Jesus Christ. The woman got up and was cured, but she accused Simon Kimbangu, 'You've just come to remove the curse which you'd put on me.'[19] That was to be expected, and is in keeping with the African way of seeing things. Illness is the result of *kindoki* (witchcraft); or it is occasioned by a curse, or as punishment from neglected ancestors from whom offerings have been withheld. Simon, a Christian, firmly repudiated the accusation.

As he was going away from the house he met Nkiantondo's husband, who asks him whether he knows any plants which could heal his wife. 'I told him that he didn't need to look any further for medicines, seeing his wife had received more than these. When I arrived at the river I met the evangelist, who was washing his feet. I said to him, "Go into your village where you preach, for a miracle has taken place there. Unspiritual people say that I'm mad, but you know the illness with which she was afflicted. She's better."'[20]

6. FURTHER HEALINGS

The second miracle is the raising to life of a child, which strikes us as dramatic. This was a child called Mafuta, a twin child, whose death, according to Kikongo tradition, could not be mourned, so that the surviving child would not be troubled. 'Bring me the coffin,' Simon Kimbangu ordered. They hesitated. Finally Nfinangani understood his intentions and brought the small coffin with the child. Simon spoke in tongues (*'je parlais une langue étrangère'*); the little child in the coffin began to cry. Then Simon heard the command of God: 'Withdraw now, and then ask the father and the mother what they are thinking concerning the child!'—'Are you sad because of your child?' Simon asked the parents. The mother replied,

[19] This scene is very impressively presented by the theatre group in the service each anniversary on 6 April, in N'Kamba.

[20] Document secret, Annexe 3, 'Histoire de l'apparition du prophète Simon Kimbangu', Suite 2.

'No. I'm not sad.' Possibly she wanted to conform to what custom required. However, the father replied, 'I'm sad about my child.'—'Because of the answer of the mother my power went from me,' Simon confessed ('*mes forces s'évanouirent*'). 'I told them to withdraw. They buried the child. God forbade me to go to the cemetery, because they had refused to believe in the power of God.'[21]

In the tradition which is passed on today by word of mouth there is a repetition of events: the child was raised a second time, died again and finally remained dead because of the unbelief of the mother. It seems that we have here, as far as religious studies are concerned, a particularly clear break with tradition: either there is an acceptance of the fact of the death of one of the twins without grief and thus the surviving child is spared, or the power of God is trusted to accomplish all things.

The people began to fear Simon Kimbangu and avoided him at first, considering him a witch-doctor. But he always answered, 'It's Christ who has performed these miracles through me. I've no power to do these of myself.' He thus firmly repudiated the suggestion that he used magic charms. He was concerned solely and completely with Christ, whose instrument he knew himself to be.

Finally, there was a change. Further healings of sick people convinced many that God was at work and wanted to do great things for his people. The people began to flock as pilgrims to N'Kamba to seek healing. We learn from Kimbangu's secretaries[22] the story of a paralytic called Matubuka who said to Kimbangu, 'I've come to you, prophet of God, to be healed.' Simon answered him, 'In the Name of Christ, arise.' The man got up. Another called Ngoma was blind. The prophet asked him, 'What do you want?' He replied, 'I want to be able to see.' The prophet spat on the ground, formed a paste of the soil and saliva, anointed the eyes of the blind man with it and sent him to the spring in N'Kamba to wash there. When he did this he received his sight and glorified God. Today the sacred spring in N'Kamba is still used. The healing of a deaf man followed, then of a cripple called Thomas from Lombo. His mother brought him and laid him at the prophet's feet. 'What do you want me to do for your child?' the prophet asked. 'I want him to be able to walk,' the woman answered. The prophet spoke to the child, 'In the Name of Jesus Christ, stand up and walk.' The child arose and was able to stand and walk. In Kinshasa I met a man called Alphonse Kiabelwa who was raised to life again by Simon Kimbangu as a seven-year-old child. Mandombe Mikala and Pierre Ndangi remember

[21] Document secret, Annexe 3, Suite 3.
[22] Op. cit., Suite 5.

vividly this event from early on in Simon Kimbangu's ministry in N'Kamba.

Did all the healings really happen as they are told by Kimbangu's secretaries and by eye-witnesses? Those eye-witnesses who are still alive confirm unanimously that extraordinary and miraculous things took place. They have no doubt that God Himself showed His power and love. The healings of which we were told are sometimes almost verbal parallels with the healings of Jesus and the apostles in the New Testament. Simon Kimbangu and those who spoke of him were obviously concerned to show that God was now revealing His power in the heart of Africa. We could speak of an imitation of Christ and the apostles. However, the purpose of this imitation was not to replace Christ by a new healer-messiah but to remain within the bounds set by the New Testament. We shall return later on to the fact that Simon Kimbangu's ministry, life and sufferings are seen again and again in terms of the ministry, life and sufferings of Jesus and His disciples. This is a fact which also strikes us with respect to other prophetic movements in Africa.[23]

7. N'KAMBA PENTECOST

As far as the followers of Kimbangu were concerned, nothing less than a new Pentecost had come. The Holy Spirit had evidently descended on Simon Kimbangu and had given him authority to heal and to preach. A wood-carving, which was given us, shows Simon Kimbangu praying and the Spirit of God descending upon him in the form of a dove. The conviction of the church that Simon preached and healed in the power of the Spirit is so strong that often to the trinitarian formula 'In the Name of the Father, and of the Son, and of the Holy Spirit' is added 'who descended upon Simon Kimbangu' or 'who has spoken to us through Simon Kimbangu'. That does not mean, as has already been asserted,[24] that Simon Kimbangu replaced the person of the Holy Spirit in the minds of his followers, but simply that he was the instrument of the Holy Spirit.

The events in N'Kamba were seen as a re-enactment of the life and sufferings of Christ: Christ had appeared through Kimbangu in Zaïre. Thus he demonstrates in a tangible way that he is the Saviour

[23] M.-L. Martin: 'Walter Matitta and His Moshoeshoe Church in Lesotho', a still unpublished manuscript.

[24] D. Buana-Kibongi: 'L'évolution du Kimbanguisme', Flambeau No. 10, Yaoundé, 1966.

from sin and Satan, but also from disease and suffering—not only the Saviour of the soul but also of the body. Like the Hebrews, the Africans are concerned with the redemption of the whole man. Salvation includes healing and sanctification.

Here was an outpouring of the Holy Spirit in the middle of Africa, and N'Kamba became the 'new Jerusalem'—just as the places of other prophetic healers in Africa have become the new Jerusalem, a pledge of the idea that Christ is the living Lord, yesterday and today and for ever.

8. SIMON KIMBANGU'S PREACHING

Simon did not only heal. He also preached. Unfortunately, little about the content of his sermons has been preserved for us, but it is possible that the material which was hidden in the forests during the forty years of persecution will one day come to light and give us more knowledge of the content of his sermons. His preaching and healing ministry was indeed only very brief. He preached that fetishes should be cast aside and trust should be placed in God alone. It is reported that along the roads that led to N'Kamba discarded fetishes were found everywhere. Did he replace them with a 'more powerful' fetish? We know nothing of such. He was concerned with faith in Christ and with repentance. It is possible that people who came to him placed their trust in the prophet or in the blessed water of N'Kamba. But that was not Simon's intention. He warned his followers not to take part in the dances of the non-Christians, which led to debauchery and lewdness, and he emphasized purity of morals and monogamy.[25] The church adheres strictly to these rules, even today in urban life. 'How can a man live in peace and find inner quiet and freedom for prayer if he is living in polygamy, which always leads to difficulties and tensions in a household?' Joseph Diangienda, the youngest son of Kimbangu, answered when I asked him why the church insists so strongly on monogamy. I asked this question because in important African independent churches in the south, for instance in the churches of Lekganyane and Shembe, polygamy is permitted. Admittedly it is today no longer practised by many for economic reasons. Kimbangu also taught obedience to

[25] 'Dès les débuts de sa mission les observateurs doivent reconnaître qu'il réussit là où bien d'autres échouent, dans la lutte contre la polygamie, l'abus des boissons alcooliques, les danses licencieuses', quotation from A. Doutreloux in 'prophétisme et "Leadership" dans la société Congo', in 'Devant les sectes non-chrétiennes', Louvain, 1961, p. 71.

The Early History of Simon Kimbangu

those in authority and love of one's enemies—repayment of evil with good—which is surprising when we think of the great injustices meted out to the blacks by the white colonial authorities. He expressly included the whites in these ethical rules of life. He preached in the general Christian way that man was created as God's good creature but was depraved by the Fall and can only be saved by the sacrifice of the one Redeemer, Jesus Christ, through faith in Him. He clung to the belief that this redemption of Christ was available to all men as a free gift through faith, for whites and blacks, inasmuch as they remained in fellowship with Christ.[26] We stress this because again and again it is said, even today (in a history book published in Nigeria and used at universities), that in Zaïre Simon Kimbangu launched an anti-whites movement.[27] We quote a prayer of Simon Kimbangu, which he is supposed to have prayed every day (although it may come from a somewhat later period, it shows that he had no hatred for foreigners): 'I thank Thee, Almighty God, Maker of heaven and earth. The heaven is Thy throne and the earth is Thy footstool. Thy will be done on earth as it is in heaven. Bless all peoples of the earth, great and small, men and women, whites and blacks. May the blessing of heaven fall on the whole world so that we all might enter heaven. We pray to Thee trusting that Thou dost receive us, in the Name of Jesus Christ our Saviour. Amen.'[28]

Simon Kimbangu never claimed to heal all those who were brought to him. More and more he asked about faith and repentance, like Johann Christoph Blumhardt in Bad Boll. He was not concerned only with healing but with sanctification of the whole man.

9. SURVEY AND REACTION

Simon Kimbangu and the movement he called forth represents the Christian African reaction against colonization and evangelization. This was not a reaction *against* missionary work. On the contrary: in retrospect, missions might be very grateful that through their preaching and above all through their translation of the Bible this fruit ripened on their tree. Admittedly, it was a movement which had not been expected and which was soon to spread beyond the

[26] From a private letter from Joseph Diangienda, based on reports of eye-witnesses.
[27] 'Africa in the 19th and 20th Centuries', ed. J. C. Anene/G. Brown, Ibadan University, 196, p. 143.
[28] From the Kimbanguist document 'Mise au point', 1957, not published.

narrow frontiers of the Protestant missionary area drawn up by the *colonial administration*. Moreover, there were manifestations which were known only from apostolic times and with which people no longer reckoned. The Africans were experiencing Christ in a tangible way as he shared their troubles, lived with them, and revealed himself as Conqueror. Now they could really believe in him. Sundker[29] of the Shembe Church in Natal writes: What Jesus once did to redeem the Jews in Palestine is re-enacted and made tangible through Shembe in his sacred city of Ekuphakameni among the Zulus. The same is true of N'Kamba. It was a matter of revelation of Christ here and now. By this is not meant a continuous revelation since Christ. That would be a dangerous way of putting things, because it was not a matter of a new revelation but of making the once-and-for-all revelation in Christ present and concrete at that time. 'It is Christ—comprehended, displayed concretely, going ahead and continuing His work—from whom we can learn.'[30] This holds for Simon Kimbangu, as well as for many a church founder and 'messiah' in southern Africa. It is a matter of redemption, the cross and resurrection, the outpouring of the Holy Spirit *here* and *now*, on African soil, not only long ago in Palestine. 'Jerusalem' epitomizes the whole work of redemption. Thus, N'Kamba became the new Jerusalem.

Is this heresy or superstition? Is not rather something emerging here and is not biblical revelation coming alive here in a way which could help us as well in intellectualized Europe? To be sure, it might lead to a new messianism, and in Lower Zaïre there was an upsurge of chiliastic and messianic groups which for the most part looked to Simon Kimbangu; but they were neither recognized by Kimbangu himself nor by his loyal followers. A sharp distinction must be drawn between these groups and the movement which Simon Kimbangu called into being. In the case of Kimbangu, it was a matter of Christ, the Christ of the Bible, whom he understood in his simple way and proclaimed after long hesitation and who is still preached today in the 'Church of Jesus Christ on Earth through the Prophet Simon Kimbangu' in song, word, social aid, and faith-healing.

The healings were admittedly questioned by some missionaries. R. L. Jennings, a missionary in Mbanza-Ngungu, had at that time the supervision of the region of Ngombe-Lutete (Wathen), to which N'Kamba belonged, because his fellow-missionary Hillard had only been in Zaïre for a short while. He reported to London that he had

[29] B. Sundkler: 'Bantu Prophets in South Africa', 2nd edn, London, 1961, p. 284.

[30] D. Sölle: 'Phantasie und Gehorsam', Stuttgart, 1968, p. 8.

The Early History of Simon Kimbangu

summoned Kimbangu to Ngombe-Lutete as early as April. 'But he was obsessed by the idea that God had chosen him for this ministry of healing.'[31] Jennings wrote to the other Protestant missions in Lower Zaïre:[32] 'On 17 May my colleague Hillard and I went to N'Kamba to see for ourselves what was happening. We were unable to observe a single miracle. Many came to be healed but many more came to the prophet to receive his blessing.' Jennings gave the urgent advice: 'Keep your folk away from here!'

Is it surprising that the Zaïrians were disappointed by their missionaries' attitude?

In a letter from Mbanza-Ngungu Thomas, a missionary, writes: 'Kimbangu is not seeking any material gain but is healing in the Name of Jesus. All our deacons here in Wathen accept all Kimbangu's claims without questioning. They told us, "You're sceptical because he's black." '[33] Were they perhaps right? On the tree of missionary work a fruit had suddenly matured which had not been anticipated... And yet the missionaries had to admit, as emerges in the same letter, that a new interest in the Word of God had arisen in the whole district. 'Our village chapels filled whilst the Catholic chapels emptied. From everywhere requests came for teachers and school materials; in three months we sold about five hundred hymnbooks.' Graham wrote in the missionary report mentioned above: 'So it seems to me that this is the most remarkable movement which the country has ever seen. The prophets only seem to have one goal—the proclamation of the Gospel.' He was thinking of Kimbangu as well as his helpers. 'I am every day receiving letters from our Zaïrian members and adherents telling of wonderful cures they themselves have witnessed, and begging us not to doubt them, for they are all of God, and are the means of bringing hundreds of hitherto careless people within the sound of the Gospel... many of our old members speak of it as a great spiritual uplift and revival.' We shall see in Chapter 9 that we have a similar missionary report from Boko, dating from the early period of the Kimbanguist Movement.

[31] Letter from the missionary R. L. Jennings, Thysville, 18 June 1921.
[32] Letter from the missionary Jennings, 19 May 1921.
[33] Letter from the missionary Thomas, Mbanza-Ngungu, 30 June 1921.

CHAPTER 5

GRIEVANCES AGAINST SIMON KIMBANGU: INTERROGATION, FLIGHT AND ARREST

1: SUSPICION AND ACCUSATIONS

Hundreds of people undertook pilgrimages to N'Kamba. They left their work as kitchen and garden boys for the whites, or their forced labour in the plantations, and made their way as pilgrims to Simon Kimbangu, which aroused the suspicion of the whites. A few days after the first healing, news of the healer-prophet spread, with the result that the people set out to see him and to receive his aid. Already on 26 April 1921 the administrator of the district capital Mbanza-Ngungu, L. Morel, told his superiors that a certain Simon Kimbangu in N'Kamba was claiming to have received the gift of healing the sick. He was laying his hands on them and uttering texts of Scripture. He was not handing out medicines and was not accepting payment for his services.[1] Undoubtedly, complaints had been voiced on the part of those who woke up one morning to discover that their messengers and workers had disappeared and gone to N'Kamba. Immediately, the white settlers thought that a revolt was brewing. Indeed, a year earlier a rebellion had broken out in Sankuru, as was mentioned above.

We possess the report which the administrator Léon Morel wrote to his superiors. In it he tells of his uneasiness with regard to the *illuminé* (enlightened one) of N'Kamba. 'From far and wide (*de toutes les régions*) people are making pilgrimages to him and bringing their sick with them.' Morel, who adopts a critical attitude towards Kimbangu in his report, writes: 'No serious-minded person has been able to observe a single healing as yet, but the natives believe in the blindest fashion that he can heal.' Nevertheless, Morel admits that Simon Kimbangu is inspired by the Bible and knows

[1] Documents secrets (belges), chap. 1, p. 2; Annexe 1: Lettre de L. Morel au Commissaire du district, 26 avril 1921.

it thoroughly. He comes to the conclusion in his report that Kimbangu is not guilty of any crime, but he sees two dangers. Did Simon Kimbangu want to found a new church? Or was he seeking such popularity that he would later be able to organize a rebellion against the colonial administration? In the same report Morel mentioned how he had asked the Protestant missionaries to be of help by keeping him fully informed about the 'visionary'. They assured him, so he claims, that they had disassociated themselves from Kimbangu: This remark of Morel's does not correspond to the facts, as source material in London clearly shows.

The second danger which Morel mentioned was the possibility of an epidemic caused by the great gatherings of the people and the presence of sick folk in N'Kamba. In his report he advised against the arrest of Simon Kimbangu because such a measure would only increase his standing. But he suggested that Simon Kimbangu be invited to Mbanza-Ngungu, where he would have him taken to hospital for observation and kept under surveillance so that no one would have access to him.

2. MOREL'S VISIT TO N'KAMBA

Léon Morel's superiors told him to go to N'Kamba to investigate the matter on the spot. On 11 May he arrived in N'Kamba from Ngungu, having covered a distance of about 70 km. In his report of 17 May (only six weeks after the first healing) Morel tells us[2] that, as he was approaching the village, Simon Kimbangu with a group of loyal followers came out to meet him with a staff in his hand. The staff is significant, as Prof. Wyatt MacGaffey has shown in an article,[3] for it represents prophetic or regal authority. Pierre Ndangi (Kimbangu's fellow-worker) verified this in a conversation with me, calling it a sign of rule or authority. The chief's staff, for instance, is equivalent to the chief himself. The chief or prophet can be called 'staff' (*mvwala* in Kikongo). The document[4] which Simon Kimbangu's secretaries drew up contains the same information, only it adds that Simon Kimbangu had had a vision at night several days before in which God commanded him, 'Arise and pray,

[2] Documents secrets: rapport d'enquête administrative sur les faits et incidents de Kamba (sic!), chefferie du Zundu.

[3] Wyatt MacGaffey: 'The Belovèd City, Commentary on a Kimbanguist Text', Journal of Religion in Africa, Leiden, 1969, pp. 129 ff.

[4] Documents secrets: Annexe 3: 'Histoire de l'apparition du prophète Simon Kimbangu', Suite 9.

your enemies are on their way to inflict suffering upon you and to kill you.' Upon this, Morel came. Simon Kimbangu went out to meet him. Pierre Ndangi, who is still ministering today as an assistant and healer, followed him. He commanded the soldier, who had come on ahead of Morel, to throw down his rifle. He did so and fell on his knees before Simon Kimbangu.

Suddenly Simon realized (so the document continues) that he had left his staff at home. He returned and came back with his four assistants (*bansadisi* in Kikongo)—Mikala Mandombe, from whom I learnt details, and Telezi (Thérèse) Mbonga, as well as the principal evangelist and the writer of the report. The fact that he fetched his staff shows that he wanted to meet the 'enemy' with prophetic authority. To the African mind, abstract concepts are made concrete and visible—in this case, in the prophetic staff. The material realm is made part and parcel of the intellectual and spiritual life.

Armed with the sign of his prophetic authority, the prophet asked the soldier, 'Have you come to fight against God?' Then he went aside and prayed. Just then Morel appeared on the hill. The prophet and his five companions sensed the Spirit of God taking control of them and they spoke in 'heavenly tongues', lifting up their voices. Morel comments in his report: 'Simon and his companions, among them two young girls, were excited and trembling and uttered unintelligible sounds' ('*des cris bizarres*'). 'I tried in vain to talk to them.'

Then Morel went to N'Kamba and pitched his tent near Kimbangu's house. Simon Kimbangu took his Bible and, according to the account of his secretaries, read a psalm to Morel—Morel himself reported that Kimbangu read him the story of David and Goliath, which must have had great significance in this situation for Kimbangu and his followers. Just as David triumphed over the giant Goliath in the Name of the Lord, the prophet would triumph over his enemy with God's help. Pierre Ndangi, who recalled this day clearly, explained that Simon Kimbangu read Isaiah 24 and Psalm 23 and Mikala Mandombe read the story of Goliath.

When Morel tried to interrogate the prophet the latter replied that he (Kimbangu) must first pray, and in prayer the assurance is given him that, in accordance with Matthew 10, not he but the Holy Spirit will speak and answer.

Whilst Kimbangu had withdrawn to pray, an uproar broke out. Both documents mention the fact that just at this moment false prophets *bangunza* arrived. They were dismissed by Kimbangu as 'prophets of the Evil One'. The document of Kimbangu's secretaries comments that the prophetess Telezi Mbonga was the first person to acquire the ability to distinguish between false and true prophets, i.e. between those who were doing the work of Christ and such as were seeking their own glory and tried to cover themselves by using the name of Kimbangu.

It is significant for the later development of Kimbangu's movement and the prophetic messianic movements in Zaïre that from the beginning there was this—conflict and distinction between them—a fact which has been too little heeded in literature until now. We must therefore re-emphasise the difference between the two movements which often show externally similar characteristics (ecstasy, speaking in tongues, healing of the sick through prayer) but which at bottom are, from the point of view of the Gospel, going different ways. Mr Thomas, a missionary, also mentions the false prophets in one of his letters:[5] 'Some think being a prophet is financially profitable. In the whole district prophets emerged and rumours reached Administrator Morel that they were telling the people not to pay any more taxes. Admittedly there is no proof of this.' Andersson as well mentions people who after, or even during, their pilgrimage to N'Kamba received the call to 'prophecy'.[6]

After he had 'dealt' with the false prophets, Simon Kimbangu returned to Morel. But when the admistrator tried to question him, Simon and his companions were seized afresh by the Spirit and spoke in tongues. Simon shouted out, I'm not afraid of 10,000 men. God, protect me from my enemies. Help me, oh, help me!' Morel reported, 'I tried in vain to interrogate Kimbangu.'

Simon Kimbangu and hundreds of his followers spent the whole night singing hymns (such hymns became one of the main features of the Kimbanguist Movement, as they are still—faith being expressed in music and art and not in theological formulations). Morel wanted to sleep and asked them to stop singing, but they continued. Thus Morel came to the conclusion that Simon Kimbangu was not quite in possession of his senses—just as the Jews in Jerusalem at Pentecost said something of the kind about the apostles, who were speaking in tongues.[7] We twentieth-century Europeans may think the same of a Pentecostal service in Africa or services in one of the many Zionist churches in South Africa in which, at a certain point, the whole congregation joins in prayer leading to ecstasy. The question is simply whether we can apply here our sober Western standards. If we do, what are we then going to do with the Old

[5] Letter from the missionary Thomas to England, 30 June 1921.
[6] E. Andersson: 'Messianic Popular Movements in the Lower Congo' Uppsala, 1958, p. 58.
[7] Acts 2:4 and 2:13.

Testament prophets like Samuel, or with Elisha who used music to put himself into a trance,[8] or with Ezekiel and his apparently pathological conditions? What are we going to do with Paul who was caught up into the third heaven and also spoke in tongues?[9] We can attempt to explain such phenomena in psychological terms. In the case of Kimbangu we can point out the enormous tensions occasioned by colonial authority and missionary activity. All these factors must be taken into account. But is that all there is to it? Can we not, like the Kimbanguists, reckon with a real outpouring of the Holy Spirit whereby miracles occurred? Could not such miracles call forth such joy as well as spiritual release that ecstasy with trembling and speaking in tongues cannot simply be brushed aside as 'pathological'? Did not something similar happen among George Fox's Quakers in the seventeenth century in England, to give just one example? Certainly such phenomena are called forth not only by the Holy Spirit. There are also other spirits, and therefore the biblical exhortation to soberness and discernment of the spirits is fitting as well as the other exhortation of the apostle Paul not to quench the Spirit.[10]

Unfortunately, Protestant missionaries in Ngombe-Lutete were unable to view the phenomenon in this way, just as the missionaries in South Africa were unable at first to understand the upsurge of prophetic movements. They convinced Morel that Simon's ecstasy was an exact reproduction of that of the witch-doctors. Indeed, we can observe in the various regions of Africa how ecstasy occurs among non-Christians and Christians alike, as well as in the nationalist syncretistic movements in which Christian elements are integrated into traditional African religion. I had the opportunity to observe this phenomenon in all three groups. The crucial thing is ultimately not the phenomenon itself but the faith which is expressed in it. Is it faith in Jesus Christ, as expressed in the Gospels and Paul, or is it faith in some supernatural power, in a 'deity', or is it faith in being gripped by ancestral spirits? The answer to this question is crucial. These phenomena of ecstasy give rise so easily to misinterpretation, and believers themselves can be led astray. In Zaïre itself, the *bangunza* movement outside Kimbanguism cultivated ecstasy in particular and still emphasizes it today. Thus, ecstasy and speaking in tongues are not forbidden in the 'Church of Christ on Earth through the Prophet Simon Kimbangu', but their use is, however, severely restricted.

[8] 2 Kings 3:15–16.
[9] 1 Cor. 14:18–19; 2 Cor. 12:2.
[10] 1 Thess. 5:19.

Morel came to the conclusion that under the influence of what he called 'religious fanaticism' in N'Kamba certain psychosomatic illnesses really were cured or sick people experienced relief. He added (and this seems to me to be important as far as the theology of missions is concerned though Morel meant it negatively): 'Kimbangu wants to found a religion which is in accord with the mentality of the African, a religion which contains the characteristics of Protestantism but with the addition of practices (*pratiques*) taken from fetishism.'[11] In the usage of that time, African traditional religion as such was frequently referred to as 'fetishism'. 'Everyone can readily see', wrote Morel, 'that the religions of Europe are completely shot through with abstractions and in no way correspond to the mentality of the African, who longs for tangible facts and protection. The teaching of Kimbangu suits him because it is supported by palpable facts.' How right Morel was, but the time had not yet come to view this insight positively! He continued, 'It is therefore necessary to oppose Kimbangu since he has a tendency towards pan-Africanism.' The natives will say, 'We have found the God of the blacks, the religion which suits the African.' Is the drama of Donna Béatrice to repeat itself?

When Morel left N'Kamba again after a few days he went to the Baptists and received from them the assurance that they would do their utmost in the struggle against Kimbangu's movement, for 'Kimbangu's religion is basically a parody of theirs.' Did the Baptists really give this assurance? It is a fact that they were by and large disturbed because the Catholics and white planters accused them of having caused the movement. However, in a letter[12] the missionaries Jennings and Hillard warned Morel against premature arrest and asked for deferment. A further letter confirms that Morel invited them to Mbanza-Ngungu, together with Father van Cleemput and the Vice-Provincial of the Redemptorists for talks.[13]

3. THE FLIGHT OF KIMBANGU

Kimbangu had chosen, besides those already mentioned, further assistants. Paul Monika proved to be a false teacher. Simon Kimbangu was angry when Monika taught that he was 'the vine', and he and others were dismissed. Another, André Mbaki, had begun his

[11] Documents secrets, Suite 4.
[12] Letter from the missionaries Jennings and Hillard to L. Morel, 16 May 1921.
[13] Letter from the missionaries Jennings and Hillard, 20 May 1921.

ministry under a false pretext and was excommunicated.[14] It is important to bear this in mind.

At this same time Thomas N'Twalani joined Kimbangu as an assistant.[15] We mention him particularly because his followers were true to him even after his death in exile, and they joined the 'Church of Jesus Christ on Earth through the Prophet Simon Kimbangu' after its official recognition by the state, but broke away from it again in 1963 to form their own church, the 'Mission N'Twalaniste', which was also called the 'Church of the Two Witnesses, Simon Kimbangu and Thomas N'Twalani'. This was banned in June 1968 for political reasons. In April 1970 a large number of its adherents returned to the Kimbanguist Church. N'Twalani himself remained loyal till his death in exile.[15a] The report of the secretaries of Kimbangu mentions numerous false prophets who wanted to enter the service of Kimbangu but who were turned away.

Genuine and would-be prophets of Kimbangu spread the movement so rapidly in May 1921 that the Belgian administration began to be afraid. On 1 June 1921 it called a meeting of the leaders of the Catholic and Protestant missions in Mbanza-Ngungu to repudiate Kimbangu and other prophetic movements. In the Belgian documents there is special reference to the insistence on the immediate arrest of Kimbangu by one of the Catholic missionaries. The Protestants hesitated, wishing to dispel the movement not by force but by persuasion. The Belgian administration agreed with the Catholics, who wanted to intervene immediately because they were afraid that Kimbanguism could turn into a political movement.[16] On 2 June the District Commissioner ordered that Kimbangu and his four assistants be arrested without delay.[17] It was still his intention to put Kimbangu in hospital in Boma, the port on the Zaïre estuary.

On 6 June, Morel went for a second time to N'Kamba, this time with soldiers, in order to arrest Kimbangu and his four assistants. A skirmish took place. Morel's account speaks of an attack on the part of the followers of the prophet, which endangered his soldiers and himself finally prompting him to hand out ammunition. In the skirmish a child was killed.[18] Since Kimbangu's secretary Nfinangani

---

[14] Documents secrets, Annexe 3, 'Histoire de l'apparition du prophète Simon Kimbangu', Suite 12.   [15] Op. cit., Suite 13.

[15a] While this book was being printed, NTwalaui's son Kiamusi, the man who had caused the secession, returned at Christmas 1973 to the Kimbanguist Church and got reconciled to its spiritual head Diangienda.

[16] Documents secrets, p. 7.   [17] Op. cit., p. 5.

[18] Documents secrets, Annexe 4, Lettre de L. Morel au Substitut Procureur du Roi à Boma, 6 June 1921.

was also arrested, his account breaks off before these events. Mikala Mandombe, whom I questioned about what happened, accuses Morel's soldiers of brutal action in the course of which Zaïrians in colonial service took the side of the followers of Kimbangu. This eye-witness account agrees with the report of Mr Jennings, in which the missionary wrote: 'Our Christians confirm that the crowd was not hostile towards Morel but Morel's soldiers hit out with their rifle butts. Through their action two soldiers and a woman were injured and a child was killed by a soldier.'[19]

In the general confusion the prophet and his assistants, along with his seven-year-old son Charles Kisolokele, managed to escape. The Kimbanguists still regard this flight as a miracle. Kimbangu went to Mbanza-Nsanda where he stayed for three months and from where he apparently went on a number of secret presumably shortish evangelistic tours.

During his stay in Mbanza-Nsanda, Kimbangu, so Mikala Mandombe tells us, gave instruction to his assistants and the twelve apostles whom he called. Not all the twelve remained subsequently loyal. It was a time of great deprivations; they had to remain in hiding. They were often short of food, and had to sleep in the open at night. (The report that during these three months Kimbangu went as far as Kinkole on the shores of Stanley Pool—now Lake Malebo—seems to be unfounded, though it is probable that he visited local and more distant places from Mbanza-Nsanda.)

During these three months the Belgian administration tried in vain to gain information from the Zaïrians about Kimbangu's whereabouts. There was an uncanny silence. People were arrested and interrogated. An élite group of natives, principally Protestants, was accused of preparing and leading the movement, and the Protestant missionaries were unable to gain permission to visit those under arrest. Rumours were heard that the Zaïrian railway workers would go on strike if Kimbangu was arrested. A letter of the Belgian administration of 6 July reported that numerous children had left the Protestant mission of Ngombe-Lutete.[20] A further letter of 23 July recounted that new Kimbanguist groups had arisen as far up river as Kinshasa.[21] Confirmation of this is found in the Annual Report of the Baptist Missionary Society, which was completed in March 1922. In the districts of Mbanza-Ngungu and Luozi many arrests were made, whether of followers of Kimbangu, of Protestants or supporters of other prophetic movements is not clear, but in the

[19] Letter from the missionary Jennings to missionary HQ in England, 18 June 1921.
[20] Documents secrets, p. 8.   [21] Op. cit., p. 9.

eyes of the Belgian administration all blame was laid at the door of Simon Kimbangu. Finally on 12 August a state of emergency (*régime militaire mitigé*) was declared in the districts of Mbanza-Ngungu and Luozi.[22]

Also in August, the missionaries H. Ross Phillips and Lawson Forfeitt went to Brussels to make a request of the Belgian colonial minister to treat the prophetic movement in a wise and benevolent way.[23]

4. THE RETURN OF SIMON KIMBANGU TO N'KAMBA AND HIS ARREST

In September Simon Kimbangu heard God's voice saying to him, 'Return to N'Kamba to be arrested.' He tells his followers in Mbanza-Nsanda that his hour has come. They try to restrain him but Kimbangu obeys the voice of God.[24] This is reminiscent of the words of Jesus and His readiness to undergo His passion. It can be assumed that Kimbangu felt constrained to re-enact in this way the passion story without, however, posing himself as the Son of God. J. Chomé has depicted the whole episode of the persecution, arrest and sentence of Kimbangu as a parallel to the passion of Jesus, with the inclusion of the traitor Judas, namely Romain Nkaya, who is supposed to have betrayed the prophet in Kinkole to the Scheut Father Pollé, though this episode is not supported by the facts.[25]

Kimbangu returned on 12 September 1921 to N'Kamba. He gave himself up voluntarily to the military after exhorting his followers to face suffering courageously, not to use violence and not to repay evil with evil. Those who were not able to do this should go away. The refusal to use force within the Kimbanguist Church presumably stems from this exhortation of Simon Kimbangu. He was arrested below N'Kamba with four assistants, among them the young Mikala Mandombe, by the territorial agent Snoek, at the spot where today the wide flight of steps begins leading up to his last resting place in

[22] Op. cit., p. 10.
[23] Baptist Herald, January 1922, Vol. 104 and letter from the missionary Thomas, dated 7 October 1921. 'Sur la requête des Missions protestantes du Congo et conformément à l'avis des juristes du Ministère des Colonies, le roi des Belges commua la peine de Kibangou (sic) en détention perpétuelle.' Quotation from N. Poivre. 'Fils et Filles d'Afrique', Paris and Geneva, 1946, pp. 137–40.
[24] Eye-witness report.
[25] J. Chomé: 'La Passion de Simon Kimbangu'; Présence africaine, Paris 1959.

the mausoleum.[26] Mr Thomas, the missionary, reports that no one was armed and no one fired shots except the soldiers. Kimbangu handed himself over willingly.

Kimbangu and the four arrested with him were chained and, without being given food or drink, were taken to Nzundu, and from there to Mbanza-Ngungu. Followers and friends who tried to give them water or food on this wearisome journey were driven away.

In Mbanza-Ngungu there were demonstrations of sympathy for the arrested prophet, and Thomas N'Twalani is mentioned in this connection.[27] One of my informants, Pierre Sungudilwa, took part. They sang hymns to express their loyalty to the cause of Kimbangu, for which many were punished with deportation. A few days later Nfinangani, the secretary of Kimbangu, was arrested whilst teaching Kimbangu's eldest son, Charles Kisolokele.[28] Kimbangu's wife Mwilu Marie and her three children Charles Kisolokele, Solomon Kiangani Dialungana and the youngest, Joseph Diangienda (at that time three years of age), were also brought to Mbanza-Ngungu. Charles was questioned by the court (a seven-year-old child!) and courageously testified that his father had performed miracles.[29] He was put in the Catholic school colony of the Christian Brothers in Boma. Kinzembo, Simon Kimbangu's aunt, travelled from Mbanza-Ngungu to Matadi and Boma with Charles Kisolokele, who was at first imprisoned at Boma and later transferred to the school colony. As for Kinzembo, she was sent to Banana, near the Atlantic, where she stayed until about 1925. Then she was taken to Boma, to be kept in confinement, since—her gift of tongues being misinterpreted—it was assumed that she had gone mad. Kisolokele often visited her at Banana between 1921 and 1925, since it was there that the authorities sent orphans for their school holidays.

Kinzembo died in 1927 at Boma; and a modest memorial was erected to her, which we saw when we visited the town in 1968.

5. SENTENCED TO DEATH

On 3 October 1921, Simon Kimbangu was sentenced by a court martial to 120 strokes of the whip and then to be put to death. The judge was military commander Rossi. Kimbangu was accused of

[26] Documents secrets, p. 11.
[27] Op. cit., pp. 11–12.
[28] Op. cit., p. 12.
[29] Oral information via Charles Kisolokele.

sedition and hostility towards the whites. The sentence was based on a false charge.[30] Arbitrary procedure on the part of the military court led to this false verdict. Neither witnesses nor counsels for the defence were admitted. J. Chomé (*op. cit.*) calls the whole procedure, on the basis of the documents which he has studied as a lawyer, a monstrous legal travesty.[31] The Redemptorist priest Braekman, who was present at the trial, says of the prophet during the hearing: 'Kimbangu is an intelligent man and spoke and answered in a dignified manner.'[32] The missionaries Ross Phillips of the British and Joseph Clark of the American Baptist Missionary Society went to the Governor-General at Boma to hand in a petition for pardon. The British Baptist Missionary Society sent a similar petition to the Belgian king.[33]

In November the death sentence was commuted by King Albert to life imprisonment.[34] Evidently there were doubts in Brussels with regard to the trial in Mbanza-Ngungu, though Catholic missionaries had been in agreement with the death sentence. The newspaper *L'Avenir Colonial Belge* protested vehemently against the clemency of the king.

To them it was a question of a political revolutionary movement, whereas the Baptists were convinced, as clearly emerges from their reports, that Kimbangu's movement was purely religious. It can be seen from the Annual Report of the Baptist Missionary Society of 1921[35] that one of the most regrettable factors was the attitude of certain white merchants who placed their business interests above all else and demanded the execution of Kimbangu; thëy maligned in the most shameful way both the Protestant missionary societies and their missionaries. The 'militant songs' of the Kimbanguists, to which the Belgians had taken exception and which they had misunder-

---

[30] C.R.I.S.P.: op. cit., p. 6. The actual accusation reads: '(1) Rébellion contre l'ordre établi. (2) Atteinte à la sûreté de l'Etat. (3) Outrage à un fonctionnaire dans l'exercise de ses fonctions.' (This last charge probably refers to L. Morel, whereas the second has in view the Belgian (white) colonial administration.)

[31] 'Son procès se déroula devant le Conseil de guerre de Thysville, comprenant un juge unique, le commandant Rossi. Un acte d'accusation faussé, une procédure arbitraire aboutirent à la condamnation à mort du prophète' (C.R.I.S.P.: op. cit., p. 6).

[32] Documents secrets, Annexe 5, 'Rapport d'enquête sur le Kimbanguisme', Janvier–Février 1925, par le Procureur général Voisin, Suite 12.

[33] See note 23 for sources.

[34] Documents secrets (belges), 'Apparition de Simon Kimbangu', p. 13.

[35] Annual Report of the BMS, London, 1921.

stood,[36] referred according to the testimony of the Baptist missionaries to spirtual armament. 'They (the Belgians) know nothing of Protestant worship and its treasury of hymns,' the Baptists reported.

Before he was transported off to Elisabethville (present-day Lubumbashi) in November 1921, Simon Kimbangu managed, after many difficulties, to bid his wife and his three sons farewell. He blessed all four of them, and directed that the seven-year-old Charles should care for his family (which the little boy could not as yet understand). He also predicted that Joseph Diangienda would head the movement. Charles Kisolokele recalls these words clearly.[37] Then a train took Simon Kimbangu, only thirty-two years of age, to Kinshasa (Léopoldville) where he was given his 120 strokes of the whip and then taken from there by ship and rail to the prison of Lubumbashi (Elisabethville) in Shaba (Katanga), thousands of kilometres away from his village of N'Kamba. He never saw N'Kamba or his family again. He spent the next thirty years for the most part in solitary confinement. Only rarely was he allowed to work in the kitchen. He had his Bible with him—and when, a few years after his transportation to Lubumbashi, the translation of the whole Bible into the Kikongo language was complete, he asked the Baptist missionaries to send him a copy. Only very seldom was he visited. A Belgian employee who took a photograph of him was immediately dismissed, but it is to him that we owe the well-known photograph from Kimbangu's imprisonment. Kimbangu's witness in suffering was so exemplary that the governor of Shaba, and the prison director recommended in 1935 in Brussels that he be released. But it seems that both the colonial authorities in the Lower Congo (because of the Ngunzist Movement which had arisen in Luozi) and also the Catholic archbishop protested very strongly against this. Thus Simon Kimbangu remained in prison, and ended his life on 12 October 1951 as a martyr.

Joseph Diangienda was at the time of his father's death in the vicinity of Kananga (formerly Luluabourg). He told us how he had the following vision: he saw a young man and recognized him as his father, who said to him: 'I now live with God in heaven.' Joseph

---

[36] Documents secrets (belges), 'Apparition de Simon Kimbangu', p. 8: 'On remarque des déplacements suspects le long de la ligne, et un chant se répand dans ces régions, intitulé: 'Soldats, habillez-vous et prenez les armes."' Probably this is a translation of the well-known hymn 'Stand up, stand up for Jesus,/ Ye soldiers of the cross' or of 'Onward Christian soldiers'.

[37] Oral report by Charles Kisolokele and Joseph Diangienda.

Diangienda spoke to his Belgian superior, who 'phoned to Lubumbashi and indeed received the information that Simon Kimbangu had died a few days before. No one had even thought it necessary to inform the family! Luckily some friends from Lower Zaïre had been in Lubumbashi at the time, and they had paid for his coffin and burial—otherwise the very whereabouts of his grave would have been unknown. As soon as he had confirmation of his father's death, Joseph Diangienda went to Lubumbashi, where he established that his father had been admitted to hospital on 3 October and had indeed died on 12 October 1951.

While he was there, Joseph heard the story of his father's conversion to Catholicism, and went to the Catholic nuns who had tended his father to pursue the matter further. They maintained that Simon Kimbangu had remained to the last *méchant* ('wicked'), although a Zaïrian Catholic priest, F. Sekoto, had evidently tried to convert him or had even baptized Simon Kimbangu when he was no longer fully conscious. However, a Zaïrian prison warder, who was with Simon Kimbangu till he died, categorically denied that any Catholic baptism had been administered. Unfortunately, this man lost his life in the troubles of the '60s in Zaïre and could not therefore endorse this testimony. Joseph Diangienda calls the story of his father's conversion to Catholicism a downright lie intended to bring discredit on the Kimbanguist Movement and to split it.

However, we have anticipated developments and now return to the early years. The question arises as to how the movement could survive after Simon Kimbangu was placed, after such a short ministry, under lock and key and all his fellow-workers, including his family were so rigorously persecuted and oppressed. Looking back on the years of persecution and on the loyalty and pertinacity of the followers of Kimbangu, we can indeed say that the call, the ministry, and also the suffering of Simon Kimbangu were not of man but ultimately of God.

CHAPTER 6

THE HISTORY OF SIMON KIMBANGU'S MOVEMENT AFTER THE PROPHET'S ARREST (1922-4), AND THE RISE OF NGUNZISM

'Just as the work of Jesus was carried on by the apostles after His death, the same was true of the work of the prophet Simon Kimbangu'—Solomon K. Dialungana, son of Kimbangu and Custodian of N'Kamba-Jerusalem, 6 April 1968 at the celebration of the 47th anniversary of the beginning of the work of Simon Kimbangu.[1]

1. THE FATE OF SIMON KIMBANGU'S FAMILY

N'Kamba was completely destroyed by the Belgian administration, and the people of the chief of Nzundu had to build a house, which is still standing, for military or police guards. When they were offered payment for their work they refused to accept it, giving as their reason, 'We are not going to sell N'Kamba.'[2] They had learnt in the meantime—a lesson which had cost an enormous amount of blood and tears in Africa—that when the white man pays he lays claim to the land, which is an alien concept to African tradition. The refusal to accept payment was chalked up against them as rebellion. Simon's wife Marie Mwilu had already settled with her two sons Solomon Kiangani Dialungana and Joseph Diangienda in neighbouring Ngombe-Kinsuka, which lies opposite N'Kamba and is only separated from there by a narrow valley in which the sacred spring is situated. According to her sons, she lived in miserable circumstances and was constantly kept under surveillance, and several times the

[1] A copy of the Kikongo original, translated into French, was placed at my disposal.
[2] Documents secrets (belges), 'Apparition de Simon Kimbangu', p. 17.

safety of her children was threatened; yet she was the secret focal point, the spiritual mother, of the followers of Kimbangu, whom we shall now call Kimbanguists and from whom we shall distinguish the Ngunzists. During this time of hardship, Simon Kimbangu often appeared to his family to comfort them although he was imprisoned thousands of kilometres away. This is a phenomenon of which we as Westerners can only take note: it is certainly very doubtful whether our rational explanations (such as telepathy) are adequate. Marie Mwilu prayed with those who came to her in their need and sent them to the spring. Always, however, faith founded on the Gospel and prayer remained central. The water of N'Kamba, in which the believers dipped themselves (as they still do today) in the Name of the Father, and of the Son, and of the Holy Spirit, was never to take on magical quality.

Charles Kisolokele compulsorily placed in the school colony of Boma, was left at first in the belief that his whole family had perished and that, as an orphan, he owed the Christian Brothers, who directed the school, his gratitude for all their kindnesses, until he found out that his family were still alive. For twelve years he was not allowed to see his mother. Joseph, the youngest son of Kimbangu, entered in February 1934 (at the age of sixteen) the boarding-school in Boma, which his older brother had already left in 1932. He was allowed to visit his mother now and again, but on condition that at least each Sunday he attended mass at the Catholic mission station of Ngombe-Matadi about 26 km. away! In the boarding-school reading of the Bible was strictly forbidden. Despite this the two sons of Kimbangu secretly had their Bibles and read them all the more eagerly for that. Hence their sound knowledge of the Bible. At school they received in addition an excellent education and their good knowledge of the French language.

The middle son, Solomon Kiangani Dialungana, remained all the time with his mother, and later as a young man he was compelled to work for the Belgians as a porter, carrying the heavy luggage of colonial agents on transfer over distances of more than 150 km. Despite that, he learnt to read and write. He is the author of various texts in the Kikongo language which are used in the instruction of the church.[3]

---

[3] All this information comes from Charles Kisolokele and Joseph Diangienda.

2. PERSECUTION—TOLERANCE—NEW PERSECUTION

As early as November 1921 military patrols of 150 men began to watch over the areas of the 'prophetic disturbances'.[4] In 1922, the Belgian authorities forbade Kimbanguists to hold further meetings. The spring near N'Kamba was strictly guarded and, in order to make access to it impossible, bushes and trees were planted, but these in fact offered protection to the followers who bathed there and prayed at night. In remote huts, along rivers, and especially near waterfalls there were gatherings to sing those prayerful hymns which have become so important to the Kimbanguists right up to the present day. Finally, all the roads leading to N'Kamba were checked by military patrols. The mission station of Ngombe-Lutete was almost deserted, for followers of Kimbangu accused the missionaries of being partly to blame for the arrests and deportations which were now instigated.[5] Relations between the Baptist missionaries and the Kimbanguists became strained. Bowskill, a missionary who returned to Ngombe-Lutete in the autumn of 1921, wrote in a letter to London that of 1,500 church members only 600 now remained. Work in the school, outpatients department and among the women had suffered severely. Mr Hillard, a missionary, told me in conversation that the Kimbanguists had 'boycotted' the mission. By the end of 1921 he could not find in Ngombe-Lutete a single black porter who was prepared to help carry a sick lady missionary to Mbanza-Ngungu.

The missionary conference of all Protestant (not only Baptist) missionaries decided in November 1921 in Bolenge[6] to make an appeal to all 'the native congregations to abstain from participation in a movement harmful to the progress of Christianity and the normal development of the native population'. By this was meant the prophetic movement. Government measures were justified at this conference by saying that 'We believe that the authorities had to take severe and immediate measures to check the Prophet Movement which rapidly became favourable soil for propaganda hostile to all white men, endangering civilization itself.' The missionaries were asked to oppose the prophetic movement, even though this would draw upon them the distrust and hostility of their church members. Even the harsh sentences of the Belgian administration, about which the Baptists had been indignant, were now excused: 'Although the

[4] Documents secrets (belges), 'Apparition de Simon Kimbangu', p. 14.
[5] Op. cit., p. 15.
[6] Baptist Herald, 22 March 1922.

punishments are harsh, they are the punishments of a military court which was faced with an extraordinarily difficult situation. Mitigation will be possible later when the danger is past.' Is it then surprising that the followers of Kimbangu were bitterly disappointed? One of their documents from this period voices the lament, 'We have been forsaken by both Catholics and Protestants.'[7]

How are we to view this attitude of the missionary conference? The missionaries thought the fruit of their labours was destroyed. They could not at the time see that there were Africans who were spiritually mature and wanted their own independent, self-governing, self-directing and self-propagating church with its own forms of life. It is true that there were already such churches, the 'Ethiopian' churches in South Africa,[8] but in central Africa Ethiopianism had met with extreme suspicion since the Chilembwe rising in 1915 in Malawi (then called Nyasaland) and since the attempts of Marcus Garvey to gain a footing in Liberia.[9] The colonial authorities and white settlers were afraid of this first sign of African national consciousness. A further reason for the severe resolutions of the missionary conference was presumably the fact that Roman Catholic and Belgian circles constantly held the Protestants responsible for all the aberrations of the prophetic movements—the Ngunzists.

In 1922 the massive banishments and deportations of Kimbanguists began and were to continue until 1957. An official report of the colonial authorities of 15 July 1922 confirms that 244 people (i.e. heads of families, not counting women and children) had been deported, quite apart from those who had already been arrested and exiled at the time of Simon Kimbangu's sentence.[10] Many followers had at that time made plantations in the area around N'Kamba in the hope of the speedy return of the prophet so that they would be able to feed the pilgrims streaming to him, and this naturally incensed the colonial authorities.

More and more deportations followed. Those who were deported

---

[7] The document (handwritten), which also contains the hymns of the early period translated in the next chapter, is in the possession of Joseph Diangienda and is at present not accessible. I was only able to write down this quotation and the hymns at my special request as I was preparing a microfilm of the document for the archives.

[8] G. Shepperson: 'Ethiopianism Past and Present', article in the omnibus volume 'Christianity in Tropical Africa', Oxford, 1968, pp. 97–113.

[9] G. Shepperson/T. Price: 'Independent African', Edinburgh, 1958, pp. 230 ff., 321 ff., 430.

[10] Documents secrets (belges), 'Second mouvement de Kamba', Mars 1922–Sept. 1923, p. 16.

were settled in over thirty regions of Zaïre in what were like concentration camps. In the struggle against disease and wild animals they usually lived together in groups, cleared the land for cultivation, devoted themselves to their faith, prayed for the sick, and thus proclaimed the Gospel to the non-Christians. Belgian documents dated 1922 speak of the Ituri forests in Upper Zaïre. 'Led by a follower of Kimbangu they (the exiles) are evangelizing. Sick folk are brought to him in the hope of being cured. In this way the revolutionary ideas from Lower Zaïre are spreading.'[11] Ultimately, even these harsh measures of the Belgian colonial authorities became a blessing for the movement. It spread from now on to all tribes and was not limited to the tribe of the Bakongo. In the course of the thirty-six years from 1921 to 1957, altogether 37,000 heads of families were banished, which probably means that more than 100,000 were sent into exile. Only a few, around 3,000, returned to their former homes after the declaration of Zaïrian independence in 1960. Many had died in the meantime.[12]

Despite this systematic suppression and persecution many *chapelles* (i.e. meeting places consisting of posts with palm roofs and no walls) were erected as well as schools, where children learnt to read the Bible and sing the hymns of the Kimbanguists. Bibles were bought at the Protestant missionary stations—although to begin with only the New Testament, the Psalms and parts of the Old Testament had been translated (by Dr Bentley and his helpers, particularly the blind Nlemvo). For a time no more hymn-books could be bought, and thus began the production of a very remarkable collection of hymns with Africanized or completely African tunes, and these are a special feature of the life of the Kimbanguist Movement and Church.

The exiles wrote letters and exhorted Kimbangu's followers to be loyal. They were to have confidence in the future. Only a few of these letters have been preserved since, for fear of the police, they were burnt after they had been read.

A document of the colonial administration of 12 February 1923 mentions a man of the name of Kitoko, who is supposed to have promised the believers that the exiles would soon return. It quotes

[11] Op. cit., p. 18.
[12] This figure is taken from Kimbanguist data. The figures given by the Belgians are smaller, but the Belgians had no interest in publishing high figures for these measures which offended against all human rights. The number of those who were deported seems in any case to have been very great. More than thirty 'concentration camps' were counted to which Kimbanguists and Ngunzists were banished during the years 1922–57.

the Kimbanguists as saying: 'We know that the state is against it but we shall never give up' (*'nous continuerons toujours'*). The movement was contagious, and constantly even ministers and evangelists of the Protestant missions were joining it. A climax was reached at Christmas 1923.[13] Everywhere people gathered together.

3. NEW INCIDENTS[14]

On New Year's Day 1924 the Catholic missionary from Tumba complained to the administrator of Mbanza-Ngungu that a Kimbanguist group apparently led by chief Tumansangu had come and sung their hymns. It emerged that, in various villages in the vicinity of the Catholic station, of Tumba such services had indeed taken place on Christmas Day 1923. But two followers of Simon Kimbangu had in fact been whipped by the people of Tumansangu (who was in reality hostile towards the Kimbanguists), whereupon the crowd went to Tumansangu and declared, 'We want to sing our hymns. We're neither Catholic nor Protestant. We're singing to our God, and if the administrator wants to banish us to the Upper Congo we're ready to go.'[15]

Acting on the complaints of the Catholic missionary, the administrator took twelve 'ringleaders' with him to Mbanza-Ngungu. Amongst other things they said, 'We're disappointed with the Protestant missionaries because they've left the Kimbanguists to their fate and our leaders have been deported. The Protestants complained about Simon Kimbangu when he was called to be a prophet so that he would be deported.'[16] We have seen, of course, in the last chapter that things were not as simple as that. 'Our God is the same as that of the Protestants. We no longer need any missionaries because we're mature and intelligent enough to lead ourselves ... We want to open Kimbanguist churches everywhere. Of course, we don't pray to Simon Kimbangu—we pray to God. Kimbangu is the ambassador of God.' For the theology of missions this early testimony is important in the light of the fantastic messianic notions which were at that time current in Ngunzist circles.

A delegation, led by Chief Gungu, went to ask the administrator in Mbanza-Ngungu what was now going to be done with the twelve 'ringleaders'.

[13] Documents secrets, p. 17.
[14] C.R.I.S.P.: op. cit., p. 7.
[15] Documents secrets (belges), 'Troisième mouvement Kimbanguiste', p. 19.   [16] Op. cit., p. 20.

4. THE REPORT OF NOIROT

The assistant commissioner of the district of Boma, Mr Noirot, was summoned to an inquiry in Mbanza-Ngungu; and on 10 January, he reported the following to the governor of the province of Congo-Kasai: 'I can't discern the slightest insubordination (*insoumission*). On the contrary, all assure me of their loyalty towards the government. Indeed, they no longer want to have any dealings with the Protestant missionaries.'

On being asked the reason for this emphatic repudiation of the Protestant missionaries, Noirot replied, 'One of the reasons which they give is the rejection of Kimbangu by the missionaries in 1921. They don't want to pay any further contributions to the missionaries for the support of evangelists. They've their own evangelists, they've the Bible, they will also set up their own schools. They don't want to be interfered with any further by the missionaries. They'll instruct their children in the religion which is the same for all people, whites and blacks, and they'll teach them to respect the government.'[17]

What has today become a matter of course in the third world where indigenous churches have grown up out of missionary work was at that time an unheard-of novelty, in central Africa and elsewhere in the world.

A further missiologically important reason which Kimbanguists give for the creation of a completely independent church (a reason which is found in similar form in South Africa) is the fragmentation of the Christian church, the lack of ecumenicity. 'The Catholics claim that they alone are the true ambassadors of God. The Protestants say the same about themselves. So we hold that we can worship God just as well in forgoing the support of missionaries, who can't agree among themselves anyway.' This is a serious condemnation of denominational differences, which have created divisions in Africa even within hitherto united tribal groups.

Noirot reported further that in places as yet unreached by missionaries daily services are regularly being held. He came to the conclusion, 'I cannot stop the natives from meeting for prayer in the way the whites have taught them just because they now want to do this without the help of the whites.' Noirot was pleading for tolerance although even in the same report he stressed that the colonial government would suppress without mercy any rising propagated (!) by Simon Kimbangu and his disciples.

In a second report to the provincial governor[18] Noirot added,

[17] Op. cit., p. 21.   [18] Op. cit., p. 22.

'Those under arrest have been liberated. Tempers have calmed down.' Of course, restrictions followed: 'Censorship of letters, if not the prohibition of correspondence, must be introduced to stop all communication between the exiles and their friends and followers.' Noirot accused the Protestants of stirring up fanatical elements by recommending Bible-reading and by their hymns, and he found Catholic missionary practice better suited to conditions. He claimed, 'The Protestant missions [the scapegoats of the Catholic Belgian administration] have made the blacks into fanatics by their unthinking kind of religious instruction and so they bear the blame for the rise of the Kimbanguist Movement.' In conclusion, Noirot expressed the fear (which turned out to be justified with regard to the Ngunzists) that ambitious fanatics could turn the hitherto religious movement into a political movement. However, he said at the end of his report, 'It seems that at present the movement still has a purely religious character.'

Following Noirot's report the provincial governor recommended caution.[19] Religious freedom was granted the people so long as the hymns (so feared by the administration) did not occasion disorder. He made the important comment: 'Kimbanguism is a fact which we can neither ignore nor suppress. We must examine the possibility of adapting it to the structure of our organization.' He admitted that there were dangers in Kimbanguism. 'They are presumtuous to think that they can dispense with the leadership of the white missionaries ... Our administration must be strict and at the same time paternal.' Here we find the usual colonial paternalism. But 'it is best to grant the Kimbanguists freedom of worship.' We shall see that, to begin with, this advice brought the Kimbanguists a brief period of respite throughout the whole country as far as Kasai, but then there were vehement attacks on Noirot's 'superficial report'. Before turning to this reaction which eventually led to the total suppression of the Kimbanguist Movement, let us look briefly at the Ngunzist Movement.

5. THE NGUNZISTS

The Kikongo word *ngunza* means 'prophet', and the biblical words for 'prophet' (*nabi* in the Old Testament and *prophetes* in the New) are translated in the Kikongo Bible by the word *ngunza*. Originally the *ngunza* was the hero, or the man who spoke in the name of the chief. We shall use the word in our context with reference to what

[19] Op. cit., p. 23.

Kimbangu called 'false prophets', fully aware, however, that this is a one-sided use of the word and that *ngunza* can just as well be used of Simon Kimbangu, and indeed is used of him. We do so in order to draw the firm distinction between the pseudo Kimbanguist and the genuine Kimbanguist movements. This is all the more necessary since the two have hitherto been confused in literature on missions for lack of a history of the Kimbanguist Movement based on source material which observes the distinction. The Kimbanguist Movement led to the foundation of the 'Church of Jesus Christ on Earth through the Prophet Simon Kimbangu' with the exclusion of syncretistic, 'paganizing' tendencies.[20] As has already been remarked, since the source material was not accessible, we cannot reproach the missiologists who have confused the two movements. Two instances from the extensive material on the subject will serve to show how Kimbanguists and Ngunzists have been confused. We are taking these intentionally from literature in German, although both are based on information in English and French (on Andersson's detailed account and Balandier's studies). For example, we read, 'Simon Kimbangu was a helper, but what is far more important he was one of their own (people) . . . Simon Kimbangu was, in the face of his arrest, no longer viewed as a prophet but was seen as the "God of the blacks". And now there are strivings for an independent African church. After Kimbangu's deportation; all kinds of legends were rampant: Kimbangu was to be shot, but out of the soldiers' rifles came nothing but water; Kimbangu was then put in a great cauldron, but whilst the fire was burning beneath him he calmly continued to read; he was sent by rail to Boma, but the train could not move so long as Kimbangu was sitting in it. Finally, his parousia was expected.'[21]

Or again, 'After the second arrest of Kimbangu, in which he this time imitated the self-surrender of Jesus in Gethsemane, he is sentenced for life to penal servitude in mitigation of the original death sentence. He died in 1950 [sic] in prison in Elisabethville. From now on there evolves around Kimbangu nothing less than a myth. He is apotheosized [deified] and his return in apocalyptic form is anticipated. At the head of the heroes of the ancient Kingdom of Kongo he is to return in richly-laden ships as the *ntotila* (the title of the ancient kings) and re-establish the independent Kingdom of the Kongo. However, his movement develops from its religious aspect

[20] G. C. Oosthuizen, in 'The Theology of a South African Messiah', Leiden, 1967, calls this tendency to go back to pre-Christian religion 'nativistic'.

[21] H. J. Margull: 'Aufbruch zur Zukunft', Gütersloh, 1962, p. 57.

in secret meetings at night into a libertine, neo-pagan cult in which all Christian elements are rapidly cast aside.'[22]

These assertions by Margull and Beyerhaus are not pure invention but the ideas presented in them are by and large those of the Ngunzists, which we must distinguish from those of the Kimbanguists. Admittedly, the formation of legends around the person of the imprisoned prophet began early. I heard from leading Kimbanguists who were present when Kimbangu was arrested and taken away the story that the rifle bullets of the Belgians turned into water (perhaps this is a reference to dud, defective ammunition) and that the train which was to take Simon Kimbangu from Mbanza-Ngungu to Kinshasa (not Boma!) did not set off until he had taken leave of and blessed his family, Marie Mwilu and the children. Was this some easily explicable delay which (as happens by the way in the Old Testament as well) appeared as a miraculous intervention of God? Such incidents can be 'demythologized', but we cannot deny that ultimately they are evidence of God's work. *However*, the neo-pagan developments which now began are another matter and they had already begun during the period of Kimbangu's short ministry. We have already noticed in Chapter 5 how, when Morel had come to N'Kamba for his investigations, Kimbangu drove away false prophets as 'prophets of the Evil One'.

The Ngunzist movement now gathered momentum, and many looked to Simon Kimbangu in their neo-pagan activity and their apocalyptic expectations and finally made him the 'God of the blacks', the new messiah, just as has happened with prophets in South Africa. Kimbangu had become a kind of 'catalyst' for all the dissatisfactions and insecurity which had come through the social and colonial upheavals in Zaïre, changing the old order and partly destroying it. He was expected to bring salvation, liberation from sickness and witchcraft, but above all freedom from the yoke of colonial power. He would drive the whites into the sea—an ever-recurring motif of reaction in Africa against conquest and colonization. No longer thinking in Biblical categories, people projected a glorious past into the future and thus sought a return to the past. This was not genuine eschatology. The Cross of Christ—the heart of the Christian faith—was by-passed, as I have tried to show in my first study.[23] People were clinging to the myth of the returning

[22] P. Beyerhaus: 'Kann es eine Zusammenarbeit zwischen den christlichen und den prophetisch-messianischen Bewegungen in Africa geben?', Evangelisches Missions-Magazin, 111. Jahrgang, Heft 1, 1967, Basle, pp. 21–2.

[23] M.-L. Martin: 'The Biblical Concept of Messianism and Messianism in Southern Africa', Moriah, 1964, pp. 157–61.

ntotila, the king of the ancient Kongolese Kingdom, idealizing both him and the time of the old kingdom.

Shortly before his death, Simon Kimbangu heard what the people of the Ngunzist Movement had made of him. Missionary H. J. Casebow of Ngombe-Lutete reports[24] that in July 1958 at a conference of the Baptist Church in Ngombe-Lutete the Kimbanguist Movement was discussed. 'A woman whose husband had been in the army told us that when they were in Elisabethville (Lubumbashi) she managed to get into the prison and saw Kimbangu not long before he died. On her first visit she was too overcome to say much to him, but on later occasions she had a chance to talk. He remembered her as a child. She told him what people (Ngunzists) were saying about him. He replied, "I was, and am simply a servant of Jesus Christ and nothing more." He was perplexed to know where and how all the stories about him had originated. He had never urged that blacks and whites separate.' This inconspicuous incident is indeed of great importance historically and to the theology of missions.

It must be admitted that even today not only do such Ngunzist groups continue to exist, and to disseminate their fantastic stories about Kimbangu, but some on the periphery of the 'Church of Jesus Christ on Earth through the Prophet Simon Kimbangu' even claim to be true Kimbanguists. They look to the head of the church, Joseph Diangienda; but he (very wisely) does not regard them as officially belonging to the church, as he is aware of the danger of syncretism and repudiates it. After the declaration of the independence of Zaïre in 1960, he was faced with the onerous task of deciding which of the scattered independent groups should be integrated into the intentionally elastic framework of the Kimbanguist Church and which should be excluded. Thus in 1966 an anthropologist, Prof. Wyatt MacGaffey, could still describe a visit to one such 'periphery group',[25] which shows that the sifting process was not yet complete. The tendency, however, is apparent: only where the name of Jesus Christ is clearly recognized as that of the only, unique Saviour and where the Bible remains central do we have true Kimbanguism. What is more, the rite of healing has been restricted: only the head of the church and, in his absence, his oldest brother and those assistants of the initial period who are still alive and were engaged by Simon Kimbangu may lay on hands, along with some few of those who were at one time exiles and to whom the miraculous gift of healing was given during their suffering; I am

[24] Oral information.
[25] Wyatt MacGaffey: 'Kimbanguist Diary', unpublished manuscript.

thinking in particular of John and Clementine Mayanga in N'Kamba. The water of N'Kamba must not be abused. All aid that is asked for is based on faith, prayer and intercession. Church members do not lay hands on the sick. They pray for them. These issues are important because of the efforts of the Kimbanguist Church to establish ecumenical contacts; for, as Beyerhaus has remarked, the question of co-operation with the independent African churches is one of the most crucial for missionary activity in Africa today.

We now return to the years 1922–4 and investigate the early development of those Ngunzist groups. The prophets who already appeared in the time of Simon Kimbangu and continued their activity after his arrest were very different from him. Some were adventurers, rogues and charlatans, performing their healing for payment—contrary to all that Kimbangu had taught. They exploited the gullibility of the people and the name, the 'renown', of Kimbangu and based their activity on the superstition and the religious longings of the people. They were the chosen ones of the 'Holy Spirit' to replace the traditional *féticheurs*, the witch-doctors.[26] They resembled the many South African Zionist healers who took the place of the non-Christian healers of earlier African tradition, the *dingaka, izangoma,* and *tinyanga* who worked with magic bones and herbs in conjunction with the ancestral spirits.

The drive of the Belgian colonial power against Kimbangu and the Kimbanguists went hand in hand with the campaign against these 'false' prophets. The records discuss the case of one after another; some of them urged the withholding of taxes, preached hatred of foreigners, encouraged resistance to the compulsory labour ordered by the state; and made fantastic promises. The expectation of the Kimbanguists that Simon Kimbangu would return soon after his arrest (that is, either that he would be miraculously freed from prison like Peter, or that he would be released in the ordinary way) was translated into apocalyptic expectations: he would return like Christ 'through the air' to N'Kamba and would then become the great king of the Kongo. The Ngunzists were a religious and political movement, and the political element was important until 1959 and then again from 1963 to 1966. The risings in Matadi, Kinshasa and elsewhere in 1959 and the hunt for white missionaries shortly before the declaration of independence of Zaïre, of which the Kimbanguists have been falsely accused, were caused by the Ngunzists.[27]

The Ngunzist Movement stressed from the beginning the element of ecstasy, and that is why they are also called *trembleurs* (quakers)

[26] C.R.I.S.P., op. cit., p. 5.
[27] Op. cit., p. 15, 'Note sur les mouvements de ngounza'.

or *bantu ba Mpeve ya nlongo* (people of the Holy Spirit). C.R.I.S.P. (*op. cit.* p. 5) enumerates the following five points which distinguish it from Kimbanguism:
1. The Ngunzist Movement is not ecclesiastical in character. Ngunzists form small groups which (like certain South African Zionists) were founded by a local prophet and exist without any fixed organization—following the inspiration of the Spirit.
2. They developed particularly in the districts of Luozi and Mayumbe, to the north of the lowest course of Zaïre. From there they penetrated easily to the former French Congo, the present-day People's Republic of the Congo, where they joined up in the 30s with the African splinter group of the so-called independent Salvation Army and the political movement of *Amicalism*, founded by André Matswa.
3. Christian hymns, prayers, and Bible-reading are of secondary importance—as in many of the South African Zionist groups and certain independent churches in Kenya and Rhodesia.
4. The main emphasis is placed on 'organized quaking' (*tremblement organisé*) to the beating of drums. This leads to collective ecstasy, accompanied by speaking in tongues and wild shrieking.
5. The practice of healing and exorcism of the *ndoki* (the exorcism of magic powers and demons) in accord with non-Christian African ritual. Return to the old order.

It has already been mentioned that a political and anti-whites tendency has characterized the Ngunzist Movement. Membership cards were discovered entitled, 'The King of the Kongo'. In this movement all stress is laid on the 'Holy Spirit' and his manifestations.

Documents from the archives of the Belgian administration tell how these *trembleurs* appeared particularly in 1930 in the district of Mbanza-Ngungu and of Luozi[28] (which we have already mentioned). Documents were found at that time on the arrest of such Ngunzist leaders which prove that (perhaps influenced by Kitawala) they spoke of a great apocalyptic king who was to come. Clearly chiliastic (i.e. millennial) tendencies were asserting themselves. A sign of fire and rain would proclaim the arrival of the king.[29] A new John the Baptist (*Yoani Mvubi* in Kikongo) exhorted the people in the district of N'Kamba: 'Smear your houses with the blood of a lamb as at the time of the exodus from Egyptian bondage. All those who don't do this will perish in the imminent war. Only those who've smeared

[28] Documents secrets (belges), 'Menées prophétiques de 1925–1931', pp 35–6.
[29] Op. cit., p. 37.

their houses will be saved ... Rejoice when you pray, for God gives great power to triumph over all whites. The prisons will be shaken (as in an earthquake) and our captives will be liberated ... Simon Kimbangu and all those who were arrested with him are already on their way back to your country to fulfil the task they have been given. Kinshasa is the place where the new kings, who will win the war, will unite.' So ran the appeal of Yoani Mvubi![30]

Later in 1931 there was a rising in Sankuru and Kinshasa. A certain Pierre Lubaki of what was then the French Congo declared himself to be Simon Kimbangu who had come again and claimed that the whites would become black and the blacks white. This was originally a saying of Kimbangu, who meant by it that there would be before God no distinction of race. But Lubaki meant it differently and was really saying that now the blacks would be the rulers and the whites the subjects. In Kinshasa a certain Pierre Nganga appeared.[31] Was this the same man who, as one of the three men commissioned by André Matswa, used to collect contributions in the French Congo, particularly in Brazzaville, for his social campaign on behalf of the blacks?[32] Nganga held a meeting in Kinshasa with about 300 people; later the rumour went round that Kimbangu lived with him. Nganga claimed that he often dreamt of Kimbangu. He made the same claim when interrogated, and the Belgian administration made a note of it on 3 March 1931. If he was really the same Pierre Nganga, this could mean that there was much earlier than E. Andersson supposes[33] a connection between the followers of André Matswa and the Ngunzists, who also looked to Kimbangu, albeit falsely.

We have anticipated things a little and now return to the events of 1924 in the district of N'Kamba where the Kimbanguists were enjoying a measure of tolerance in December 1923.

[30] Op. cit., pp. 37–8.

[31] Op. cit., p. 39.

[32] Documents secrets (belges), 'Kimbanguisme-Ngounzisme en A.E.F., p. 46.

[33] E. Andersson: 'Messianic Popular Movements in the Lower Congo', Uppsala, 1958, pp. 139–45; G. Balandier: 'Sociologie actuelle de L'Afrique noire', revised edn, Paris 1963, pp. 465–77.

CHAPTER 7

THE RADICAL SUPPRESSION OF THE MOVEMENT IN 1925

1. THE REPORT OF FATHER DUFONTENY[1]

We have seen that as a result of Commissioner Noirot's inquiry a certain tolerance was shown towards Kimbangu's followers which reached its climax at Christmas 1923. The movement was gaining ground and had by 1921 spread into what was then the French Congo.[2] This toleration encouraged the Kimbanguists. However, their spread and growth disturbed the administration. According to one report only those chiefs in Lower Zaïre who were themselves Kimbanguists could maintain order.[3] In October 1924 there arose in Belgium a fierce press campaign as a result of a long report by Father Dufonteny.[4] He claimed that the Kimbanguists wanted to rid themselves of the white administration in Zaïre. He accused the Protestant missions of pulling the strings behind the Kimbanguist Movement. The colonial administration, he said, was in league with them through ignorance or anti-clerical feeling. Such an accusation called for a careful inquiry. Thus, in December 1924, a new inquiry was opened under Solicitor-General Voisin, who went to the scene of events and drew up a long report in which he discussed the accusations of the priest.

[1] Documents secrets (belges), Article du R. P. Dufonteny—'Enquête du Proc. Gén. Voisin', pp. 27 ff.; Documents secrets, Annexe 5, 'Rapport d'enquête sur le Kimbanguisme', Janvier-Février 1925.

[2] Documents secrets (belges), 'Apparition de Simon Kimbangu', p. 9.

[3] Documents secrets (belges), 'Troisième Mouvement Kimbanguiste', p. 26.

[4] Bulletin de la Ligue pour la Protection et l'Evangélisation des Noirs, No. 2, 1924.

Meanwhile, the edict of tolerance continued in force, and in December 1924 the Kimbanguists were able to hold publicly, for the last time for many years, their Christmas services without fear of being arrested and deported. This fact, we noted, had impressed itself deeply into the memory of the Kimbanguists.

2. THE FINDINGS OF THE SOLICITOR-GENERAL'S INQUIRY[5]

Voisin's report gives the impression that he had little sympathy for Father Dufonteny, whom he called a fanatic who had confused the anti-Belgian manifestations of 1913 with those of the Kimbanguists and Ngunzists (which he had indeed done). Voisin reproached him further overlooking the fact that not only Protestants (to whom Father Dufonteny ascribed all the blame) but also Catholics and non-Christians had joined the Kimbanguists. This comment is important as proof that Zaïrians of both confessions, as well as non-Christians, were converted through Kimbangu's witness and the preaching of his assistants.

Voisin's report makes apparent the difficulties in which the Protestant Baptist missionaries had become embroiled through the rise of the Kimbanguist Movement. They had not only lost control over the movement (indeed, they had never had such control) but they were also made responsible for it: they were the scapegoats. Father Dufonteny was all the more hostile towards the British Baptist missionaries because he was, as Voisin put it, a chauvinist, and one could see that it was he who was stirring up the xenophobia of which he accused the Kimbanguists!

In his report of February 1925, Voisin stressed that the inhabitants of the district of N'Kamba, who had disassociated themselves from the missions and paid their taxes promptly, were exemplary subjects (*'se montrant d'une soumission exemplaire'*.). In this they differed from the Ngunzists. And yet they were, said Voisin, convinced of God's commission to Kimbangu and hoped for his return, as well as for that of the exiles. In every village there was a Kimbanguist evangelist who was also a teacher.

Because the Kimbanguists did not want white missionaries, and blamed the Baptist missionary Jennings for Simon Kimbangu's arrest, Voisin described the origin of the movement as rebellious, though at that time they were not thinking of violence and were expecting the release of Kimbangu through a miracle. Mr Jennings of Mbanza-

---

[5] Documents secrets, Annexe 5.

The Suppression of the Movement

Ngungu was in a difficult position: since he felt compelled by the decisions of the missionary conference of 1921 to excommunicate those Baptists who attended Kimbanguist meetings, he was considered by Kimbangu's followers as an enemy of the movement.

Father Dufonteny had expressed the view that the Kimbanguist Movement was directed from headquarters in Kinshasa. Voisin proved that this was not the case and said, 'The leaders are certain chieftains and evangelists who have become Kimbanguists.'

Nevertheless, Voisin expressed disapproval of Noirot's clemency and demanded a strict watch over the Kimbanguists. Looking back on his observations, Voisin remarked, 'They show the inner unity and solidarity of Simon Kimbangu's followers—and that is a grave danger.' What danger was he thinking of? For him, as a Belgian Catholic, Kimbanguism was the religious fruit of the 'individualism of the Christianity taught by the Baptist missionaries'. He was thinking of the fact mentioned already that (contrary to the practice of the Catholic Church of that time) every Protestant was given a Bible and instructed to read it. He came to this conclusion, 'We must continue the struggle against Kimbanguism as one of our civilizing tasks.' He suggests measures against every manifestation of xenophobia and also positive evangelism aimed at eradicating Kimbanguist ideas and opposing all new creeds (*croyances nouvelles*). 'It seems to me quite impossible', he wrote, 'to allow an independent religious movement [*culte*] to develop further in which evangelists "entertain" the natives with crackbrained notions, which we know all about, and turn them into fanatics by using texts from the Bible, which they interpret in their own way.' The signal for suppression had been given.

3. SUPPRESSIVE MEASURES

On 6 February 1925 the subjects of the governor of Kasai Province, which at that time included those who lived in the Lower Zaïre, were forbidden once and for all to have anything to do with Kimbanguism, the so-called 'religion of the country' (*religion du pays*), for it was seditious and constituted a danger to the European occupation.[6] All the Kimbanguist churches and schools were closed.[7] Offenders were deported. In a circular, dated 24 February 1925, the governor asked the Catholic and Protestant missions to co-operate

[6] Documents secrets (belges), Article Dufonteny—'Enquête Voisin', p. 28.
[7] Op. cit., p. 29.

in the suppression of both Simon Kimbangu's movement and that of the Ngunzists.⁸ From then on soldiers patrolled the districts of Mbanza-Ngungu and Madimba (on the road between Mbanza-Ngungu and Kinshasa). These measures led to new deportations.⁹ It was assumed that at that time about two-thirds of the population were under the influence of Kimbanguism or Ngunzism.

4. KIMBANGUIST HYMNS FROM THE PERIOD 1922–1925

The following hymns were collected by the Belgian colonial authorities. They are written in French though they were sung in Kikongo. We shall render the French word *misère* by 'suffering' or 'misery', and the word *palavre* by 'conflict'.

I

Come Jesus, our Redeemer,
Come with Thy power!
We have run into difficulty.
With Thy Name 'Jesus' help us, help us.
The enemy is persecuting us.
We are resisting him with our prayers
In which we ask for Thine aid.
The Devil is persecuting us all the time,
But when he sees Thee he will flee.
When Satan surrounds us
Do snatch us from his hands!
In times past we did not know Thee, O Jesus,
We did not know Thee in our hearts.
Today we know Thee.
Let no evil befall us.
All our evangelists have been deported
For the sake of Jesus' Name.
We shall do our utmost so that they [presumably referring to the authorities] will let us alone.
Jesus, come, help us
If we must go to the Upper Congo [into exile].
Jesus, Thou wert the First to go,
We are following Thee.

⁸ Op. cit., p. 31.
⁹ Documents secrets (belges), 'Menées prophétiques de 1925–1931', p. 40.

II

God has created the heavens and the earth,
None is mightier than He.
God will end the conflict of these days.
Come quickly, let us pray.
We are following Thee.
Someone wants to inflict evil on us.
Our God, Jesus, our Brother,
Jesus, snatch us from misery.
Come, Jesus, help us here on earth.
We are listening to Thee.
For our enemies we are performing all the labour
They demand of us.
But they do not see the truth about our cause [a reference to Kimbanguism].
Our Father and Mother [?], we are obedient.
If conflict arises
Then we shall resist with our prayers.
Jesus was a prisoner,
Jesus was smitten.
They are smiting us, too,
We, the blacks, are prisoners.
The whites are free.
The enemy has snatched from us the staff [the sign of prophetic power, the prophet himself].
All kinds of suffering befall us.
We are afflicted, our tears flow.
Come, help us, Holy Spirit,
Come, come, come, help us!
We are all following Thee.
Blacks and whites are praying,
And we do not know the day of Thy Return.

III

We who are carrying on our cause [Kimbanguism],
Let us be clothed and armed! [This is a reference to spiritual armament.]
Jesus will protect us.
Let us clothe and arm ourselves!
The Holy Spirit will protect us

Through the power of the Redeemer.
The enemy is watching us, wanting to frighten us
And make us give up our cause.
But we are looking only to the Saviour,
He will give us strength
For the struggle which will befall us.
Let us clothe and arm ourselves!
We are praying to the God of our fathers,
This God has sent us a Redeemer,
Jesus Christ, the Redeemer,
Let us clothe and arm ourselves!
God is in [or 'with'] this Jesus:
Jesus was crucified, His blood was shed.
We wash away the sins of our hearts with His blood.
We have to suffer much down here.
We become afflicted, our tears flow.
Come, help us, Holy Spirit,
Come, come, come and help us!
Starvation is afflicting us.
Lead us not into temptation!
Come help us!
There is much conflict in our country.
We want to be true to our cause,
But the enemy does not want this.
Come, help us, we are following Thee!
Blacks and whites persevere in prayer,
We do not know the day of Thy Return.

IV

We are going to Heaven,
When Jesus is there [where Jesus is].
He loves us all.
We have seen Thee by believing in Thee.
Today we shall behold joy with Jesus and His angels.
We are all meeting to pray to God.
We are suffering at present
And we desire to be with Thee again.
That is why we sing and pray to God.
Jesus is holding us fast.
We are suffering inexpressibly,
But through Thy power
No one can hold us back.

V

All of you, our brethren, stand firm,
Jesus will come and help us.
His conflict is known, pray for him. [This refers to someone in difficulties.]
The one who has done evil will go to Hell.
Follow His [Christ's] counsel,
He was crucified and the people watched it.
Those who did it do not know God.
This is a conflict born of revenge,
Caused by the Devil.
Pray to God! He will love you.

VI

Persevere in your work as evangelists,
For the Redeemer is coming.
The time is no longer far off.
There are people who have much power. [Enemies?]

VII

Suffering is encompassing us because of the Name of our Chief, Jesus.
May He come and strengthen us!
His name is Chief.
May He strengthen us all!
Pray to the Redeemer!
We are encompassed by suffering.
We pray Thee for forgiveness.
Our sufferings are great.
We pray for forgiveness!
We are fleeing the Devil.
We pray for forgiveness.
The Redeemer will come to all of us
And will help us.
We pray Thee for forgiveness.
Forgiveness! strengthen us. We pray Thee for forgiveness.
The enemy is encircling us.
We pray Thee for forgiveness.
Jesus, Forgiveness, do not depart from us!

I commit myself into Thy hands.
The enemy does not want this.
We pray Thee for forgiveness.
We still have hope.
We pray for forgiveness.
Forgiveness! Come to our aid!
We pray Thee for forgiveness, our God.
Hear our words! Jesus, help us!
May no misfortune befall us!
We pray Thee for forgiveness.

These hymns show in what extremity the followers of Kimbangu were and how they turned in their affliction in prayer to God, to Jesus, and the Holy Spirit. In the express hope for the return of Christ and for salvation there is no doubt included the hope for the release of Simon Kimbangu and his fellow captives. In the first hymn they sing, 'In times past we did not know Thee ... Today we know Thee.' This presumably refers to the mission of Simon Kimbangu, through whose word and healings and through whose suffering Christ has come alive, 'existential' for his followers—no longer only a distant 'pale' Christ, but the Christ who has revealed himself in Zaïre. In later hymns, too, this one theme occurs again and again: 'We have received Jesus, the Son of God, through the prophet who has appeared among us. In Africa He has revealed Himself through Simon Kimbangu.' 'The intention here was to use hymns as a means of instruction; ... man is all rhythm and music, in Africa more than elsewhere,' says R. P. Masson.[10]

5. THE OUTLOOK

The suppression, which began in 1925, was so radical that in the years 1925–30 few new 'prophetic manifestations' were observed. Yet the movement continued to survive, but underground. Before his sentence Kimbangu is said to have exhorted his followers (and we were told this on various occasions) to become members of the existing churches for the time being. Thus, many returned to their churches but remained in their hearts—as 1959 was to prove—loyal to Kimbanguism.

[10] Masson, R. P.: 'Simples réflexions sur des chants kibanguistes', in 'Devant les sectes non-chrétiennes', Louvain, 1961, pp. 88–9.

However, they gathered in secret, sang their hymns of faith, and occasionally went on pilgrimages to the sacred spring of N'Kamba. We know this because the Belgian documents report that in 1932 Chief Lutunu denounced in Ngombe-Matadi followers of Kimbangu who had secretly gone to N'Kamba to fetch water and soil (water as a pledge of healing and soil as a sign that in N'Kamba, on earth and in the heart of Africa, God had revealed Himself to them).

CHAPTER 8

THE ARRIVAL OF THE SALVATION ARMY; SIMON MPADI

1. THE MOVEMENT LIVES ON

Despite all the measures of the Belgian administration the movement begun by Kimbangu was not stamped out. Documents from the years 1934–7 speak of a new revival of both groups, the Kimbanguists as well as the Ngunzists. Of the region around N'Kamba it was reported: 'No one hides his allegiance to the old Kimbanguist Movement: no palm wine is drunk, nothing is willingly accepted from the whites, not one person is to be found living in polygamy ... All the regulations of Kimbanguism are scrupulously observed.'[1] At that time, in 1934, many Kimbanguists were deported from Mbanza-Ngungu. Their behaviour never gave cause for complaint. On the contrary, their employers were by and large satisfied with them. As a result the administrator called them together and told them to seek as individuals reprieve from deportation and to give the assurance that they would never again give themselves to 'prophetic proselytism'. Hardly had the administrator made this suggestion when their spokesman declared, 'We're unable to make such a promise, we can't pledge ourselves to anything of the sort, even at the risk of being deported once and for all.' The acceptance of this suggestion would have been tantamount to a repudiation of all the Kimbanguists believed. The same suggestion was made to various other groups, but each time without success. The report came to the conclusion: 'None of them will ever drink a glass of palm wine; never will they join in dances; none of their children will follow a school course organized by the administration.'

[1] This quote and the ones which follow come from Documents secrets (belges), 'Recrudescence de 1934–37', p. 49.

The Arrival of the Salvation Army

This attitude alarmed the administration. It feared that, as soon as there was an opportunity, Kimbanguism would reappear. In order to avoid new difficulties, a colonial official suggested that communications between the exiles in the region of Thysville and their families in and around N'Kamba be severed. In addition, the exiles should be moved every two years to another place in order to counteract the spread of their faith.

The situation was apparently similar in Matadi on the Congo estuary and in Kasai Province: the followers remained loyal to Simon Kimbangu and resisted categorically the attempt to prevent them from spreading their teachings, which they regarded as God's cause.[2] The strongest prophetic activities were in the Luozi district where Philip Mbumba, a follower and disciple of Kimbangu since 1921, had great influence. As a result he was deported to the Province of Lake Leopold where he again became the leader of the exiles. In Luozi, however, there were just as many pseudo-Kimbanguists and Ngunzists at work.[3]

2. THE ARRIVAL OF THE SALVATION ARMY

The Salvation Army arrived in Matadi in 1934 and made a great stir with its uniforms, its fanfares, and its methods of evangelism. It was popular, and led a great religious revival throughout Lower Zaïre. But a great misunderstanding had arisen, for many of the followers of Kimbangu thought that the Salvation Army had come in his name. Did not the 'S' on the Army uniforms stand for Simon? Some (doubtless Ngunzists who looked to Simon Kimbangu) went so far as to claim that the Salvation Army was Simon Kimbangu himself who had returned to his country and his people.[4] Captain Becquet himself was regarded as the reincarnation of Simon Kimbangu.[5] It was assumed that Simon Kimbangu had become a white, a not unusual idea among the Bakongo, who believed that the ancestors returned to their kin in white form. For these reasons people flocked to the Salvation Army who, to begin with, were delighted with their success. Gradually the officers realized that there had been a misunderstanding.

In Brazzaville, in what was then the French Congo, the Salvation

[2] Op. cit., p. 50.
[3] Op. cit., pp. 50–1.
[4] E. Andersson: 'Messianic Popular Movements in the Lower Congo', Uppsala, 1958, pp. 126 ff.
[5] C.R.I.S.P.: op. cit., p. 8.

Army became for many Congolese an anti-magic movement. Those who were suspected of witchcraft, or thought they were bewitched, went to the Salvation Army. They shook hands with the officer. Those who could do that without any harm befalling them on their way back home proved that they had nothing to do with witchcraft.[6] People thronged to the Salvation Army in tremendous numbers, particularly in what was then the French Congo, to free themselves from the curse of witchcraft—the manifestation of the Evil One both in the individual and in society. The non-Christians and even many nominal Christians believe that people (not only women) fly through the air as witches without knowing it or make use of wild animals to enter the huts of their victims at night to inflict harm upon them and 'consume' them. The fear of evil; of the unknown; of 'fate'; the awareness that a man so often wishes evil on his fellows; and all antisocial behaviour, as well as the consciousness of personal inadequacy and the possibility of being 'evil' oneself, find their expression in this belief in witchcraft. Crude as it is, the belief in witchcraft has deep psychological roots, and was prevalent in 'Christian' Europe until not so long ago.

3. THE BEGINNINGS OF AN 'INDEPENDENT' AFRICAN SALVATION ARMY

Unfortunately, the Salvation Army employed assistants who had been excommunicated by the other missions partly because of Ngunzism, which increased the misunderstanding. From what was then the Belgian Congo Ngunzists from the district of Luozi went to the French Congo. Eventually the Salvation Army, as a letter from Captain Becquet of 28 November 1942 shows, had to ward off those who were coming forward to free themselves from the curse of witchcraft.

Consequently an independent African Salvation Army, or, as E. Andersson calls it, a 'Ngunzist Salvation Army', arose in both Congos and rapidly spread from 1942. Its teaching was far removed from what Kimbangu had ever taught: if a person had been to the Salvation Army he was perfect—no witch could put a spell on him. He could attain health.[7] Salvation had become entirely a thing of this world, as in so many syncretistic groups in southern Africa.[8] The Salvation Army proposed that such movements be not called 'Salva-

[6] Andersson: op. cit., pp. 132 ff.
[7] Op. cit., p. 134.
[8] See Ch. 6, note 20.

tion Army'. In Brazzaville it had the name of *Nzambi ya sika-sika*, 'the very new worship' which leads us to the figure of Simon Mpadi.

4. SIMON MPADI AND HIS 'MISSION OF THE BLACKS'

Simon Mpadi, still alive today in the district of Madimba and head of the 'Mission of the Blacks', comes from Madimba, an area in which Simon Kimbangu had many followers. At first he belonged to the American Baptist mission which was working there and became a village schoolteacher. Around 1937 (the year when the Belgian administration decided to stamp out completely Kimbanguism and Ngunzism) Simon Mpadi was dismissed from the employ of the mission for adultery. He went to the Salvation Army and, after a period of probation, entered the officers' school, after which he was stationed in the district of Madimba.[9]

The turning point came in 1939, the time of the outbreak of the Second World War in Europe and shortly before Belgium was overrun. Already during his training Mpadi received gifts from his adherents in Lower Zaïre, and unknown to his officers, was hailed as their 'spiritual head'. One day he came to see Becquet with a ready-made constitution of the Mission of the Blacks and was immediately dismissed.[10] Thus the independent 'Mission of the Blacks' is founded, its uniform being khaki. His first supporters are probably former Ngunzists or Christians excommunicated by the missions. The moral standards of Mpadism were very low, and both because of this and the quality of its membership, the movement should not be compared with Kimbanguism.[11]

Mpadi could not continue for long. Because it was not permitted to found a new church at that time, he was arrested and deported. The Ngunzist Movement had spread to Angola—as had Kimbanguism—whence Mpadi seems also to have fled before going to the ex-French Congo.[12] He claimed to have the confidence of Simon Kimbangu and looked to the prophet.

In his stay in the French Congo, Mpadi met with Philippe Kufinu (also known as Mavonda Ntangu) and Thomas Ngoma. There he laid the foundation-stone for the amalgamation of Ngunzism, the so-

[9] Oral information from Alexandre Kimu.
[10] Information received from the sister of Major Becquet.
[11] C.R.I.S.P.: op. cit., p. 9.
[12] M. Merlier: 'Le Congo de la colonisation belge à l'indépendance', Paris, 1962, pp. 239 ff.

called 'independent Salvation Army', and the *Amicale Balali* of André Matswa which was seeking to help the Africans to better social standing and ultimate freedom.[13] Matswa was already dead by that time, having died in Prison in 1942 in Mayama in the French Congo after one of his envoys, Pierre Nganga, had already established contacts with the Ngunzists and had talked of visions of Simon Kimbangu. Through this amalgamation with the *Mission of the Blacks* (also called *Mpadism* or *Kakhism*), *Amicalism*, which had been at first a socio-political, purely secular group, now took on messianic religious features.

Either in 1944 or—according to Massamba-Débat—on 3 August 1949, Mpadi was handed over to the Belgian colonial authorities and also deported to distant Lubumbashi (Elisabethville), where he was put in the same prison as Simon Kimbangu.[14]

According to Balandier's and Andersson's accounts, Mpadi's Khakists, who also invoked the names of Matswa and Kimbangu, became fully syncretistic again and, at the time when Balandier was conducting his investigations, showed few Christian characteristics.[15] Nevertheless, Philippe Kufinu, who carried on a 'mission' after Mpadi's arrest, looked to Kimbangu, whom he saw in a vision and from whom he claimed to have received his commission. Kufinu came from Luozi in the ex-Belgian Congo, the centre of the Ngunzists, but he worked for the most part in the French Congo.

In Zaïre Mpadi's Mission of the Blacks had its main sphere of influence in the region of Madimba, Kasangulu and Mbanzu-Ngungu, where the Kimbanguists had been vigorously suppressed since 1937. Because the Mission of the Blacks in this region involved the name of Kimbangu, their activities and their manifestations of religious syncretism were often laid to the charge of Kimbanguism—although the Kimbanguists survived only in secret.

Simon Mpadi remained in prison in Lubumbashi until 1960, when Zaïre became independent. He then returned to the district of Madimba and Kinshasa, where I saw him briefly in July 1968. He

[13] E. Andersson: op. cit., p. 140.

[14] A. Massamba-Débat: 'De la révolution messianique à la révolution politique', Brazzaville, 1968, p. 66; G. Balandier: 'Sociologie actuelle de l'Afrique noire', revised edn, Paris, 1963, p. 449. Balandier tells us that S. Mpadi was arrested both in 1944 and 1949.

[15] G. Balandier (op. cit., pp. 431 ff.) describes above all the church of Galaboma in Congo-Brazzaville, in the district of Mayama, which was founded by E. Nganga and has Kimbanguist, Mpadist, and Ngunzist elements. The church is strongly syncretistic, and its ritual is borrowed from Catholicism. See pp. 465–77.

was wearing a splendid red robe embroidered with golden crosses, so very different from the members of the Kimbanguist Church, who—apart from the almost military dress which the *service de surveillance* (supervisory service) wear at special services of worship—have no religious vestments or uniforms. Mpadi returned along with 3,000 Kimbanguists who had survived deportation. Despite his appeal to Simon Kimbangu, there is no connection between his Mission of the Blacks and the Church of Jesus Christ on Earth through the Prophet Simon Kimbangu. In contrast to the Kimbanguists, Mpadi has reintroduced polygamy. He stresses ecstatic elements much more than the Kimbanguists, who keep them under fairly strict control.

CHAPTER 9

SIMON KIMBANGU'S MOVEMENT IN THE FORMER FRENCH CONGO

1. THE BEGINNINGS IN BOKO, AND SAMUEL MATUBA

Whilst Simon Kimbangu was preaching in N'Kamba in April and May 1921, there also came vast numbers of Congolese to N'Kamba from the other side of the River Congo, from what was then the French Congo. It is a good day's journey on foot from Boko to N'Kamba. The Swedish missionaries, whose main station in the district of Boko is still Musana, saw that great crowds from the whole region were going to Simon Kimbangu.[1] They sent to N'Kamba Samuel Matuba of Boko, a man who had first been an evangelist and then, after being trained in the college of Kingoyi in the region of Luozi, had become a minister. His task was to find out the nature of the movement which Simon Kimbangu had started. The missionaries wanted to know in particular whether there was here true prophecy in the New Testament sense. Samuel Matuba told me in May 1969, 'I was the last person in Boko to go to N'Kamba.' He heard the biblical message of the prophet, witnessed healings and returned to his missionaries to—as he himself put it—'witness to the truth' concerning Simon Kimbangu.[2]

To begin with the missionaries were open to Simon Kimbangu's movement, and saw in it the possibility of a great revival. It is true that many supporters of the mission in Sweden had become convinced that the revival in Musana featured those unhealthy elements of organized ecstasy which marked the Ngunzists. However, a missionary in intimate contact with the movement put that right and

[1] Documents secrets (belges), 'Kimbanguisme-Ngounzisme en A.E.F.' (Afrique Equatoriale Française), p. 44
[2] Oral information, recorded on tape.

reported what had really happened:[3] 'In 1921 there was news of the prophet' [Simon Kimbangu] 'and his miracles. Two of the professeurs [presumably Congolese schoolteachers] went to N'Kamba without first asking permission of the white missionaries. However, no one stopped them and they were simply given the advice to discern between good and evil. After their return, in May 1921, a great interest in the prophetic movement was noticeable among the population. The heathen were throwing away their fetishes.'

In an article written in 1939,[4] Andersson claims that the faith of these people had its roots in traditional notions concerning *nzambi* (the term for 'god' in Kikongo), but the zealous opposition to fetishes showed the Christian, or at any rate the biblical, character of the movement. And Ekstam, a missionary in Kinyogi, writes: 'Along the roads you could see idols and magic pouches which had been thrown away, showing that the people were moved in their heart of hearts.'[5]

Our account continues: 'The chiefs sought the aid of the missionaries, sending people to Musana to obtain teachers and schools—presumably to teach the population how to read the Bible. All the teachers were filled with a great desire to save souls and proclaimed the Gospel powerfully. They had only one great aim, and that was to win the Congo for Christ.' A great revival movement began. Thousands went to testify that they had forsaken their pagan beliefs and wanted to serve the living God. The supply of hymnbooks had just run out. So the hymns of the prophet and his followers were introduced and sung. In their enthusiasm, those touched by the revival wanted to sing night and day. 'Everywhere hymns and prayers were heard.' There were no signs of xenophobia or political propaganda—which proves that genuine Kimbanguists, not Ngunzist elements, were at work. They prayed for the sick, always doing so in a dignified way.[6] The exhortation to be willing to die, to be loyal in persecution, and not to repay evil with evil, was not lacking either. Nowhere in Congo were taxes paid more promptly than in the region of Boko. When missionaries visited the villages, they were welcomed and the Gospel was heeded. The hymns were sung lustily and really enjoyed. The people came in such throngs to

---

[3] Unfortunately, I was unable to discover the name of the missionary. He wrote the letter on 16 December 1922, in Mariestad (Sweden). A photocopy of it (or rather, of an unsigned carbon-copy) was placed at my disposal by Mr F. M. M'Vuendy, who is writing a sociological study of Kimbanguism.

[4] Svensk Missionstidskrift 1939, pp. 24–5.

[5] G. Balandier: op. cit., pp. 435 ff.

[6] 'mais toujours restant dans les formes les plus dignes'.

be baptized that the writer of the letter admitted that he doubted whether he would ever experience anything as great again.

And yet, he remarked, enemies were also at work. Some of the heathen chiefs were afraid of losing their influence, and they were supported by their superiors in the French colonial administration. That the drums no longer called people to dance but hymns rang out instead, and that a third of the population had been converted, was not welcomed. The writer exclaimed at this point, 'O, you Satanic power, when will you be destroyed and when will justice triumph?' He closed the letter thus: 'It seems to us, who have seen all that has happened, beyond doubt that what is now being done to suppress this revival is tantamount to religious persecution, for in the name of justice we must say that there is nothing to justify what is now happening.'

It is therefore clear that the missionaries were at first open to the movement triggered off by Simon Kimbangu and had reason to hope that it could be integrated into the church. Soon afterwards, however, the missionaries adopted a reserved and then a negative attitude towards the movement.[7] Had Ngunzist elements crept in? Samuel Matuba does not know the reason. Were perhaps the French colonial authorities responsible, since they co-operated with the Belgian authorities and adopted the same sceptical and hostile attitude towards the Kimbanguists and Ngunzists as the Belgians?

Samuel Matuba was excommunicated by the Swedish mission, but he was not intimidated and continued unswervingly with his evangelism. In 1922, he was arrested by the French colonial authorities in Boko and taken to prison in Brazzaville, some 140 km. away. From Brazzaville he was deported to Fort Archambault in what is now the Republic of Chad and put into prison there. He was freed in 1927 and returned to Boko. Despite all the dangers, he courageously held secret Kimbanguist meetings and undertook evangelism. In 1930 he was imprisoned for the second time. It was the heyday of the Ngunzists who, inspired by Yoani Mvubi of Luozi were proclaiming that the final conflict was at hand, thus gravely compromising true Kimbanguists. Samuel Matuba was again deported to distant Chad, this time to Crebedji, where he spent five years in prison. Up to his death on 4 September 1970, he often wore a loose, white, shirt-like dress of the people of Chad. Although he was brought back home to Boko in 1935, he remained until 1940 under close police surveillance.

At the famous conference of Free French forces in Brazzaville in

[7] Oral information from Samuel Matuba.

1944, de Gaulle was fêted by Matswaists and Ngunzists as a 'saviour'. From now on in the region of Congo-Brazzaville Kimbanguist meetings could be held without police interference, although the Kimbanguist Church was not officially recognized until 1961. But from 1948 on there was limited religious freedom—'a merely camouflaged freedom',[8] as it was called.

2. THE SPREAD OF THE KIMBANGUIST MOVEMENT IN THE PEOPLE'S REPUBLIC OF THE CONGO

From Boko the Kimbanguist Movement spread very rapidly to the capital Brazzaville and to Pointe Noire on the Atlantic coast, albeit secretly, and a little later to Dolisie and finally to Libreville in Gabon. As in the Belgian Congo, the Kimbanguists were the 'quiet ones in the country', whereas Ngunzists, followers of Matswa, and the Khaki Movement of Simon Mpadi were much more noticeable and caused confusion.[9]

How Kimbanguism arose in what we know as the French 'Haut-Congo' (Upper Congo) is interesting.[10] Two Kimbanguists, banished to the then Belgian Upper Congo and now settled in Kwamouth at the confluence of the River Kasai and the River Zaïre, met one day in 1924 Fadouma Antoine, a hunter who had crossed the river in a dugout. They asked him, 'Do you want us to give you something which you don't yet have?' When the huntsman said he did they told him the message which Simon Kimbangu had preached and lived. The huntsman was impressed, and the two exiles urged him, 'Go back across the river and proclaim there what you've heard. Fadouma Antoine's testimony was heeded and accepted, and thus there arose in the French Upper Congo (in Ngunzulu) the first Kimbanguist congregation, quite independent of the groups which already existed in Boko, Pointe Noire and Brazzaville. This short episode is also an eloquent testimony to the evangelistic zeal of the exiles and shows their simple method of evangelism. What impressed people again and again was the fact that God, the Father of Jesus Christ, had chosen an instrument in Africa and had thus shown himself the merciful Saviour of the despised African, who was suffering under the yoke of colonialism.

One of the men who accepted the message of Fadouma Antoine

[8] 'liberté camouflée seulement'.
[9] Oral information from David Nsomi, leader of the Kimbanguist church in Brazzaville.
[10] Oral information from P. Obambi.

was Paul Obambi, one of my informants. Paul Obambi went to Gamboma and Kundjulu, in the district of Djambala, and taught there in the heart of the Congo what he had heard. He had the fortune not to fall into the hands of the colonial authorities.

In 1930, when Samuel Matuba was imprisoned for the second time, David Nsomi (the present leader of the work in the People's Republic of the Congo) was also deported, first to Gamboma and then to Djambala, though as a prisoner he was unable to establish any contacts with the congregations there. So it took quite a while before contacts between the Kimbanguists in the Upper Congo, in the centre of the country, and in the old congregations of Boko and Brazzaville were established. There was not even any contact between Ngunzulu, Gamboma and Djambala, and this was not rectified until 1956. Until then the congregations in the Congo lived in almost complete isolation.

Although from 1948 there was religious freedom on paper in the French Congo, the Kimbanguists could not appear openly as the 'Church of Jesus Christ on Earth through the Prophet Simon Kimbangu' until 1956, the year in which the movement in the Belgian Congo was first granted limited 'freedom', as we shall see. From 1956 on, Kimbanguists from Kinshasa (among them Joseph Diangienda) attended services in Brazzaville or Boko on various occasions, though not without the risk of criminal action being taken against them. The Kimbanguists of Kinshasa came and systematically taught their hymns, written and set to music in the long years of exile and persecution, to the Brazzaville Kimbanguists, thus establishing closer contact between the Kimbanguists of the two countries, separated by the European powers. In 1962, André Mayunga, a successful Brazzaville businessman, began to build at his own expense a church in the centre of Brazzaville, and it was consecrated at Easter 1969. In Boko, the administrative centre of the Kimbanguist Church in the Congo, another church was also built.

3. THE MISSION TO THE PYGMIES

In 1966, in the district of Gamboma, in Ngafura, and in the district of Djambala, the Kimbanguist Church began work among the pygmies, who are today still despised by the Bantu, and who lived until recently from hunting and catching fish and, like the bushmen in the Kalahari, spent their lives as nomads. It is extremely difficult to reach such nomadic tribes with the Gospel. The Kimbanguists found the pygmies living in great poverty because, with the advance of civilization, animals that can be hunted are becoming increasingly scarce, and the first of the early evangelists was sent to begin agricultural work. He showed the people how to plant manioc and other crops, as well as how to keep poultry, easing the transition from hunting to agriculture. At the same time the Gospel was preached to them. In 1968, when I made a brief visit to a pygmy village near Ngafura, there were already a hundred candidates wanting to become Christians. Because the pygmies lacked everything—not only clothes, which they wanted, but more importantly hoes and other simple agricultural implements—the Kimbanguists in Zaïre and the Congo took up collections in order to help these, the poorest of the poor in Central Africa.

The Kimbanguist Church has at present about 10,000 members in the People's Republic of the Congo, very few in comparison with Zaïre, where by 1959 there were a million members, and where there are today probably more than three million Kimbanguists.[11] But it is important to remember two facts. In the first place, the Kimbanguists in the Congo had until recently only one Land-Rover, and most of the roads into the interior were extremely bad: this was a real hindrance to evangelism. In the second place, the population is only one million strong, many of whom are non-Christians, whereas there are probably more than twenty-two million people living in Zaïre.[12]

[11] Unfortunately, there are no statistics, though every member of the Kimbanguist Church has a membership card.

[12] Statistics were published during the course of 1971–2 based on the census which was made at the beginning of 1970.

CHAPTER 10

TOWARDS TOLERATION AND INDEPENDENCE

1. THE REVIVAL OF KIMBANGUISM

After the War the Belgians proposed to assert their authority and to continue in their Colony as before. But it was inevitable that as time went on Belgium should lose its position in Zaïre.

C.R.I.S.P.[1] records that in 1947 the Ngunzists attracted attention once more in Kinshasa, spurred on and led by an Angolan evangelist belonging to the Jehovah's Witnesses. In the eastern Kivu Province of Zaïre there had already been a rising in 1944 led by the prophet Bushiri. Bushiri had been arrested with 73 companions and sentenced to death.[2] The name of the Africanized movement (which is a schism from the Jehovah's Witnesses) in Zambia and in Zaïre is *Kitawala*—a mutation of the English word 'watchtower', the title of the Witness periodical. In 1935 the Kitawala Movement in the Province of Shaba (Katanga) precipitated a crisis, which was probably an additional reason why Kimbangu was not liberated at that time despite his exemplary conduct.

About 1948, a certain Simão Toko began to prophesy in Kinshasa.[2] He healed people, showed signs (trembling) of being possessed by the Holy Spirit, and exerted considerable influence over his adherents. He contacted Joseph Diangienda, and referred to the teaching of Simon Kimbangu. His group was known as 'Nzambi na mapapu' (the winged god) a reference to the trembling which we associate particularly with the Ngunzists. Toko was arrested in 1949 and deported to Angola, his native country, where his 'red star'

[1] C.R.I.S.P.: op. cit., p. 9.
[2] V. Lanternari: 'Les mouvements religieux des peuples opprimés', Paris, 1962, p. 248. (Oral information by ex-adepts of Toko.)

movement—the red star being a symbol used by Toko—was later banned. Was Toko a Kimbanguist or a Ngunzist? The question is still asked today. But in my opinion, Toko himself supplied the answer in 1961. At that time, there was a conflict between Toko and the clandestine Kimbanguist movement in Angola; and both Toko and the Kimbanguists were exiled. But now Toko has completely severed his ties with Kimbanguism, and is reported to live in Portugal or Madeira. Some of his ex-followers (who had been with him in Kinshasa) are now faithful and active Kimbanguists. Several admit that Toko transmitted vital impulses to them; but since 1949, under the influence of Joseph Diagenda, they have turned to Kimbanguism.

A further figure who comes into the limelight at this time is *Emmanuel Bamba*, a native of Kasangulu. His former friend Kimu Alexandre, who now holds a high administrative and spiritual position in the Kimbanguist Church, describes him as a forceful personality, not without ambition (I was told by Charles Kisolokele), and yet deeply religious, as I was assured by a Methodist missionary who often met Bamba in Lubumbashi. From 1935 to 1941, when the Kimbanguists were under heavy pressure, he lived with Kimu Alexandre in Nsona Bata where Kimbanguism was widespread. Bamba's mother had made a pilgrimage to N'Kamba in the very early period of the movement, so he must have had contact in his youth with the teaching and ministry of Simon Kimbangu. From 1947 to 1950 he was the 'right-hand man' of Joseph Diangienda, who was then beginning to visit the scattered Kimbanguist groups and to hold services with them in secret, although he was still officially a member of the Catholic Church. Impressed by the healing of the sick, Bamba was a Kimbanguist, but he also engaged in practices which are alien to Kimbanguism. He had candles and oil sent from America, and he used the oil to anoint the sick. In 1950 he went with Joseph Diangienda and Charles Kisolokele to N'Kamba to seek healing for his sick child.[3]

The frequent assertion (see e.g. C.R.I.S.P., *op. cit.*, p. 9) that he had in 1949 a crucial influence on Joseph Diangienda and persuaded him to take on the leadership of the Kimbanguists, is not true. It seems to have been rather that Emmanuel Bamba himself wanted to assume the leadership. In 1951 he was arrested and taken to prison in Lubumbashi, where he met Kimbangu. Although he was in personal touch with Kimbangu only for a few months, as far as this was possible in prison, this meeting seems to have made a strong

[3] Oral information from Alexandre Kimu.

impression on him. After his release he abandoned syncretistic elements and the practice of healing by anointing with oil. In 1959 he was arrested again, this time because of political activities on behalf of ABAKO, the Bakongo Party. In 1960 he returned to Kinshasa and was present in April 1960 when the mortal remains of Simon Kimbangu were transferred to N'Kamba.[4]

On his return from Lubumbashi, he travelled throughout Zaïre, declaring that if he should ever found a new church, he would have taken leave of his senses. However, there was soon a rift, for Bamba was apparently seeking worldly honours. He was a businessman, became a cabinet minister, and founded in 1962 his own church, 'Le Salut de Jésus-Christ par le témoin Simon Kimbangu',[5] a church which was, as far as we can tell, orthodox in its teaching but with an intensely nationalistic streak.

2. THE ROLE OF KIMBANGU'S SONS

All religious movements continued to be vigorously suppressed in Zaïre, and the founding of churches outside the Catholic and Protestant missions was forbidden. Nevertheless, Joseph Diangienda had begun, since his arrival in 1947 in Kinshasa, to take up secret contact with the groups existing in the country and to strengthen them. He had been educated like his brother Charles Kisolokele by the Catholic 'Brothers' of the 'school colony' in Boma. Intelligent, far-sighted and deeply convinced of the divine mission of his father, which it was his task to carry on, he was a man who knows his Bible and who also has the gift of healing through prayer and the laying on of hands. He was at the time a secretary in the service of high officials of the colonial administration, finally becoming the private secretary of the Governor-General. They thought highly of him for his qualities of character, his integrity and conscientiousness. He had been married in the Catholic Church, and until 1956 he was forced to remain outwardly a Catholic. From Kananaga, where he was at the time of his father's death in 1951, he returned in 1952 to Kinshasa, still a secretary in the service of the Belgian administration. From

[4] Oral information. E. Bamba can be seen on the photo which was taken at the beginning of April 1960, when the mortal remains of Simon Kimbangu were transferred to N'Kamba. The photo hangs in the waiting-room of Joseph Diangienda.
[5] The Salvation of Jesus Christ through the Witness Simon Kimbangu (C.R.I.S.P., 1966, p. 432).

time to time he went (despite threats) on Sundays to Brazzaville to worship with the Kimbanguists.

His eldest brother Charles Kisolokele was still living in exile. After finishing his studies in Boma he first became a teacher at his school, then he too entered, as an exile, the service of the administration. After thirty years (in 1960) he was to end his administrative career as the first Zaïrian *agent territorial principal* in Maduda in the western tip of Zaïre in the Territory of Tshela. In 1960, after the release of the exiles, he went to live in Kinshasa, where, until he became ill in 1963, he served as a minister in three different cabinets (under Lumumba, Ileo, and Adoula). He is now a People's Commissioner in the National Assembly and also occupies a leading position in the church as the person in charge of schooling and social work, and 'chef spirituel premier adjoint.'

Solomon Kiangani Dialungana stayed with his mother Mwilu Marie in Ngombe-Kinsuka across from N'Kamba, which is still uninhabited. He is 'chef spirituel deuxième adjoint.'

3. LUCIEN LUNTADILA COMES TO THE FORE

In 1951, Lucien Luntadila, the man who was to become their General Secretary, joined the Kimbanguists. Though his parents were Protestants, Luntadila was at that time a student in a seminary for priests, preparing for theological training. He wrote:[6] 'We heard in 1951 of the death of Simon Kimbangu. Kimbangu's so-called conversion to Catholicism was made much of in the papers. My fellow students teased me by saying, "Well, your prophet who you say performed miracles is dead and was even converted to Catholicism!"' Luntadila told me that the accusations which were constantly hurled at Kimbangu and his movement had made him study the matter more closely. Although he could not know as yet that the story of Kimbangu's conversion to Catholicism was fiction, he replied, 'I still say he performed miracles and preached the Gospel.'

'As a result I was dismissed from the seminary,' he writes, 'but I was not the only one who lost his place, for there were others who also testified to their sympathies with Simon Kimbangu. Some of these others lost their jobs, and their children were expelled from church schools. There were hardly any state schools at that time.'

Luntadila, a gifted man (he studied for a short time in Geneva at the 'Institut Africain'), found a post immediately with the colonial

---

[6] L'Essor, No. 13, 29 September 1966, La Chaux-de-Fonds.

administration, where educated people were needed. Besides, from 1954 on the administration became more liberal when a liberal-socialist government came to power in Brussels.

When working in the section *population noire* (black population), Luntadila came across documents which told of new deportations of Kimbanguists and Ngunzists, among whom his uncle was included. 'One day', so he writes (it was between 1954 and 1956) 'a document of the United Nations, which Belgium had joined, came into my possession. Wisely, Belgium had not published this document (the 'Declaration of Human Rights') in Zaïre.' Luntadila read it with the utmost interest. As a result the Kimbanguists sent a memorandum to the UNO and a letter to the Belgian minister, van Acker. Furthermore, they contacted members of parliament concerning the fate of the exiles. The scandal was published—at last—in the press. From 1956 on Kimbanguist services and prayer meetings were held again throughout the country and other churches became empty.

Conflict with the Protestants followed. Protestant ministers and evangelists more or less announced in 1956 in their services that supporters of the Kimbanguist Movement had no longer any right to be members of the Protestant churches, though this is what Kimbangu had advised them to become. In their dismay they went to Joseph Diangienda, who confessed, 'C'était la journée la plus dure de ma vie' ('it was the hardest day of my life'). At the time he was still the secretary of Governor-General Pétillon. 'From that day on we organized our services on private plots of land (*parcelles*), and thus the Kimbanguists broke away from the Protestants.'[7]

We can assume from this that until 1956 the Kimbanguist Movement could have become a sort of spearhead and an 'Africanizing' element within Protestantism despite all that had happened in the 30s. Without a doubt, this would have brought new life into the historical churches, and many of their current problems could perhaps have been solved. But the action of certain Protestant churches in 1956 made this impossible. Since then the Kimbanguist Church has evolved its own type of church with its distinctive structure. Until 1956 Kimbanguism was a movement. From 1956 on it developed as an independent church which can be regarded as neither Catholic nor Protestant. It was now that the name 'Église de Jésus-Christ sur la terre par le prophète Simon Kimbangu' (EJCSK)—the 'Church of Jesus Christ on Earth through the Prophet Simon Kimbangu'—was coined.

[7] Oral information from Joseph Diangienda, recorded on tape.

Following these early moves to form a church, the colonial government once again took a number of measures. But now Kimbanguist young folk, under Luntadila's leadership, protested (the source for the following description is L'Essor, *op. cit.*) They held a peaceful demonstration: they hired lorries, drove through the city of Kinshasa, and sang Kimbanguist hymns. The police came and arrested them. They continued to sing.

> Go into the villages and proclaim salvation,
> Everywhere on earth preach forgiveness to the oppressed!
> Armed with the Gospel go from town to town,
> Win the whole wide world for God!
> Bear the message of hope to all sinners,
> And preach Jesus Christ!

The police began to hit out at them. The scars on the arms of Luntadila still bear witness to the ill-treatment he received. The Kimbanguists followed simply the teaching and example of Kimbangu, who had spoken out against all use of violence.

4. NEW DEPORTATIONS—THE GREAT TURNING-POINT

On 11 June 1957 there were further arrests and deportation. The newspaper *Le Kimbanguisme*, which was published for three years from 1960 to 1962, referred back to this on 15 June 1960 under the title, *Ne craignez pas ceux qui tuent le corps mais qui ne peuvent tuer l'âme* (do not fear those who kill the body but cannot kill the soul). This was illustrated with a photograph of the five congregational leaders who had been arrested including Stephen Diasiwa (at present the principal minister of Kinshasa), Jean Mantuidi (who from 1962 on was to serve in the sphere of Kimbanguist education) and Kina Paul. They were bound with ropes around their necks and were found guilty of being 'rebels', 'xenophobists', and 'deceivers'. In 1957 the Kimbanguists had reached the point where they said, 'It can't go on like this.' There followed in Kinshasa's Baudouin Stadium (now called the 20th of May Stadium) what has become a famous episode in the history of the Kimbanguist Church. Whilst Joseph Diangienda, stayed in his car to pray, a delegation of Kimbanguists went with a letter to the Belgian Governor-General Pétillon. The letter contained the signatures of 600 leading Kimbanguists in Kinshasa who were known for their irreproachable behaviour. 800 were ready to sign, but the project had to be rushed through so fast that only 600 could give their signatures. Part of the letter ran: 'We are suffering so much. Wherever we meet for prayer we are arrested by your soldiers. In order not to burden the police with added work we shall all gather—unarmed—in the Stadium, where you can arrest us all at once or massacre us.' The alternative was, though not explicitly stated, 'or you can grant us religious freedom!'

With this letter the delegation went to Pétillon whilst the Kimbanguists stayed away from work and prepared themselves for arrest or death and began to make their way to the Stadium! The Governor-General found himself in an awkward situation. 'Do you think that the government has the right to wipe out a whole section of the population without further ado?' he asked the delegates. They replied, 'What do you mean? Doesn't the government have this right? How otherwise could it have deported 37,000 families?' Pétillon hesitated. He did not want to make a decision. What would Brussels say if he turned the police on the unarmed crowd? What would the world press have to say about it? On the other hand, how would the *colons*, the white settlers, react if he granted the Kimbanguists religious freedom? The delegation was not to be fobbed off with verbiage and deferments. It wanted a clear yes or no. 'Whilst we are here all our friends are praying,' they added. Finally the Governor-General granted toleration. 'I grant you toleration, though not with the government's guarantee. I do not have the authority to give you that. But I will not arrest you.'[8]

'We were overjoyed', L. Luntadila concluded his account of the incident. Of course, negotiations were slow. Joseph Diangienda had to write several times more to Belgian government offices, stressing his political neutrality and pleading the right to practise his religion freely. The disturbances in Matadi, Kinshasa and elsewhere, mentioned earlier, and which were occasioned by politico-religious Ngunzist elements, did not make things any easier, since they were laid to the charge of the Kimbanguists. When called to account on this score, the leader of the Kimbanguists replied. 'If you can find one single Kimbanguist among the imprisoned Ngunzists, we shall admit that we are guilty.'[9] They could not find one. A Belgian parliamentary commission which studied the Matadi risings of 1 January 1959, could not find any proof of direct Kimbanguist participation. The Kimbanguists themselves published in the press a categorical denial of having had any complicity in the affair. They stressed that none of their members could be seen on any of the

[8] Oral information from Joseph Diangienda.
[9] Oral information.

Towards Toleration and Independence

many photos taken during the rising.[10] It was of course not easy to distinguish between Kimbanguists and Ngunzists, for the latter often appealed to Kimbangu as well. One of the Ngunzist rebels in Matadi actually called himself the risen Simon Kimbangu.

Joseph Diangienda has since become the legal representative (*représentant légal*) of the Church of Jesus Christ on Earth through the Prophet Simon Kimbangu. Some time after these risings, on 26 October 1959, he submitted an official petition to the President of Senate in Brussels for recognition of the church and an end to the continuing discriminatory measures, and this was finally attained at Christmas 1959.

The Kimbanguist Church was recognized by the Belgian colonial government and placed on the same footing as the Catholic and Protestant churches. Eight months before, on 27 April 1959, the widow of Simon Kimbangu, Marie Mwilu, the indefatigable counsellor and comforter, had died. She did not live to see the day the church received recognition.

Six months later, on 30 June 1960, Zaïre suddenly declared its independence. The difficult period of government crisis and risings began, continuing until 1965 (in the north-east until as late as 1967).

But let us return to 1957 when the church was at last granted toleration. Despite this, the Kimbanguists still met with grave misunderstandings and even hostility on the part of the churches. In a document *Mise au Point*,[11] dated September 1957, there is the following assertion:

'God, who is infinitely just, and merciful towards all men, was moved (*touché*) by the excellent work of His ambassadors (the missionaries) in Central Africa as well as by the great courage and the humility of our forebears, who received the word of God, and so He gave them the prophet Simon Kimbangu. It was at the beginning of 1921 that Simon Kimbangu was commissioned by Almighty God (*du Très-Haut*). He was visited by Jesus Christ, who told him to save lost souls. "Kimbangu" means the "Witness" (ed.: in Kikongo the word *kimbangi* means "witness") to faith in the Gospel of God, which was proclaimed by the missionaries, and the "Revealer" of what was still concealed.'

The document refutes in particular the false accusations that Kimbangu's followers were xenophobists, that Kimbangu had be-

[10] Rapports à la Chambre, Chambre de Représentants, Session 1958–9, March 1959.

[11] 'Mise au point', an excerpt appeared in C.R.I.S.P., 1960, op. cit., p. 18. The whole document was hectographed and placed at my disposal for these studies, but it is no longer available.

come a Catholic, or that he was a rebel. It also criticizes the Baptists, though their good work is recognized. On the other hand, it contains (as Mr Casebow, the missionary, demonstrated in a pamphlet)[12] several erroneous details, mainly concerning the visit of the missionaries Hillard and Jennings to N'Kamba, which had taken place on 17 May 1921. The particulars concerning the 'healed' Nlemvo, Dr Bentley's blind assistant who worked with him on the Kikongo translation of the Bible, are also inaccurate according to Casebow's statement.

Mise au point does, however, correct certain errors in what had hitherto been written about Kimbanguism which does not tally with the facts because much of the information comes from enemies of the movement—which is especially true of the article by the Jesuit Father J. van Wing.

By and large it is a document which shows how tense the situation still was in 1957, and it reveals a certain animosity towards the missionaries. Those who signed the document in the name of the Kimbanguists (*adeptes du Kimbanguisme*) are Lucien J. Cl. Luntadila, Yowani Albert, Diata Norbert, and Wikisi Raymond.[13]

Mr Casebow's 'reply' contains an important piece of information concerning Simon Kimbangu: when the prophetess Thérèse Mbonga died he refused to raise her from the dead. In a sober fashion, he said to those who wished him to resurrect her: 'It was God's will that she should die and so she is not to be raised from the dead.'[14] In addition, the 'reply' contains an exhortation of Kimbangu to his followers not to leave the white missionaries without help in house and garden. It was Mr Casebow's concern to help the Kimbanguists through his amendments and to present a more sober picture of Simon Kimbangu himself, which was certainly important in the controversy of 1957.

5. THE CONSEQUENCES OF CHURCH TOLERATION AND RECOGNITION

Christmas 1959 was the first time since 1924 that the Kimbanguists could openly celebrate Christmas together without fear. All those who until then had followed Kimbangu's recommendation and had become members of the Protestant or Catholic churches or the Salvation Army now publicly joined their church, the 'Church of

[12] 'Reply to Kimbanguism', 1958, mimeographed.
[13] Wikisi Raymond says that he has since left the Kimbanguist Church.
[14] Mandombe Mikala confirmed this fact. Thérèse Mbonga had died before Simon Kimbangu was arrested.

Jesus Christ on Earth through the Prophet Simon Kimbangu'. The result is that once more many of the mission churches lost a considerable number of their members and their churches empty as in 1921.

Some mission churches (but not all) reacted to this development. Thousands of Kimbanguist children were expelled from Catholic as well as Protestant schools, or stayed away because they were afraid of being expelled.[15] Despairing parents visited Joseph Diangienda, who decided on 4 January 1960 to open Kimbanguist schools, using voluntary teachers to begin with and meeting outside under trees and palm roofs. A well-qualified educationist from Brazzaville, Matthieu Ouatoula, and his young assistant, F. M'Vuendy, were entrusted with the organization. From these modest beginnings a considerable educational system has developed in the last ten years, so that in 1968 93,600 pupils were receiving education in state-supported schools as well as many thousands of children and young people in Kimbanguist schools not yet recognized by the state. Some schools teach up to university entrance. The leaders of the church want to give good schooling to the best of their people and make a university education possible for them. Thus, in October 1970 the *Institut pédagogique et théologique* (Institute of Education and Theology) should have been opened in Kinshasa and to have university status; as this was not possible for various reasons, a theological seminary was opened the same year to train Kimbanguist theologians. (see Appendix, page 182).

Although the Kimbanguists were not wealthy after all the persecution they had suffered, and the civil disturbances in the country, they paid for everything out of their own pockets and continued to build up the church, the educational system, and their social work (see below, Chapter 11) without any financial help from abroad or from a missionary society. They fulfil the ideal, long since formulated by the missionary societies, of being a self-propagating, self-supporting, and self-governing church, as they would have wanted to be way back in 1923 and 1924.

6. THE CONSTRUCTION OF THE MAUSOLEUM IN N'KAMBA

The exiles were permitted to return, but of the 37,000 deported *families* only 3,000 people came back. Charles Kisolokele, who had

---

[15] This harsh measure may have been taken because the church schools (there were only a few state schools) could only take a limited number of pupils and they had in the first place to give preference to their own members.

been living in exile since 1921, left Tshela for good on 3 June 1960 to settle in Kinshasa. Joseph Diangienda had set up headquarters amongst the working-class population of the city and lives in a modest house in the Ngiri-Ngiri zone, formerly a native township'. He gave up his post as a secretary of the administration in 1959 and has since devoted himself full-time to the church. He receives no payment, and his older brother supports him, his wife, and his children. Yet N'Kamba remains the administrative centre of the church, and is of course more than simply that, since it is still the new Jerusalem, which has been repopulated since 1960.

On 24 August 1959, during the period when the church was tolerated but not yet recognized by the state, Joseph Diangienda petitioned the colonial administration, asking for permission to transfer the mortal remains of his father Simon Kimbangu to N'Kamba. This was refused. 'The time had not yet come,' he now says, looking back. In March 1960, shortly before Zaïre became independent, the petition was granted.

A delegation, made up of the three sons of Kimbangu, Emmanuel Bamba and other leading Kimbanguists, went to Lumbumbashi. The coffin was dug up, the mortal remains were placed in a sarcophagus and taken to Matadi Mayo near Kinshasa, arriving on 2 April 1960, and on the following day Simon Kimbangu was taken to his final resting place, a simple mausoleum in N'Kamba, where an impressive ceremony was held. A moving hymn was written for this occasion: 'Now we rejoice greatly in the Lord, although He has taken from us the one who was so dear to us. But now, as we see him again and he returns to us, we sing hallelujah, praise the Name of the Lord!' The hymn gives voice to feelings of joy and hope for resurrection. The exclamation 'Hallelujah' rings out repeatedly. This hope and joy is a feature of all worship in the Kimbanguist Church.

7. ANCESTOR WORSHIP?

Twice a year the simple mausoleum in N'Kamba-Jerusalem is opened so that pilgrims can see the sarcophagus and offer a prayer of thanksgiving. This happens particularly at the great annual festival on 6 April, commemorating the first miracle which Simon Kimbangu performed. Is this ancestor worship? There are ethnologists who are quick to find traces of non-Christian religion in everything to do with an independent African church. However, they rarely ask how far the old has been transformed and thus become new. The African lives far more in the dimension where time and eternity meet. The living and the dead (or, in Christian terms, those who have passed on believing) are united as the *communio sanctorum,* the communion of the saints in heaven and on earth. The crucial question as to whether there is here a vestige of non-Christian tradition must be answered in the affirmative if the veneration of the departed replaces Jesus Christ as the only Mediator and if offerings and prayers are made to them. But this is hardly the case in the Kimbanguist Church.

Simon Kimbangu is a living reality for the Church of Jesus Christ—he is the sign, even yet, that Christ has made, and continues to make, his work tangible and evident in Central Africa. Simon Kimbangu is not dead, he has risen, he is with God and Christ and leads his own through Joseph Diangienda. No offerings are taken to the mausoleum, except for plastic flowers. But followers may occasionally turn to the prophet in prayer or song—just as Catholics may turn to Mary or a saint. This parallel is indeed the closest and also expresses best the heart of the matter. In times of crisis and before important decisions Simon Kimbangu has appeared to Kimbanguists as a messenger of God and has brought them a concrete message from Jesus Christ and borne their prayers before Him. Are we perhaps faced here with a dimension which has by and large been lost to Westerners? This possibility must be seriously considered before we conclude precipitously that we have here a 'pagan way of thinking'.[16]

8. THE CHARACTER OF KIMBANGUISM IN 1960

At the end of 1959 Joseph Diangienda, as head of the church, made a statement, which was published on 1 May 1960 and from which we take the following:[17]

1. The aim of our movement is to spread the Gospel of Jesus Christ throughout the world. We differ from the Catholics, Protestants

[16] See Ch. 12, Section 2. This dimension, known as 'communication', is being given great emphasis at present by African Christian theologians. As I was revising this manuscript for publication, I came across an article by A. D. Mabona, a lecturer in the Dominican seminary in Hammanskraal (South Africa) entitled 'Africanisation of the Church' in Pro Veritate, 15 March 1970, Vol. VIII, No. 11 (Johannesburg), in which Mabona speaks among other things of the notion of 'two-way communication' between the believing ancestors and their descendants. 'African spirituality seems to be based on the feelings of gratitude, of solidarity, and of universal participation or communion.'

[17] Cf. R. P. Decapmaeker: 'Le Kimbanguisme', in the omnibus volume 'Devant les sectes non-chrétiennes' Louvain, 1961, pp. 63 ff.

and the Salvation Army, who enjoy the protection of the central government in accordance with colonial status [the text was written before 30 June, Independence Day, on which all the churches were put on the same footing]. Kimbanguism welcomes all people on condition that they accept the principles of Christianity in their entirety and submit themselves to our rule of life. [In other words, people of all races, classes, and tongues can become Kimbanguists, but there can be no compromise in matters of faith and living. What is being particularly thought of here is the prohibition of alcohol, the principle of non-violence and the moral commandments, which we shall allude to in the penultimate chapter.]

Our movement is concerned with the sphere of religion. That does not mean that Kimbanguists should not fulfil their duties as citizens of the country. No law on earth can forbid the adherents of a denomination or religion from joining a political party. We have seen, of course, how in other regions of the Congolese church leaders expressed their political views without being punished for this by the administration, but the leaders of our church will refrain from any political interference. However, it is impossible to stop people taking an interest in social questions, for instance the question of education of the young. [Here Diangienda is demanding that the Kimbanguist Church be given the same right of social action as other churches and that its members be able to join the political party of their choice without pressure being brought to bear upon any of them, as unfortunately happens occasionally in other African states where churches exert political pressure on their members.]

2. The Kimbanguist Church gives every member the freedom to go to a doctor in case of illness. [This point is important with respect to other independent churches in Africa which practise faith healing and forbid their members to seek medical treatment. But the Kimbanguist Church demands that sick people should have the right to seek help other than from a doctor—and here faith healing and the sacred spring in N'Kamba are being thought of.]
3. The Kimbanguist Church has no material interests, nor must its members use fetishes.
4. At this point it is reiterated that the Kimbanguist Church welcomes people of all races and draws a line of demarcation between the sphere of religion and that of civil life, and indeed in the sense that the church will not interfere in the realm of state government but also does not grant the government the right to

interfere in church affairs. [This is not, of course, concerned to teach that church and state are completely separate but, in 1960 before Zaïre became independent, to stress religious freedom and to repudiate the claim that Kimbanguists had taken part, or ever would take part, in subversive activities.]

At the same time, around 5 March, the statutes of the church were published. It is evident that in 1960, despite state recognition of the church, the problem of religious freedom was still prominent and that it is closely bound up with the problem of 'church and politics'. The Kimbanguists were still regarded with a measure of suspicion.

Part Three

THE CURRENT POSITION, ACTIVITY AND PROBLEMS OF THE KIMBANGUIST CHURCH

CHAPTER 11

THE ATTITUDE OF THE KIMBANGUIST CHURCH TO POLITICS

We have seen how Simon Kimbangu's movement was suspected from the beginning of being seditious, and the Kimbanguists are still unjustly reproached today for anti-foreign feeling. This may be true, of course, of certain Ngunzist circles with political and messianic expectations. However, we have already pointed out how important it is to distinguish between Kimbanguists and Ngunzists in this respect, too. This distinction is made complicated when politicians who do not belong to the Kimbanguist Church now describe Kimbangu—the martyr and the founder of a great, purely African church—as the 'first great nationalist of Zaïre', as has been said from time to time. Certainly he longed for freedom from the colonial yoke and seems to have foreseen the day of the independence of his country, but during his brief ministry he was concerned simply with preaching repentance, with forgiveness and healing in the name of Jesus Christ. Thus Joseph Diangienda found it necessary on 7 April 1962 (not quite two years after Zaïre had become independent) to make a statement concerning 'Church and Politics', which we reproduce in translation (along with a short commentary) in the second section of this chapter. It must be seen in relation to the political events in Zaïre at that time.

1. POLITICAL EVENTS BEFORE AND AFTER THE LIBERATION OF ZAÏRE[1]

After the Second World War, the Belgians did not realize how

[1] Cf. Colin Legum: 'Congo Disaster', Penguin Special, Harmondsworth, 1961; R. Anstey: 'King Leopold's Legacy', Ch. XII, XIII; R. Segal' 'Political Africa' (article on Lumumba, Kasa-Vubu, Mobutu, and Gisenga),

rapidly they would lose influence in Zaïre. Elementary schools were widespread and received state aid. But the official view was that the Zaïrians should not be given university education for a while. Not until about 1980 were Zaïrian university graduates intended to take over leading positions in Zaïre, being supported by a broad mass of people with elementary education. Belgium pointed to the way the French and the British trained African students at their home universities and regarded this as premature. Not until 1949 was the Catholic Lovanium University founded in Kinshasa, and the state university in Lubumbashi in 1958. Thus it was that on Independence Day there was only a handful of Zaïrian university graduates in the country—a circumstance which was to have catastrophic consequences.

Officially there was no racial discrimination, but in practice whites and blacks in Zaïre were not equal. In the cities the Zaïrians lived in the native quarters, separated from where the whites had their houses and villas. In Kisangani, formerly Stanleyville, there was a Belgian-built power station which could have easily supplied electricity to all parts of the city, thus forming a valuable basis for industrial development. But the generation of current was limited, and only the 'white' part of the city was supplied with electricity. The native quarters had to make do with paraffin lamps, candles and open fires. Whites, except for the missionaries, hardly shook hands with the Zaïrians. The Zaïrians and the whites seldom met socially.

From 1946 the Zaïrians began to demand equal pay for equal work and the slogan 'Zaïre for the Zaïrians' was heard, with demands in 1950 for social, economic and political reforms. The first cultural and social organizations arose at this time—mainly in what was then the Lower Zaïre—from which ABAKO ('Alliance des Bakongo') developed in 1954. In 1955 J. Kasa-Vubu, who died in 1969, became president of ABAKO which by 1959 was one of the most important political parties in Zaïre. In ABAKO the memory of the ancient Kingdom of the Kongo was kept alive, and it aimed at the reunification of all the tribes which belonged to the Bakongo people, separated as they had been by the European powers in 1885 in Portuguese Angola and the Belgian and French Congos.

Since Simon Kimbangu was a Mukongo, there were those who saw in Kasa-Vubu the emissary of Kimbangu and related Kimbanguism and ABAKO, though this was completely contrary to the intentions of the leaders of the Kimbanguist Church. It seems that

London, 1961; A. Massamba-Débat: 'De la révolution messianique à la révolution politique', Brazzaville, 1968, pp. 45–50; Ruth Slade: 'The Belgian Congo', Oxford Univ. Press, 1961.

there were even some Zaïrians who saw in Kasa-Vubu a 'reincarnation' of Kimbangu.² Kasa-Vubu himself did not show any special sympathy for the Kimbanguists though he was present at the ceremony when the mortal remains of Kimbangu arrived at the beginning of April 1960 from Lubumbashi.³

Because a liberal-socialist government was in power in Belgium from 1954, there was a relaxation in what had been hitherto the strongly paternalistic attitude of the rulers, although until 1958 the Belgians did all they could to keep politics out of Zaïre. Only social and cultural organizations were allowed. Not until August 1959 was legislation introduced giving the Zaïrians the right to form political parties.⁴ But before this, from about 1955, an anti-clerical trend was noticeable, and the methods and the preferential treatment of the Catholic mission schools were criticized. The *évolués* (educated Zaïrians, some of whom had received their education in France) finally saw an opportunity to express their national feelings.

Governor-General Pétillon foresaw the necessity of decolonization, and a study commission, consisting entirely of Belgians, was called into being and worked in Brussels—there was apparently no readiness as yet to enter into a dialogue with the Zaïrians. In 1956 there was published in Zaïre the first political manifesto to express Zaïrian nationalistic feeling. The demand for political independence was in the air.

In August 1958 de Gaulle made his famous speech in Brazzaville, in which he gave the Africans living in the French Congo the choice between membership of the French *Communauté* or an autonomous republic and assured them, 'Whoever wishes independence can have it as soon as he wishes.'⁵ The people in the neighbouring Belgian colony, particularly the *évolués* in Kinshasa, were highly delighted at this and sent a letter to the Governor-General in which they asked why no Zaïrians were allowed to participate in the discussions of the study group on the decolonization of the Congo. The leader of this group was Patrice Lumumba, the son of Catholic parents, whose home was in Kisangani, where he was on friendly terms with a Protestant minister with Kimbanguist sympathies. Lumumba was at

---

² P. Raymaekers: 'L'Eglise de Jésus Christ sur la terre par le prophète Simon Kimbangu', Zaïre Vol. XIII/7, Brussels, 1959, p. 682.

³ E. Bazola: 'Le Kimbanguisme', Cahiers des religions africaines, No. 4, July, 1968, Lovanium-Kinshasa, p. 328.

⁴ Catherine Hoskyns:: 'The Congo since Independence, January 1960 to December 1961', Oxford, 1965, pp. 21–2.

⁵ A. P. Merriam: 'Congo, Background of Conflict', Northwestern Univ. Press, 1961, p. 81.

that time still moderate and perfectly willing to co-operate with the whites. He often sought spiritual advice and support from his Protestant–Kimbanguist friend. Only later, when he met with strong resistance, did he become violent. He was, however at this time, moving towards the foundation of his *Mouvement National Congolais* (MNC).

Lumumba's party took a negative view of Kasa-Vubu's ABAKO party. Two irreconcilable ideologies were expressed in these parties. Kasa-Vubu was interested at heart in the re-establishment of the ancient Bakongo kingdom, and this was a regional tribal interest. Lumumba supported pan-Africanism, which strives for unified states to the exclusion of regional and tribal interests. The unity of the various tribes and parts of the country was to take precedence over all other interests.

At the end of 1958 Lumumba attended the Pan-African Conference in Accra (Ghana), which demanded the independence of the African peoples. In January 1959 nationalistic riots broke out in Matadi, in Kinshasa and elsewhere. We have already mentioned that although Ngunzists were involved in these risings, Kimbanguists—contrary to what was said at the time—were not. In Kinshasa 30,000 unemployed people held a demonstration. The colonial government arrested the ABAKO leaders, and Kasa-Vubu was taken by air to Belgium, though he was not detained there. Reforms were promised. These disturbances drew the attention of the world to Zaïre.[6]

Towards the close of 1959 there was a split in Lumumba's MNC, and he himself was arrested in Kisangani because of disturbances and conflicts within the party.—Meanwhile other parties had also arisen, among them M. Tshombe's Conakat (*Confédération des Associations de Katanga*) which proposed that Zaïre become a federation of six states. Though each party formed its own picture of the future Zaïrian state, they were all against white rule and paternalism, but (and this must be stressed) they were not necessarily against the whites as such.

In 1960 Belgium called a Round Table Conference in Brussels. All parties were represented, including those called into being and financed by the Belgians. All of them demanded the *immediate* independence of Zaïre. Following this decision Lumumba had to be released, and he went straight from prison in Kisangani to Brussels, still bearing the marks of the maltreatment he had suffered in prison. The two strong personalities at the conference were the opponents Kasa-Vubu and Lumumba. Tshombe had by that time lost popularity

---

[6] C. Hoskyns: op. cit., p. 33.

because it was known that he had connections with high finance. Lumumba emerged as the victor and an agreement was signed bringing into being a unified state with a central government, in accordance with Lumumba's ideas, certain jurisdiction being left to the provinces.[7] But between February and May 1960 there was for some strange reason a breach between Lumumba and Brussels. Meanwhile elections were held in Zaïre. No party achieved a clear majority so a compromise was unavoidable. Kasa-Vubu became the president and Lumumba the prime minister. Two rivals were harnessed together, and that in itself would surely have sufficed to pave the way for further conflict.

On 30 June 1960, in the presence of King Baudouin of Belgium, the independence of Zaïre was declared. But only a few days after the celebrations, on 5 July, the risings began. Against all the expectations of the Belgian officers the *force publique* (Zaïrian armed forces), on which they had counted, mutinied. This led to outrages against whites, and the Catholics in particular. In Mbanza-Ngungu the whites were in great danger. Charles Kisolokele, at that time a cabinet minister and a member of Kasa-Vubu's ABAKO, went with G. Diomi and General Mobutu to Mbanza-Ngungu, where, because of his standing as Simon Kimbangu's son and his loyalty to his father's principles, he was able to save them.[8] Kisolokele's involvement cannot be taken to suggest that there was any alliance between the Kimbanguist Church and ABAKO. Even before independence, Joseph Diangienda had quite explicitly said that the Kimbanguist Church would not interfere in politics, and that it left it to each individual to join the party which seemed best to him. The civil war which followed independence led to a long period of devastation in some parts of the country, continuing until 1967 in Upper Zaïre.

Meanwhile, General Mobutu had come to power on 24 November 1965, a military government was formed, and order was gradually restored. In these years of political ferment the Kimbanguist Church had to develop and to fulfil its mission. The statement 'Church and Politics' must be viewed against this historical background.

---

[7] A. P. Merriam: op. cit., p. 343.
[8] C. Hoskyns: op. cit., p. 90.

2. JOSEPH DIANGIENDA'S STATEMENT 'CHURCH AND POLITICS'[9]

In its public attitude towards state authority, the 'Church of Christ on Earth through the Prophet Simon Kimbangu' cannot deviate from the principle voiced by Christ Himself, 'Render unto Caesar the things that are Caesar's and unto God the things that are God's'. According to our view, a line must be drawn between spiritual (i.e. ecclesiastical) and secular (i.e. state) authority. For this reason, the Church of Christ on Earth through the Prophet Simon Kimbangu will be careful not to interfere directly in problems which are the province of secular government. This does not mean, of course, that we cannot draw up guiding principles for the conduct of our members as citizens of the state, for as such they are confronted with secular problems. These guiding principles are based on the teaching and the heritage of the founder of our church, the prophet Simon Kimbangu.

Now follow the guiding principles given to church members:

The 'Church of Christ on Earth through the Prophet Simon Kimbangu' is against every political, economic or social ideology, doctrine or theory which denies God as the Source of life and thus the human progress. The believer of the 'Church of Christ on Earth through the Prophet Simon Kimbangu' cannot spread or accept an ideology, doctrine or theory on which a political, economic or social system is based which seeks to explain the historical development of the world without reference to the activity of God.

This statement shows clearly that the Kimbanguist Church is directly opposed to all kinds of atheist thinking and influence.

The believers of the 'Church of Christ on Earth through the prophet Simon Kimbangu' are obliged to fulfil all the duties which are placed on them as citizens of the country in which they live.

This is a principle which the Kimbanguists consciously observe so that they cannot be accused of subversion. Although they repudiate

[9] Cahiers de la Réconciliation, Eglise et Politique, Paris, May–June, 1966, pp. 40–1; Joseph Diangienda: 'L'Eglise du Christ sur la terre par le prophète Simon Kimbangu face aux problèmes politiques, économiques et sociaux tels qu'ils se posent au Congo, en Afrique et dans le monde', Kinshasa, 1962.

violence, members of the Kimbanguist Church do military service, and we noticed on various occasions on our travels with Joseph Diangienda how military vehicles stopped and soldiers who belong to the church, or are well-disposed towards it, got out, greeted the head of the church and asked for his blessing.

> Because the 'Church of Christ on Earth through the Prophet Simon Kimbangu' knows that the fate of all countries of the world can only depend on their mutual co-operation, it condemns every policy which seeks to introduce in a country or a part of the world a political structure which is based on excessive stress on belonging to a tribe, region or race. The spirit of such excess destroys and annihilates not only all attempts at human rapprochement, which the teaching of Christ urges upon us, but it also hinders every form of economic and social progress which promotes the development of the human personality. Thus the 'Church of Christ on Earth through the Prophet Simon Kimbangu' condemns all tribal, regional and racial arrogance. It hopes for the furtherance of a new humanity in the world, which brings people closer together irrespective of their race, tribe or regional loyalty and whatever their colour of skin or their social position may be.

This emphasis on a new humanity which condemns all kinds of racial arrogance shows clearly that the Kimbanguists cannot be accused of 'hatred of foreigners' or 'hatred of the whites'. It also shows that the church is not the prerogative of the Bakongo tribe, as is sometimes still claimed today. This is a church which is conscious of its 'world mission', hence its name 'The Church of Jesus Christ on *Earth* through the Prophet Simon Kimbangu'.

> That we are against excessive stress on region (*région*), tribe and race does not mean that we are against the formation of politico-juridical entities (*entités politico-juridiques*) which fulfil all conditions of viability and unite people belonging to the same nation, traditions and culture, provided that these entities are set in a wider framework in which they can cultivate mutual contacts and thus promote the development of the entire population. This will first involve a particular country, then a part of the world and finally the whole earth.

Thus, Diangienda sees that people of particular cultural groups—Bakongo, Africans, Belgians, Swiss, or whoever they may be—constitute such entities. As far as I can see, that was to begin with the object of the South African government with its 'ethnic grouping'.

But—and this 'but' must be carefully noted—these groupings are not, and must not become, self-sufficient entities aloof from others but in a world which is becoming smaller and smaller, must always be open to others, keeping the whole in view. They have their contribution to make to the development of humanity, and to this end they must be ready for cultural and economic exchange and for integration into a wide and open world. Every narrow demarcation particularly 'apartheid' is contrary to the principles of the Kimbanguist Church. Joseph Diangienda goes on:

> Since all men are created in the image of God they should treat each other as brothers ... 'The Church of Christ on Earth through the Prophet Simon Kimbangu' considers that the observation of the 'Universal Declaration of Human Rights' in all countries is appropriate and necessary, particularly with regard to the fundamental liberties.

With regard to inter-denominational dialogue, Diangienda has this to say:

> The Church of Christ on Earth through the Prophet Simon Kimbangu' forbids its members to enter into controversies and disputes on a denominational level. It is of the view that, as soon as all religions [i.e. Christian churches] are steering towards the same goal, namely to serve God for the benefit of man, nothing can keep those religions which are based on the teachings of Christ from moving parallel to one another.

Here is indicated the possibility of ecumenical dialogue, which has since begun, and ecumenical action is left open.

> 'The Church of Christ on Earth through the Prophet Simon Kimbangu' hopes that the political and civil thinking in each country will develop in such a way as to bring people closer together. It condemns the use of violence to settle disputes between people.

This is a declaration of non-violence and a repudiation of armed resistance which is not being voiced in a country like Switzerland but in a country which at the time was being led to the edge of the abyss through civil war and armed intervention. We have already mentioned that, though Kimbanguists do not refuse to do military service, they would never defend themselves with force of arms if persecuted or otherwise oppressed. True to the instructions of their founder,[10] they do not repay evil with evil. We shall see in

[10] Cf. Lanzo del Vasto: 'Simon Kimbangu et la non-violence africaine', Jeune Afrique, No. 385, 1968, Paris, pp. 64–5.

the following section what this meant at the time of the fighting in Kisangani.

In the final section, however, Joseph Diangienda returns to the fundamental liberties which are stated in the Declaration of Human Rights:

'The Church of Christ on Earth through the Prophet Simon Kimbangu' does not consider it fitting to express views concerning the political system that a country should support. But it is against any political system which deprives the citizens of the fundamental liberties, namely freedom of thought, freedom of speech, freedom of religion and worship, freedom of the press, freedom of opinion and freedom of movement.

This document shows how, when it was being formed and built up, the church gave an account of its political involvement. It has thus borne witness to its openness to the world and shown that the striving for personal sanctification, which we shall be discussing later on, does not make it at all self-centred but makes it open to the secular issues which dominate present-day Africa—namely the desire for freedom from dictatorship, discrimination and oppression; the repudiation of armed intervention and the use of force; interest in social involvement, and concern to develop its various groups and to promote ecumenical dialogue.

3. THE CONSEQUENCES OF NON-VIOLENCE

When in 1964 the Zaïrian army, supported by Belgian troops and mercenaries, penetrated Kisangani to drive out the rebellious 'Simba', the Kimbanguist congregation was gathered under the palm roof of their improvised 'church' (not really a building) in the yard of their manse, horrified at the bloody fighting between the rebels and the army and on principle having nothing to do with it. About 170 people had gathered and were praying whilst the fighting went on in the immediate vicinity. Shells burst, and the fleeing Simba fired shots at the praying Kimbanguists. A small reconnaissance aircraft of the government troops saw the worshippers, and thinking them to be a gathering of rebels, opened fire. Attacked by both sides, by rebels and government troops, what could the Kimbanguists do? They did not flee. They stayed where they were, exposed to all shooting, ready to die but not to kill. They prayed. At length a Belgian officer, accompanied by soldiers, intruded into the prayer meeting and asked menacingly, 'What are you doing here?'—

'We're praying,' came the answer.—'Yes, you're praying for the rebels,' the officer continued.—'We're praying for all God's children and for peace,' the minister answered, showing the Belgian officer the Bible. The officer took it, looked at it, put it in his pocket and commanded his men to move on. No on was injured. This factual report was given to Rev. Lasserre on his 1966 visit.[11] It was repeated to us when we were on the very spot where these events took place. It impressed the Kimbanguists greatly that God's protective hand was over them so noticeably in this critical situation.

4. THE TEMPTATION TO BECOME THE STATE CHURCH

Because Simon Kimbangu was praised by certain Zaïrian politicians as a national hero, the Kimbanguist Church was open to the temptation to become the state church of Zaïre. But the leaders were categorically against this. The church could not be dependent on the state; it must be founded solely on Jesus Christ. If it pledged itself to the state it would no longer be in a position to raise its prophetic voice—even in opposition to the state, were it necessary to do so.

As a result there were schisms. We have already referred to the group which looked to Thomas N'Twalani. Graver still was the secession of the influential Emmanuel Bamba. There were differences of opinion between him and Kimbangu's sons concerning their position in the church—which in accordance with ancient royal tradition, in many African independent churches transferred to church leaders[12]—was described as that of crown princes. Bamba, who apparently wanted to be the head of the church himself, founded his own church. 'The Salvation of Jesus Christ through the Witness Simon Kimbangu'.

In 1962 and 1963, in the western tip of the country, in the region of Mayumbe, there first arose a division in the evangelical Alliance Mission which was working there: young Zaïrians in Mayumbe wanted to rid themselves of the white missionaries and to take over the state-aided mission schools. They called themselves 'Procos', 'pro Congo'. Soon after, a split occurred within the Kimbanguist Church there. The Kimbanguists in the district of Mayumbe wanted a 'Mayumban vicariate', independent of the leadership of Kimbangu's sons, who belonged to another district. Petty regional interests and

[11] Cahiers de la Réconciliation, Voyage au Congo, pp. 18 ff.
[12] M.-L. Martin: 'Afrikanischer Messianismus und der Messias der biblischen Offenbarung' in Weltmission heute, Heft 33–34, ed. P. Beyerhaus, Stuttgart, 1967, p. 47.

local patriotism were here being brought into the Kimbanguist Church. Because of his opposition to Joseph Diangienda, Emmanuel Bamba seems to have given financial support to this schism.[13] Joseph Diangienda was threatened in letters and telegrams that his life would be at risk if he set foot in the port of Boma, the place from which the district of Mayumbe is reached. When we visited Boma in May 1968, two years after the death of Bamba, things were still unsettled. Since then, however, some of the separated brethren have joined the Protestants and some have asked to be received back into the Kimbanguist Church. There remained, however, still some tension, stirred up by a small militant group, as we discovered in a painful way in July 1970.

In 1966 there was almost a catastrophe when Bamba, at the time a cabinet minister under General Mobutu, apparently planned with other ministers a *coup d'état* which failed. They intended to bring about a change of government by force. Bamba and his accomplices were condemned to death by the military court and publicly executed.[14] He refused Diangienda's offer of reconciliation before his death.[15] When the plot became known, persecution of the Kimbanguist Church began afresh since people were unclear about the distinction between Bamba's church and the Kimbanguist Church led by Joseph Diangienda. Kimbanguists were attacked, schools and places of worship (there were then, as now, hardly any church buildings as such) were set on fire. Fortunately the mistake was discovered, and Radio Congo announced every few minutes: 'Leave the "Church of Jesus Christ on Earth through the Prophet Simon Kimbangu" and its adherents in peace: they have had nothing to do with the *coup d'état*.' This was one of the most critical moments experienced by the Kimbanguists since 1960. Because, even in this situation, the members of the church kept strictly to the principle of non-violence, the Zaïrians noticed that there was a great spiritual, satisfying power in this church. (The struggles in the north-east of the country were still going on.)

When we laid the foundation stones for church buildings in Matadi and in Kisangani in May 1968, civic and military dignitaries

---

[13] Information from Charles Kisolokele.
[14] C.R.I.S.P. 1966 gives details concerning the conspiracy in Ch. VII, 'Les oppositions intérieures: le procès de Pentecôte', pp. 431 ff. According to this account, E. Bamba contended to the last that he, as a religious leader, had no part in the assassination conspiracy but he and his accomplices had merely wanted to replace the military government of Mobutu with a civil government.
[15] Information from Joseph Diangienda.

have been present at these ceremonies. The Governor of Kinshasa attended a great festive service in July 1968, and presented the Kimbanguist Church with a small coach to be used for taking secondary school teachers to their work.

When, in July 1968, General Mobutu invited the representatives of the various churches (Catholic and Protestant) to, as he put it, discuss the country's progress, he also invited the Kimbanguists along, and, as an observer of this six-hour dialogue, I was delighted to see grievances so frankly discussed. By early 1969, the Kimbanguist Church was recognized as the largest denomination in Zaïre after the Catholic Church.[16]

Although the Kimbanguist Church rejected the idea of becoming the state church, it remained very much aware of its special mission to Zaïre as a trust from God. 'The prophetism kindled by Simon Kimbangu was the first voice to be raised against the power without religion and religion without power, which the Europeans brought.'[17] Behind this statement lies the conviction that Simon Kimbangu in particular came as God's ambassador to the Zaïrians and that God made the life and sufferings of Christ vital again in Zaïre as a present reality. It has often been repeated in Kimbanguist sermons that if the Gospel proclaimed by Kimbangu were repudiated, then the Zaïrian people would be stricken.[18]

The Zaïrian people is made up of more than a hundred tribal groups and dialects, and, by preaching this faith, the movement has created what Bazola called a 'national conscience' (*une conscience nationale*). But the vision has extended beyond Zaïre to all Africa—across to the Afro-Americans in North America, where the Kimbanguist church recently formed a congregation, and from there to all peoples. Behind this there may be the belief that, though this time salvation does not come *from* the Africans, it is nevertheless God's will that it should be proclaimed to the world afresh through them on the basis of what he accomplished through Simon Kimbangu. There is very evident joy that God used an African for his purpose. And behind this, there is a great sense of mission. Through this awareness the church was, and is, fortified, and it is not prepared to renounce its own mission or to efface itself by being assimilated again into the various Protestant churches. Though there is no crude proselytizing, where people break away from the older

[16] International Review of Missions, January 1969, Vol. LVIII, No. 229, Geneva, p. 39.

[17] E. Bazola: :'Le Kimbanguisme', op cit., pp. 322 ff. ('un pouvoir sans religion et une religion sans pouvoir'.)

[18] E. Bazola: op. cit., p. 329.

churches and want to join the Kimbanguist Church they are received with joy and thanksgiving. It is inevitable that this should occasion tensions between those churches that have arisen through missionary activity and the Kimbanguist Church.

CHAPTER 12

THE RELIGIOUS AND SOCIAL LIFE OF THE KIMBANGUIST CHURCH

1. THE ORGANIZATION OF THE CHURCH THROUGH THE UNIFICATION OF ISOLATED GROUPS

During the long period of persecution there had been no official church leadership to give directives. Thus, when the exiled John Mayanga, an early witness, sent exhortations to the Kimbanguists left behind at home and wrote '*we* say to you', he was not referring to a governing body of the church but merely to himself and a few fellow-believers who were sharing his lot.

Since 1960, the church leaders, and particularly Joseph Diangienda, have been trying to unite the Kimbanguist congregations, which had hitherto been led by their local catechists and 'prophets', and to give them the *hierarchical structure and ecclesiastical system* which in the African setting best promote the organization of an orderly congregational life. This was no easy task. In order to embrace as many believers as possible, the Kimbanguist Church has not drawn up a rigid basis of faith in the form of a binding creed. It is only just beginning to formulate its theology, which so far has been expressed as a living reality in the hymns and the communal character of the church. The leaders have tried to be magnanimous and not to exclude people unnecessarily, and yet they have been aware of the danger of Ngunzism—of aberrations where everything is left to the spontaneity of the Spirit. They were concerned to steer clear of syncretistic elements.

Joseph Diangienda sought to promote unification in three ways. In the first place, he founded in 1962 a preacher training college, so that future ministers and evangelists would receive an education which would unite them by a common training and personal contacts created during that training. The college staff were trained either by the Salvation Army or at a Bible college of one of the Protestant churches. In 1970, the Kimbanguist School of Theology was founded at Kinshasa, which accepts candidates with at least five years' secondary schooling. This college is in process of development (see Appendix).

The church leaders know that in the present rapid development and social change in Africa the church needs well-trained workers who also have a thorough cultural grounding. The missionary societies are being asked for staff who will no longer be in any way under the direction of the sending society but who will adapt themselves completely to the life of a particular church and place themselves under its hierarchy. That is not always easy for Europeans and requires a large measure of understanding of African tradition and life. It demands adaptability and sacrifice. Missionary societies as well as ecumenical organizations will have to restrain themselves from seeking unduly to influence such independent churches.

The second step was to draw up a constitution[1] for the church, which would establish its eligibility for the recognition of the new Zaïrian state. The new statutes were introduced on 6 March 1960. Among other things they say that

> Kimbanguism is founded on the Christian faith. Its evangelistic methods and its teachings are in harmony with the Gospel. Kimbanguism is at work in Zaïre and can spread to other countries without being bound by national frontiers. The cornerstone on which the 'Church of Jesus Christ on Earth through the Prophet Simon Kimbangu' rests is the Law and the Prophets. Its message is what is revealed in the Bible. Through the power of the Holy Spirit, it teaches:
> (a) love, worship, mercy, and imitation of Christ;
> (b) abhorrence of evil and love of all that is good;
> (c) justice and moral purity;
> (d) every religious practice (*pratique réligieuse*) which serves the cultivation of mutual respect and unity between people and nations, which comprise the essential basis for harmony and peace in the world.

The 'Church of Jesus Christ on Earth through the Prophet Simon Kimbangu' confines itself to the relationship of man to God and does not interfere in interdenominational conflicts. It refrains from all political activity, since this is contrary to its

[1] 'Les Statuts', 6 March 1960 (mimeographed).

spiritual role in the world. Kimbanguism acknowledges and worships God, the Almighty Creator, and lives according to His commandments, opposing all forms of discrimination based on race or colour. It follows the Ten Commandments as set out in Exodus 20:1–17. In addition Kimbanguism demands that all its members observe the following commandments:
(a) obedience to state authority, in accordance with Romans 13:1–3;
(b) mutual love and love of one's enemies, in accordance with Matthew 5:43–5;
(c) abstinence from alcoholic beverages;
(d) abstinence from smoking, especially from narcotics;
(e) avoidance of dances;
(f) no swimming or sleeping naked;
(g) non-interference in quarrels;
(h) abstention from fetishism;
(i) payment of taxes;
(j) non-retaliation;
(k) confession of sin before specially-appointed members of the congregation;
(l) no ban on foods, except for pork and monkey-meat.
Kimbanguism is a church of the Holy Spirit, so all its members are obliged to walk in the Spirit.

In the following chapter we shall look at these statutes in detail and try to throw theological light on them. What is important here is that these statutes are binding on all groups who wish to join the Kimbanguist Church. 'Moral purity' also involves the observance of monogamy. From the outset Kimbanguism has opposed polygamy, unlike many Ngunzist groups, including Simon Mpadi's 'Mission of the Blacks'.

Joseph Diangienda's third step for the reunification of the various groups is his work of travelling throughout the country by air, car, lorry, train, ship and on foot, accompanied by a whole team of assistants and singers and a brass band. On such journeys he has visited the various congregations, spoken with the leaders, settled disputes, gained insight into local problems, given advice, admonished and healed. These journeys have been perhaps the most important means of binding the various groups together to form an organic whole. We accompanied him on such travels. Diangienda and and those who went with him were welcomed everywhere by great crowds—by numerous members of the church but also by Protestant, Catholic and Orthodox sympathizers who respect the

Kimbanguist Church and its work of upbuilding. Wherever Diangienda goes he makes time for every single individual who has a request to make or who is seeking his advice or healing.

He continues to live in Kinshasa, and people come from all over to see him when he is not on his travels, so he is kept busy day and night as a counsellor, comforter, interpreter of dreams, admonisher and healer. Dreams and their interpretation play an important part in African as in Hebrew thinking. Like Blumhardt he also exorcises demons, especially when people think that they are bewitched or that they are bewitching others in spite of themselves. I never came to Joseph Diangienda's home without there being at least twenty to fifty people waiting for him in the forecourt and in his room. Even at night he is often visited and is always ready to help, except for the hours which he reserves each day for meditation and prayer, during which no one is permitted to disturb him.

2. CHURCH SERVICES

Public worship is at the heart of the life of the Kimbanguist Church. Each day in smallish groups there are short morning and evening devotions, and at noon a time of prayer is held. In all these devotions passages of Scripture are read—often psalms, which occupy an important position in worship, as they do in the Catholic and Anglican Churches. Then an individual, designated in advance (a man or a woman, young or old), prays extemporarily. At the beginning and at the end a hymn is sung. On Wednesdays, which many Kimbanguists voluntarily set aside as a day of fasting, men and women have separate meetings for worship. The church members also meet on Fridays.

Every Saturday little prayer groups meet in homes and spend the night in prayer. Throughout the country there are small cells which submit themselves to an extremely rigorous discipline of prayer. They spend from Sunday evening to Thursday morning, or from Thursday morning to Sunday evening, in intercession, praise, meditation and fasting, and forgo their sleep. The spiritual strength of the church, and of the spiritual retreats, may well lie in this.

In the Sunday service the various choirs sing for about half an hour and an orchestra, consisting of indigenous flutes and drums, plays. Sometimes there is the brass band as well, or a group of singers accompanied on guitars. Then follow community singing, prayer, Bible reading, the presenting of children, a collection followed by a prayer, and, at the heart of the service, the sermon preached by a minister or evangelist, male or female. Women are on an equal footing with men in the Kimbanguist Church, because from the beginning Mwilu Marie (the wife of the prophet) and Mikala Mandombe were such outstanding assistants. Moreover, women occupied a not insignificant position in the ancient matriarchal Bakongo society. At present the Kimbanguist Church has among its number a few trained women ministers.

The sermon is made less formal by some ministers and evangelists by asking the congregation questions, which are answered spontaneously or by a suitable hymn. The opening and closing prayers are offered by members of the congregation. Bible readings are chosen from the Old and New Testaments, and sermon texts are taken from one or the other. We were able to notice a good balance in the choice of texts from the Old and the New Testaments. In the sermons there is often reference to Simon Kimbangu and his short ministry and the forty years' persecution of the church. After the sermon—towards the end of the service—visitors from outside the community are particularly welcomed and this is done with music or singing and with restrained hand-clapping 'in the Name of the Father, and of the Son, and of the Holy Spirit'.

Attendance at service is remarkably good. That was especially exident when we appeared unexpectedly at a Sunday service in one of the various congregations in or outside the city of Kinshasa. I was particularly impressed by a small congregation in a part of Kinshasa when the church was full despite the fact that a festive procession had taken place at 9 o'clock that morning to commemorate the Declaration of Independence of the country on 30 June. Whilst the whole of Kinshasa gathered in the centre of the city to secure a good place to watch the 'défile', hundreds of men, women and children were gathered to hear God's word. Not infrequently there are 3,000 to 8,000 people attending special services in which all the individual congregations are represented.

Most of the services must still be held in the open air under palm or corrugated iron roofs on large squares where later churches are to stand. The uniformed supervisors (*surveillants*), men and women, take care of order and (mainly in the cities) keep troublemakers away from the services. Twice a month in Kinshasa there is a special service in which the members bring their gifts—for the building of schools, clinics, churches and a guest-house. These special services, called *nsinsani* (competition), which we attended on a number of occasions, last till sunset. The band plays, and groups (of ministers, evangelists, mothers, fathers, girls, youths, children) form spontaneously, bringing their gifts in rhythmic movement to the front, where they are collected in a large enamel basin. To begin with a small gift is brought, then after a while a bigger one, and so it continues until the fixed goal has been reached. Groups compete with one another, and finally the winners are applauded as in a performance and are congratulated with shouts of *oye* (bravo). The sum so far collected is announced from time to time by loudspeaker and the people are encouraged to bring more. People give gladly—this is the African way of giving. There is singing, laughter, a chance to speak to friends, and people meet and spend the whole Sunday in good and happy fellowship. It is clear that there is no strict division between divine worship and secular social gathering. Both belong together, and man is encompassed in his totality.

Such festivities have great social significance in that the often questionable Sunday amusements in the many 'beer halls' are not simply forbidden but are replaced by a gathering which offers something better and presents the opportunity to cultivate friendship and fun (rhythmic movement). The traditional historical churches, too, may have something to learn from this kind of practice—some, indeed, are already beginning to do so.

When Joseph Diangienda attends a service he occupies the place of honour. When he arrives he is welcomed by everybody kneeling, in accordance with African tradition, and when he is officially welcomed after the sermon there is an enormous outburst of jubilation, a sort of ovation. He himself does not preach, but he exhorts the congregation after his welcome. At the close of the service he is asked to lead in prayer and to tell the congregation of the latest developments within the church and about its social work. In this way, everyone in the congregation gets to know what is happening.

When the service is over people seeking help and healing come to him and he talks to them unobtrusively and lays his hands on them in prayer for healing and blessing. But all this is peripheral rather than central. There is no propaganda and there are no testimonies to healing. The sensationalism so common in churches which practise faith-healing, is absent in the Kimbanguist Church.

Moreover, no special vestments are worn for worship, either by the ministers and high dignitaries of the church or by members of the congregation—in contrast with the practice in the many other independent churches of Africa, in which many-coloured vestments embroidered with crosses and other symbols are a feature. Even Simon Mpadi (as we saw) wears a red gown embroidered with numerous gold crosses. In the Kimbanguist Church normal clothes are worn—the women are draped in their long, colourful fabrics and the men folk wear light clothing suited to the tropics. Women in mini clothes are not regarded with approval: they offend the sense of dignity of the African woman.

3. GENEROSITY AND VOLUNTARY WORK

The Kimbanguist Church has no missionary society behind it and yet it has managed within the space of ten years to build up a considerable educational system. Work among women and young folk, clinics with trained nursing staff, a college for ministers, and a more or less functional church administration with representatives in every province, in every region, in every district, and in every village and municipal ward, are features of the church. Files and statistics are kept, and a small number of books (mainly catechisms) are produced in the church's own little, primitive printing press in N'Kamba. In 1966 the large church of Matete-Kinshasa, holding 3,000 people, was built. In Boko in the People's Republic of the Congo the congregation received its church as far back as 1959, to be followed ten years later by the one in the capital. In Matadi and Kinsangani the foundation-stones for churches were laid in 1968.[2] Apart from its agricultural colony, which was given a tractor by the Oxfam organization and three more by the government, the Kimbanguist Church has received up to 1969 no substantial financial aid from any source. That has its advantages, but also its drawbacks: more agricultural colonies for the unemployed and for the young offenders might have been established and the schools and workshops might have been better equipped. Above all, better trained staff might have been employed.

To build up a large church, with its many branches of work without funds from abroad, in such a short time in a country which was going through a great crisis and was having to make considerable sacrifices in order to reform its finances, was only possible through the voluntary efforts of hundreds and thousands of members. Many of the full-time staff receive no fixed salary. Without being asked, those who have a good living give contributions to the church so that at least some of the voluntary church-workers can be supported. Others suffer privation, and there is a lack of active and talented, dynamic staff. Far too great a burden of responsibility and work rests on Diangienda and his brothers.[3]

Most of the ministers and evangelists like the Apostle Paul, have a vocation, earning their living in the administration of the country, or as teachers, tradesmen, merchants, farmers and housewives. Their

[2] The Matadi Church was inaugurated in December, 1973.
[3] There is, however, an improvement lately.

free time is devoted to church work. The congregations are relatively small, and every member is given some responsibility, no matter how small. When a building is being put up, there are volunteers who go on certain evenings after work and make bricks and help with the bricklaying, joinery and other jobs. Office workers go after their work to help the church leaders with correspondence. Women from Kinshasa regularly go on a voluntary basis to Lutendele farm to work in the fields and plantations. For every village and every street in a part of a town there is a 'deacon' or 'deaconess' who is voluntarily available and is there should a member of a family fall ill or die or when unexpected worries arise. Everybody knows that he is not on his own. The new brotherhood within the church replaces the traditional kinship and family group. This is of great social importance in the cities of Africa. The African in the town is often distressed because he is isolated, suddenly cut off from the wider family community, so important in African tradition. This isolation can have grave consequences in the breakdown of the whole social order, leading people into poverty, prostitution and crime. The Kimbanguist Church is making a serious attempt to put something new in the place of the old which cannot hold its own in Africa's social revolution. There is a sense of security within the church, just as in the old tribal order people stood up for one another. There is a willingness to help, and to give of one's substance and share one's possessions with one's brothers and sisters. Sometimes a wealthy Kimbanguist will give a hundred Zaïres (about £100) at the *nsinsani*.

4. WORKSHOPS AND AGRICULTURAL COLONIES

The African thinks of the individual as a totality, seeing no dichotomy between body and soul, Sunday and weekdays. When therefore the political and social upheavals in Zaïre brought unemployment, with its grave consequences, to thousands and thousands of victims, the Kimbanguist Church did not look on inactively but set about establishing places where workmen could be employed and founding agricultural colonies in and around Kinshasa, as well as a school in Mbanza-Ngungu to teach people trades. This could be called a mere drop in the bucket, but had the church had greater financial resources more could have been done.

A tailor's shop was opened to make all the green and white uniforms for the schoolchildren. The church has a garage for vehicle repairs—particularly useful since the church uses cars and lorries for travelling around the country. A joiner's workshop produces furniture to sell.

On the agricultural settlement of Lutendele, about 22 km. from Kinshasa, a *kibbutz* is run along Israeli lines with plantations of oil-palms, banana and manioc, a chicken farm, fish-ponds, market gardens and some cattle. Unemployed people are thus introduced to agricultural farming, on which the economy of Zaïre basically rests. In 1967 young offenders were also accepted to work in Lutendele, either on release from prison or instead of serving a prison sentence. The religious convictions which are expressed in every aspect of Kimbanguist life have deeply affected many of these youths.

In April 1969 Lutendele had 313 settlers, including children, these being taught by three teachers. The Kimbanguist uniformed supervisory service in Kinshasa had, when we were there, just launched a similar scheme. Wasteland had been cleared and the first harvest was growing. In all these enterprises, as well as in the offices of the church administration and the educational system, the times of prayer are strictly observed, namely in the morning before work begins, at the stroke of twelve and, in the settlements, also in the evening.

Round about N'Kamba, a great plan of development will be carried out in the next few years. Volunteers have built a bridge across the torrential River Mpioka so that market produce can be taken into the surrounding area. In N'Kamba a generating station is being built, and a brick-works is producing the necessary bricks for all buildings (mainly schools and housing). N'Kamba itself, which has been populated again since 1960, will be a place where people can spend times of spiritual retreat, and those who live there will build better dwellings in the district round about and farm the land.

Agriculture has a not insignificant potential in this district. There are plans to improve the approach road to Mbanza-Ngungu so that produce can be sent there and further still to the cities of Matadi and Kinshasa. This development will have repercussions on industry and trade.

A few years ago the Kimbanguist Church formed an association to help small farmers and tradesmen, but unfortunately the necessary capital is not available for this enterprise to be really successful. Moreover, in almost all of these special undertakings of the church there is a lack of suitable, trained leaders who are able to take the initiative and make the enterprises financially profitable to the church. Much is still going to waste (as elsewhere in Africa) which could be turned to the benefit of the community.

5. WORK AMONGST WOMEN AND YOUNG FOLK

Zaïrian women had, on the whole, little chance of being educated until the country became independent, so all the more is now being done to give the women a better education. The Women's Associations of the Kimbanguist Church do not only meet for devotional purposes—although such associations are numerous—they also provide literacy courses for the unschooled, and also teach French. Instruction in housewifery and child care naturally occupies an important position in the programme of the Women's Associations and of the Women's Social Centres. The courses make great demands on the women. There are also classes for wayward young girls. The national president, Mrs Kaku, recently took a course in Switzerland, and several young girls and women are being trained in Montmirail by the Swiss branch of the Moravian Church, which is the first church in Switzerland to take a special interest in the Kimbanguists. Since Mrs Kaku's return from Switzerland there have been regular Bible studies and Bible weeks for women, using modern methods, particularly spiritual retreats.

The Kimbanguist boy scouts were affiliated with the national scout movement in Zaïre.[4] The uniformed supervisory service has its own youth branch to ensure that there are future recruits. The brass bands in Kinshasa and Brazzaville and the various flute orchestras in N'Kamba, Kinshasa, Boko and elsewhere are mainly made up of young folk, as are the choirs, which cultivate African hymn-singing. Particularly impressive are the youth drama groups with their own organization and workshop, which stage Bible stories and episodes from the history of the Kimbanguist Church in true African fashion. The drama groups perform on special occasions as part of the service. Thus in 1968 in N'Kamba one of these religious amateur plays formed part of a special open-air service: on 27 April, the anniversary of the death of Marie Mwilu, the young folk presented impressive scenes from the closing years of this great 'mother of the church'. One is reminded to some extent of the medieval mystery and passion plays (which indeed are still performed today in Europe).

[4] Since then all boy scouts and similar groups have been incorporated in the JMPR [Jeunesse du Mouvement Populaire de la Révolution].

CHAPTER 13

THEOLOGICAL CONSIDERATIONS

1. THE PROBLEMS

We have already referred to the fact that it is not easy to describe the theology of the Kimbanguist Church because it is lived and sung and not formulated. It is expressed in pictures, wood-carvings and music. Here there is a basic difference between the intellectualist West and intuitive Africa. There are few texts on which we can rely, apart from the catechisms which were written by Solomon Dialungana, the second son of Kimbangu and the Custodian of the Holy Place, N'Kamba-Jerusalem. He has had comparatively little contact with the outside world and he is the only son of the prophet not to have had any higher education. These catechisms are written in Kikongo. I rely on a translation of the *Catéchisme du Kintwadi*[1] ('Congregational Catechism') written in 1957 and on an article by Prof. Wyatt MacGaffey,[2] which contains the translation of a pamphlet published in 1961 by Solomon Dialungana under the title *Zolanga Yelusalemi dia Mpa*, which means 'Meditation on the Theme of the New Jerusalem' (or, as MacGaffey translates it, 'the Belovèd City'). These timid beginnings of Kimbanguist theology are written in Kikongo and naturally use the religious language of the Bakongo. Thus, at every step we are faced with the problem of whether a phrase or particular word expresses the new reality of

[1] P. Raymaekers: 'L'Eglise de Jésus Christ sur la Terre par le Prophète Simon Kimbangu', Zaïre XIII, 7, 1959, Brussels, p. 737. The word 'kintwadi' was later no longer used, because it led to confusion with Ngunzists.
[2] Wyatt MacGaffey: 'The Belovèd City, Commentary on a Kimbanguist Text', Journal of Religion in Africa, Leiden, 1969, pp. 129 ff.

Theological Considerations

the Gospel of Jesus Christ (just as, for instance, the Greek word 'logos' in the New Testament is given a completely new meaning, which differs from the philosophical use of the term) or whether there has been a twisting of the biblical message so that the ancient non-Christian beliefs are being given new force. In other words, we need to ask whether we are dealing with syncretism—a blend of Christian and traditional African belief, in which Christian elements might become a vehicle for a revival of traditional African religion in Christian garb. This occurs in many Ngunzist groups and is a frequent phenomenon in certain, though not all, Zionist groups in southern Africa. A new fetishism, a new form of magic emerges, in Christian clothing: water and pieces of fabric or paper touched and blessed by the prophet have a magic healing property, for instance, in the Zion Christian Church of Edward Lekganyane. Similarly, the cross was used in the ancient Kingdom of the Kongo as a new and more powerful fetish and as a fertility charm. In such syncretistic groups the Spirit of God is confused, or identified, with the ancestral spirits, for both can manifest themselves through a certain specially-chosen medium and both can occasion ecstasy. Thus, the prophet can be a mediator of the triune God or he can also be a 'false' prophet of the ancestral spirits. Both the Old and the New Testaments are familiar with this problem, and the Apostle Paul therefore made it clear that 'no one can say "Jesus is Lord" (*Kyrios*) except by the Holy Spirit' (1 Cor. 12:3). That leads us to the heart of the theological problem. Is Jesus Christ the absolute Lord in the teaching of the Kimbanguist Church or does He have rivals in the person of Simon Kimbangu, regarded as a messianic figure, or in the prophet's sons. In order to answer this question we shall not only refer to the texts of the catechisms, but also to sermons which we heard and recorded on tape, to hymns, and to carvings and pictures which we were shown and which relate to Kimbangu and his sons. Some things already mentioned in passing must be discussed again in this chapter.

It was said in Ngunzist circles that 'We prayed to God and He sent us in Simon Kimbangu a Saviour who belongs to the black race. He is the Chief and Saviour of all the blacks and has in fact the same authority as the saviours of other races, such as Moses, Jesus Christ, Mohammed, and Buddha. God gave us Simon Kimbangu, who is to us as Moses is to the Jews, Christ to the other races, and Mohammed to the Arabs.'[3] In the hymns of the Nazarite Church of

---

[3] G. Balandier: 'Sociologie actuelle de l'Afrique noire', Paris, 1963, p. 431.

Isaiah Shembe in South Africa, Shembe appears as a new messiah.[4] He stands at the gate of heaven and holds the key in his hand, locking the whites out (who are like the rich man in the parable of Dives and Lazarus) and letting his faithful followers in.[5] The ancient African ideology of the sacred kingship, which indeed is analogous to the Davidic dynasty in the Old Testament with its Messianic hope, can lead to a new African messianism.[6] Just as David conquered his own royal city and made it into the City of God by bringing in the ark of the covenant, so the new prophets and messiahs also have their Jerusalem, their Zion, their Moriah (2 Chron. 3:1), their Holy City, with a temple in it.

Does all this apply to the Kimbanguist Church, too, and is it thus indulging in a form of pseudo-messianism? Or, and this is the alternative, are the Kimbanguists using these concepts and notions to express the reality and presence of Jesus Christ today in Africa, made manifest through the ministry and suffering of Simon Kimbangu? Has God, through the prophet, shown mercy on the blacks in their sufferings? If this really is the case, ought we not then perhaps also to approach the messianic churches of South Africa with fresh presuppositions and to look again at the questions that confront us?

We are faced here with difficult and crucial problems. They are difficult, because the Kimbanguist Church, like similar churches in Africa, is not familiar with the current theological terminology and therefore uses, particularly in sermons, misleading expressions which can border on the 'heretical'. The problems are crucial, because on the basis of a re-examination of the facts we may come to new conclusions which are of relevance to missionary studies. Let us now examine this problem in the Kimbanguist Church by considering: what is taught concerning the person of Simon Kimbangu; the significance of the Holy Place, N'Kamba-Jerusalem; the symbolism of the church and its attitude to the sacraments; and the question of sanctification and legalism. In the final chapter we shall be concerned with the problem of whether Kimbanguism is a church or a sect.

---

[4] G. C. Oosthuizen: 'The Theology of a South African Messiah', Leiden, 1967, hymn supplement.

[5] B. Sundkler: 'Bantu Prophets in South Africa', 2nd edn, London, 1961, p. 291.

[6] M.-L. Martin: 'Afrikanischer Messianismus und der Messias der biblischen Offenbarung', in Weltmission heute, ed. P. Beyerhaus, Heft 33–34, Stuttgart, 1967, pp. 40 ff.

2. THE TEACHING CONCERNING THE PERSON OF SIMON KIMBANGU

In the catechism of 1957 the question is asked, 'Who is Tata Simon Kimbangu? (*Tata* is a respectful form of address meaning 'father' and is used of any adult man.) 'Tata Simon Kimbangu is the ambassador of our Lord Jesus Christ,' comes the answer. The second question reads: 'How do we know that Tata Simon is the ambassador of Christ?' The answer is that 'Jesus promised us that He would pray the Father for a comforter to do His works and even greater works than He did.' This is a reference to John 14:12–18 where Jesus, in his farewell discourses, speaks of the coming of the Holy Spirit. Then the miracles which Kimbangu performed are mentioned and his lifestory is given briefly in question and answer form. He is the son of Kuyela and Lwezi, both of whom had an untimely death, and was brought up by Maman (respectful form of address for a woman) Kinzembo. As a young man, he married Marie Mwilu. He died in the Upper Congo, he was raised from the dead, and he is with us in spirit.[7] This answer in fact explains the difficult eleventh question and answer: 'Will Tata Simon Kimbangu return? Certainly he will come back, for all that he has begun must advance towards its fulfilment', and there is reference in this connection to John 16:19–33, a passage of Scripture in which Jesus is speaking about the tribulation which will befall the church and about His Return, that is primarily His return in the Holy Spirit. In the Section 'Ancestor Worship?' (Chapter 10) we referred to the communion of the saints, encompassing both those who are alive and those who have died in the Lord. This dimension of communion and communication with departed believers is of great traditional importance to the African, as Taylor has shown in particular.[8]

But there is also talk of a more concrete return of Kimbangu: now and again it is claimed that Simon Kimbangu will appear at the last with Jesus Christ to take part in the Last Judgement, or that he sits with Christ in Judgement on the day a Kimbanguist dies. This approaches a certain messianism, but such statements must not be regarded as absolute.

Question 19 asks, 'Why is the name of Tata Simon Kimbangu given such prominence? Does this mean that Tata Simon Kimbangu is God?' The answer comes: 'No, Tata Simon Kimbangu is not God,

---

[7] Catechism, 1957, Question and Answer 13.
[8] J. V. Taylor: 'The Primeval Vision', London, 1963, Ch. 11, pp. 154–61.

but in all ages and for every race God has chosen a person to enlighten his people.' In this connection there is reference to Exòdus 3:7–17, where Moses is chosen and sent to lead his people out of Egyptian slavery to Canaan. We shall return briefly to the importance of the parallel between Moses and Kimbangu, just as in other independent African churches a parallel is drawn between Moses and the new prophet.

Question 20 asks, 'When did Tata Simon Kimbangu begin his work?' The answer to this asserts that 'He was from the beginning with God.' There is reference to John1:1: 'In the beginning was the Word and the Word was with God.' This reference could give rise to misunderstandings. But we must realize that the writer presumably had hardly the faintest notion of John's theology of the Logos. In fact he made it clear in the previous question that Kimbangu is not God.

Question 22 speaks of the death of Kimbangu. 'We know that he is dead. But', the writer asks, 'when our Lord Jesus Christ died, in whom we trust, did His work die with Him?' Reference is made to John 3:16–17: whoever believes in Jesus has eternal life.

These statements taken from the 1957 catechism show clearly that we cannot take the Kimbanguists at their word in isolated statements because they are still unfamiliar with standard theological terminology. We must try to see what is meant, and this can only be done when one has lived with them for a while, won their confidence, talked to them at length and, most of all, when one has attended their services and devotions and is familiar with their hymns and pictures.

It is also interesting to note that the 1957 catechism has since been replaced by a new one in which Simon Kimbangu is not mentioned. This catechism is solely concerned with the life, teaching and redeeming work of Jesus Christ.

In the second part of Solomon K. Dialungana's booklet *Tanginina Fu Ya Klisto*,[9] which can be loosely translated as 'The Imitation of Christ', Simon Kimbangu again occupies a fairly important position. This booklet presents a kind of ethical code or guide to life, with many quotations from the Bible. Simon Kimbangu is held up as an example. After he had begun his work there was no turning back for him. He was loyal in his obedience to God despite various temptations.[10] In the booklet great emphasis is laid on the Bible. 'When Simon Kimbangu was taken captive the elders (*bankulu*) asked him: "What are you leaving behind for us?" Simon answered:

[9] Solomon K. Dialungana: 'Tanginina Fu Ya Klisto', N'Kamba, 1966.
[10] Op. cit., pp. 22 ff.

"We who have been arrested are going with the Book (the Bible) and you who remain behind also have the Book. Thus, in all things we must seek counsel from the Bible."' A little later on it is explained: 'Tata Simon walked in the very footprints of our Lord Jesus Christ. We must follow him, for our Lord has chosen him to show us the way.' Again and again it is reiterated that the followers of Kimbangu must keep the commandments of Christ. Simon Kimbangu appears here as the great example. The 'imitation of Christ' and of Kimbangu hold an important place in the preaching of the church.

The pamphlet 'The Belovèd City' says this of Simon Kimbangu:

Through Simon Kimbangu, who was obedient to God, the promises of Jesus have been fulfilled and the Name of the Father and the Son has been glorified. Through him the Congolese realized that God and Jesus had turned to us in mercy. The sorrow and suffering of our fathers had been heard by God the Father, and our tears were wiped away.

In an address which he gave in 1969, Joseph Diangienda supplemented this formulation by saying that there existed between Simon Kimbangu and Jesus Christ a particularly close relationship, so that one could sense in Simon Kimbangu, through the fulness of the Holy Spirit granted to him, the presence of the living Christ.

Simon Kimbangu was chosen by Jesus, so his followers regard him as the prophet of Africa. Here it must be noted that, until the present, the Kimbanguists knew nothing of other similar outstanding prophets in Africa but only of the *bangunza* (false) in their own ranks. They have neither been informed of W. Harris nor of the important founders of churches in Nigeria,[11] and it is therefore of great importance that today efforts are being made to establish contact between the church leaders of the large African independent churches in the various parts of Africa.

The pamphlet 'The Belovèd City' continues:

God gave Simon Kimbangu assistants, just as He gave Jesus disciples. Through him God did His work in the Congo, healing the sick, giving sight to the blind and raising the dead. He called upon people to repent and be converted, and he banished the false gods or fetishes.

[11] Cf. H. Turner: 'African Independent Church. The Church of God Aaladura)', Vols. I and II, Oxford, 1967; D. B. Barrett: 'Schism and Renewal in Africa', Oxford, 1968.

In pictures he is depicted as a shepherd—as a young man such as he was when his followers knew him, before he was arrested and taken to Lubumbashi. In a very fine wood-carving which stands in N'Kamba he appears in the form of Simon of Cyrene bearing the cross of Jesus. Through his preaching, his healing and particularly through his suffering, he has made Christ manifest and a living reality to the Zaïrians.[12] Simon leads them to Christ (he is the instrument of Christ) and is not a new messiah, not the Saviour, but the chosen servant through whom Christ has revealed Himself to the Africans. 'Nous avons reçu Jésus fils de Dieu par le prophète qui nous est apparu... nous avons reçu la clémence de Dieu par le prophète qui nous est apparu. As-tu cru les révélations du prophète de Dieu?' the Kimbanguists sing.[13] ('We have received Jesus, the Son of God, through the prophet who has appeared to us. We have received the mercy of God through the prophet who has appeared to us. Do you believe the revelation of the prophet of God?') The glory belongs to the Father and the Son. When Kimbangu's name is praised—as in a popular hymn of praise in the African royal tradition, 'O Nkembo a Tata Simone uzietele' ('The glory of Tata Simon on earth')—that does not mean that Kimbangu's name puts the name of Christ in the shade. He is praised as the messenger of Christ on earth.

He still continues to be the messenger (*ntumwa* in Kikongo), i.e. the ambassador, the apostle, who is now living in the glory of Christ and along with the saints of all ages, has access to the Father and the Son. As such he appears from time to time to his followers in dreams and visions, mainly to his son Joseph Diangienda, and brings them a message—not his own, but that of Christ. We have already referred to this. Superstition? Paganism? Hardly: rather, a dimension may be open here which we Westerners have lost.

Like the Old Testament prophet, Simon Kimbangu does not only bring divine messages, but he also intercedes before God on behalf of the believers. He brings their petitions before Christ, and through Christ, before the Father. The same is true of Marie Mwilu, his wife, as was said at her grave on 27 April 1969 at the commemoration to mark the tenth anniversary of her death. In a prayer, which appears on the calendar of the church for 1969 under the picture of Simon Kimbangu, it is put like this: 'He intercedes before Jesus for the needs of the believers so that Jesus will have mercy on us.' The

---

[12] See Ch. 4.
[13] E. Bazola: 'Le Kimbanguisme', Cahiers des religions africaines, July 1968, No. 4, Lovanium-Kinshasa, p. 316.

prayer itself is addressed to Christ: 'Lord, save us. Once we were "outside" His hand, now we are "in" His hand.'

In Chapter 10, Section 7, we pointed out that Simon Kimbangu occupies a similar position within the Kimbanguist Church to that of the saints in the Catholic Church. The same is true of Marie Mwilu. Can this be traced back to Catholic influence? There may be something in this. What is more important, though, is the fact that in Africa it is the custom never to go with a request direct to the highest authority—modesty forbids it. One turns to a go-between, and it may be that he too will turn to a go-between who is more eminent still, and only the latter can bring the request before the highest authority. This thought stands by and large behind what is called ancestor worship in Africa. Is it not presumptuous, the African asks, to go direct to God or to Christ? Thus it happens occasionally that Simon Kimbangu is invoked as mediator. In one of the many hymns which we heard, prayer to God is made in the name of Papa Simon. These are, however as we were able to observe, exceptions rather than the rule. Of course, there are simple people within the Kimbanguist Church for whom Simon Kimbangu means more than Christ, but those in authority oppose these tendencies. There is also a song of praise which extols God the Father, Jesus Christ, Simon Kimbangu, Joseph Diangienda, and finally the Kimbanguist Church, leaving out the Holy Spirit. But this, too, is an exception, for the trinitarian formula 'In the Name of the Father, and of the Son, and of the Holy Spirit' is recited in all the services almost to the point of being wearisome, which may also be due to Catholic influence.

Summing up, then, we can say that, though Simon Kimbangu is a mediator, he is not a messiah; he is the great 'ancestor', who indeed precludes worship of one's own ancestors in the family, kindred and tribe; he stands in the closest relationship with Christ and leads his own to Christ and to the Father.

We were presented with a wood-carving in which Simon Kimbangu is depicted in prayer, with the Holy Spirit descending upon him in the form of a dove. Does this mean (as we could assume from the application to him of the texts concerning the coming Comforter and from the hymn we have just quoted) that the Holy Spirit so took possession of the prophet that He was, as it were, embodied in him? This is how Buana-Kibongi[14] has understood it on the basis of a clumsy remark by Samuel Matuba, as we have already seen. However, when such a comment is discussed with leading members

[14] D. Buana-Kibongi: 'L'évolution du Kimbanguisme', Flambeau No. 10, Yaoundé, 1966.

of the church the misunderstanding is cleared up. After I had preached at the Whitsun of 1968 in the large church of Matete-Kinshasa, some intellectuals came to discuss the sermon with me and actually said: 'You've preached the incarnation of the Holy Spirit in Simon Kimbangu and in the church.' I had by no means spoken of an 'incarnation' of the Spirit in Simon Kimbangu and in the church but of an indwelling of the Spirit, both in Kimbangu and in every believer on earth. They were not aware of the theological distinction between 'incarnation' (a word which we use only with reference to Jesus) and 'indwelling' (a word which denotes being filled with the Spirit of God). Such unfortunate remarks and formulations on the part of people who are not familiar with western theological terminology, can easily lead to their being accused of heresy and sectarianism when what is basically at issue is only the wrong use of a word rather than erroneous thinking. And we might even ask: is it as wrong as all that?

As we have already seen, to the invocation of the Trinity 'In the Name of the Father, and of the Son, and of the Holy Spirit' is often added 'who has descended on Simon Kimbangu' or 'who has spoken to us through Simon Kimbangu.' He is sometimes called the servant and assistant (*nsadisi*) of the Holy Spirit or the first black person to receive the Holy Spirit in His fullness.

The prayer from the calendar of 1969, which was quoted in the last Section, contains the following statement: 'God does not deceive us. Simon Kimbangu is the *nsadisi* of the Holy Spirit; he is the head of those who are persecuted; he is the witness of Jesus Christ.' Why is that? For two reasons: just as in the ancient church the Holy Spirit descended at Pentecost on the apostles of Jesus and made them ambassadors of the Gospel, so He has fallen in the same way upon Simon Kimbangu and empowered him to be the ambassador and servant of Jesus. And just as the apostles received authority through the Spirit to confirm their preaching through signs and wonders, so Simon Kimbangu received the same authority through the Holy Spirit.[15] Similar statements are found in the booklet *Tanginina Fu Ya Klisto*, mentioned above.

The same Holy Spirit is, however, at work in the church as well and in every believer in every age. The Kimbanguists do not think, as certain clumsy and perhaps polemical remarks could lead us to assume, that He is only at work in their church but they realize that He is active wherever people believe in Jesus Christ and look to Him for regeneration and sanctification. We shall see below that the opera-

---

[15] Cf. E. Bazola: op. cit., pp. 333–4.

tion of the Holy Spirit in the church is seen mainly in the work of sanctification. Theologically, we are faced here with the need to consider afresh the concept of prophecy in the New Testament and in the church. The question is whether the Acts of the Apostles and particularly the letters of Paul admit of a continuation of prophecy, and whether God still calls today special heralds who, in the power of the Holy Spirit, proclaim His word, there in the concrete situation of a nation or a class or a group, and make it so real that people realize that they are encountering the living Christ; that here and now is happening for them what happened in Christ's time in Jerusalem, in Antioch and in Corinth. That does not exclude, but rather does it include, the uniqueness of the one Prophet Jesus Christ as the fulfilment of Old Testament prophecy.

W. J. Hollenweger shows that the same problem crops up with regard to the concept of 'apostle' in the Pentecostal church.[16] This concept ought also to be re-examined because it is not used in the New Testament solely of the Twelve, nor, when we think of Barnabas, necessarily of eye-witnesses. As we think about this term, let us remember that Kimbangu is called an apostle (ambassador) as well as a prophet.

3. THE SIGNIFICANCE OF KIMBANGU'S SONS IN THE LIFE OF THE CHURCH

Kimbangu's sons have the highest rank in the hierarchy of the church, and all important decisions must be approved by them. The three are united and have been called *princes héritiers* (hereditary princes), or in Kikongo *zimvwala,* i.e. bearers of the prophetic and royal staff or sceptre. The term can mean that prophetic and royal functions are theirs within the church. The highest position is accorded to Joseph Diangienda.

We are thus faced with what is a frequent phenomenon in Africa—the prophet becomes the 'king' as well, and there is a revival within the church of the ancient royal tradition which had broken down because of political and economic factors but which had not been forgotten. We can see the same thing in South Africa in the case of James Limba, Edward Lekganyane (whose 14-year-old son has succeeded to his father after his untimely death in 1968),[17] and Isaiah Shembe and his son Galilee. In ancient African tradition, and

[16] W. J. Hollenweger: 'Enthusiastisches Christentum', Wuppertal and Zürich, 1969, p. 281.
[17] M.-L. Martin: op. cit., pp. 40 ff.

this holds in the Bakongo as well as among the Zulus and other tribal units, the king is a hallowed, sacred person, both the political and religious head of the tribe, the mediator who, for instance among the Zulus, is worshipped (*konzwa*). He is the 'Father' and thus in African thinking the source of all real life.[18] Given these notions, it is not difficult to turn the prophet into the new 'messiah' (i.e. 'annointed one'), for the Messiah of Old Testament tradition was to begin with the Davidic king in Jerusalem who, already in the Royal Psalms and particularly in the prophetic writings, becomes the eschatological 'new David'.[19]

At first it seems that this is what also happened in the Kimbanguist Church. Joseph Diangienda is called *Tata mfumu'a nlongo*, which is translated *Chef spirituel* (spiritual head) though the Kikongo actually means 'sacred head'. There was a time, in 1960, when he was called the Kimbanguist pope by enthusiastic followers.[20] It was a passing phase which one must not hold against him. The whole of Kimbanguist theology is indeed still in flux. Nor did he himself choose 'Eminence' as a form of address but it was forced upon him from outside, initially against his will, by state authorities in order to accord to him on official occasions a similar status to that of the highest Catholic dignitaries. We ourselves saw how he took an evangelist to task for calling him *saint* (holy). On this occasion in May 1968, in the presence of leading figures of the Kimbanguist Church, he stressed—and these were no mere phrases—that, just like the rest of them, he was a sinner who lived only by the grace of Jesus Christ and that he was far from being a 'saint' in the sense of having outstanding and divine qualities. On this, as on other occasions, he firmly and calmly rejected all attempts to give him 'messianic dignity'. When crowds of followers gathered at the airport of Kisangani and gave him what amounted to a 'messianic' ovation (in a situation of political uncertainty, in which his presence meant support and help and such a demonstration was psychologically understandable), he remained calm, gathered the crowd in the provisional church and pointed them to the Scriptures as the only basis of faith. After such climatic occasions it may well be (as we ourselves saw) that he will show that even he is only a servant by spontaneously handing his companions the bowl of water and

[18] P. Tempels: 'Philosophie bantou, Présence africaine', Paris, 1949 (French), 1959 (English), pp. 42 f. in both edns; J. V. Taylor: op. cit., p. 136.

[19] G. von Rad: 'Theologie des Alten Testamentes', Munich, 1958, Vol. I, pp. 317 ff.

[20] 'Kimbanguisme', N'Kamba, 21 October and 23 December 1961.

towel, which are provided before a meal so that people can wash their hands. He has the deeply religious humility to resist the temptation to be the most eminent person in the church in a worldly way.

And yet Joseph Diangienda does keep to the formal aspects of the royal tradition within the church. That is why there are the customary ovations when he is welcomed at church services. He takes his mediatorial office in an intercessory sense so seriously that no one is permitted to disturb him when he withdraws to his room, sometimes for hours. He sees this office as a spiritual gift and a commission, like that of the Old Testament High Priest and intercessor. However, he knows and says that he also needs the intercession of his friends and fellow-workers, and thus he places himself again on the same level as they.

His decisions are taken seriously and he is greatly respected—not simply because of his position, but because he deserves this respect through his humanity, his care for the poor and the sick, and through his unstinting self-sacrifice. Something of the imitation of Christ is seen in his manner of life. He stresses again and again that he possesses the Holy Spirit to a much lesser extent than did his parents, and one also senses how seriously he takes the responsibility which rests upon him. In his letters this is often apparent. He will undertake and decide nothing without being sure of God's guidance, which he always seeks in prayer. He keeps himself under strict control, which does not mean that he cannot become angry when this is called for. He demands of all church members and staff obedience and subordination, and I have occasionally heard it said that obedience to him is also obedience to Simon Kimbangu, who can be seen in his son. This corresponds to the saying of Jesus, 'He who has seen Me has seen the Father,'[21] but it is also in accordance with African tradition where the personality of the father lives on in the son. Such formulations naturally have inherent dangers, particularly for simple folk, who think in a concrete and not an abstract way, and for whom Simon Kimbangu and his son are the present embodiment of the revelation of Christ.

Joseph Diangienda is assisted in his work by his older brothers Charles Kisolokele and Solomon Kiangani Dialungana. Since 1959 Charles Kisolokele has supported the whole large family, providing for both his own family and for those of his two brothers, in accordance with traditional African custom. This enables Joseph Diangienda and Solomon Dialungana to devote themselves to full-time

[21] John 14:9.

service in the church without receiving the slightest payment for their work. Solomon Dialungana visits the congregations in the province of Lower Zaïre and organizes with his staff of assistants the great festivities which are held in N'Kamba and to which thousands of pilgrims come.

The question arises as to who will one day succeed the sons of Kimbangu. Will Kimbangu's grandchildren? Who of them will be the spiritual head? Will the 'dynastic line' be thus continued or will the church be ready to leave the question of succession completely to the leading of the Spirit of God? An election throughout the church, as is customary in many Protestant, democratically organized churches, hardly comes into question and, as far as I can judge, has often proved a failure in Africa, even in historical churches. As yet Joseph Diangienda has left the question open, but I have heard leading Kimbanguists say that they would only consider a grandson of Simon Kimbangu as successor to Joseph Diangienda. The danger of a personality and dynasty cult among simple believers is obvious, and this could one day have unfortunate consequences, particularly when we see how the mass of believers turn to Kimbangu's sons for help, advice and support, even when ministers and evangelists could give equal advice and assistance. At any rate, it is imperative that a stratum of leaders be trained as rapidly as possible as theologians and responsible head-teachers in their own spiritual tradition to assume responsibility in the theological, human, social, medical and in administrative spheres. They should also be those with whom the spiritual head can discuss the things seriously.

As far as I can see, there is not only the need for well-educated leadership but also for charismatic leader figures in whom, as in Joseph Diangienda, something of the power of Christ is evident. The lack of such figures has led many a church in Africa (and in Europe?) into grave difficulties. Africa does not live by ideas, formulations and sound creeds, but by 'incarnation' in the widest and fullest sense. That this incarnation should occur, even after the death of Kimbangu's sons, does not rest in the power of man but in divine providence, in which we can only believe but over which we have no control.

4. NEW JERUSALEM

N'Kamba occupies a central position within Kimbanguism. In N'Kamba there began a recapitulation of the life and sufferings of Christ, and this was completed in 1960 with the return of the mortal

Theological Considerations 153

remains of Simon Kimbangu. N'Kamba-Jerusalem and the reactivation of the redeeming work of Christ, which occurred once and for all in Israel, are of crucial importance, and without them the Kimbanguist Church and its theology, expressed in its hymns and art, cannot be understood. All that has happened stands in relation to the facts of the Old and New Testaments, and in this N'Kamba remains central. In his booklet *The Belovèd City* Solomon Dialungana explains this:

> Abraham came to Salem (Jerusalem) and was blessed by the priest Melchizedek (Genesis 14), who in Hebrews 6:20 is identified with Jesus. King David conquered Jerusalem and his descendants reigned there. However, Israel did not keep God's Law. God was merciful and spared His People, until they were ultimately carried off into Babylonian captivity. But God in His goodness promised a new Jerusalem. Texts in the Old and New Testaments prove this.

Where is this new Jerusalem? It is here in N'Kamba. Here God has revealed Himself to the degraded, suffering black race, and Dialungana refers at this point to the sufferings of the Zaïrians under colonial rule, particularly to the notorious forced labour and 'flu epidemic of 1918, which did not spare a village or a family in Zaïre.

> Our fathers cried for a 'chief', a saviour, but no saviour came, until they said in resignation that God did not know us black people. He only knew the whites. Then missionaries came with the light of God. They obeyed the command of Jesus to 'Go into all the world and preach to all nations...' (Matt. 28:18–20 and Mark 16:16–18). But they confined their ministry to preaching. The number of the converts was not great. The people hid from the missionaries and remained in the grasp of fetishism, of witchcraft, and of other evil practices. Then on 6 April 1921, the first miracle occurred. Simon Kimbangu of N'Kamba raised the dead, healed paralytics, gave the blind their sight, cured the sick and drove away those who had anything to do with witchcraft.

N'Kamba became the new Jerusalem. The emergence of Simon Kimbangu as a prophet endued with the power of the Holy Spirit was the new Pentecost. 'Through the events in N'Kamba God our Father and His Son Jesus Christ have come to us.'

'When this happened the hills of Satan also arose', the counterpart of N'Kamba-Jerusalem which, like the earthly Jerusalem in Palestine, is situated on a hill. What is meant by the hills of Satan are the attacks of the colonial government and the missions, which declared their hostility towards Simon Kimbangu and his followers. 'They were jealous that Jesus had given His power to the Africans and had manifested His new Jerusalem in Africa.' They had forgotten—so Dialungana continues—that Jesus was brought as a baby to Egypt (Africa!) and that Simon of Cyrene, an African, bore His cross, and that (according to Acts 10:35) God loved all nations.

The booklet concludes,

> We must therefore love the new Jerusalem (N'Kamba) just as Israel loved ancient Jerusalem. It is the city of Kimbangu just as ancient Jerusalem was the city of David. It is the city of blessing, with its Pool of Bethesda (John 5) [a reference to the sacred spring through which many believers have been healed]. It is the city to which all nations are making their pilgrimage, where God is praised night and day, where no witchcraft can penetrate, and from which the three sons of Kimbangu, the *zimvwala*, come and where they have their home. Just as the Jews used to go as pilgrims to Jerusalem, so all members of the 'Church of Jesus Christ on Earth through the Prophet Simon Kimbangu' should make their pilgrimage.

It is understandable, in the light of this theology of 'Jerusalem-N'Kamba', that great importance is attached to the visits of Christians of other nations and races. This is the fulfilment of the divine promises, which are transferred from the ancient city to the new Jerusalem—the promises that people of all nations will come as pilgrims to Zion.[22]

The centre of the new Jerusalem is the mausoleum or *kinlongo*[23] (i.e. 'sacred object', 'temple') containing the mortal remains of Simon Kimbangu, a very simple building which is opened twice a year. Steps lead from the foot of the hill, from the spot where Simon Kimbangu was arrested, to the height on which the mausoleum stands. Just as Joseph, Jacob's son, had promised his father to take his mortal remains from Egypt to Canaan and to bury them there, so Joseph, the son of Simon Kimbangu, promised his father that he would bring his mortal remains from the land of bondage and slavery—in his case, Lubumbashi—to N'Kamba-Jerusalem.[24] The steps which lead to the church and the mausoleum which stands behind it are reminiscent too of Jacob's ladder to heaven, and indeed God pronounced His blessing from above.[25] Thus, at every turn,

[22] Cf. Is. 2:1–4.
[23] 'Kinlongo' is the word used in the Kikongo Bible for 'temple'.
[24] See Ch. 10:6.   [25] Gen. 28.

reference is made to events in Israel and to Christ. N'Kamba makes the life and sufferings of Christ real *today* for the Zaïrians and, beyond the Zaïre, for Africa and the world. The years 1921–60 are compared to Israel's forty years in the wilderness. Just as Moses only stood on the threshold of the Promised Land of liberty but was not permitted to enter it but had to hand over the leadership to Joshua, so Simon Kimbangu foresaw the day of liberty but did not experience it, and in this connection Joseph Diangienda is compared to Joshua. He led the Kimbanguists to freedom, in those eventful years of 1956–60.

5. OTHER BIBLICAL PARALLELS

Simon Kimbangu (like the South African prophets) is also often seen as a new Moses. His visions and auditions are compared with the meetings which Moses had with God on Mt. Sinai. Just as Moses was a liberator, so was Kimbangu. He freed people from superstition, witchcraft and sickness, and today he is also seen in a spiritual sense as a *libérateur*, a liberator from the colonial yoke, since he dared to obey God rather than men. Liberation means to the African mind something total, namely liberation from collective as well as personal bondage to powers which will not let a human being be or become human. Thus, a political dimension in a 'higher sense' enters here, but of course only remotely in the sense in which the Belgian colonial power meant it when it sentenced Kimbangu to death.

Just as Moses led the Israelites in their wanderings for forty years in the wilderness, so Simon Kimbangu led his own people, too. Preachers apply this parallel with Moses to the present as follows: 'Many of the Israelites never entered the Promised Land because the fleshpots of Egypt were more important to them. That happens today. We cling to the past although we think we have fled from Egypt. We shall not enter the Promised Land if we do not let ourselves be led by Tata Simon Kimbangu. Let us follow his example and make no distinction between Bakongo, Bangala, and Baluba.'[26] In other words, let us leave all tribal rivalry out of it. Thus, Egypt not only stands for the bondage of colonial rule but also for persistence in sin and disobedience towards God.

Kimbangu is also compared to other biblical figures. He is like Noah, in whose day the Flood befell the disobedient—an allusion to the disturbances and civil wars which afflicted Zaïre from 1960 to 1967.

[26] E. Bazola: op. cit., p. 329.

In the booklet *Tanginina Fu Ya Klisto* there is the following parallel: 'When Jesus Christ was born Herod was displeased. The same thing happened again when Tata Simon Kimbangu began his work, for the colonial government was displeased and arrested him.' The booklet continues: 'Tata Simon Kimbangu was not loved by the world just as Christ was not.' Hence, the writer concludes, 'Whoever does not love Tata Simon, who is Christ's ambassador and witness in Africa, does not love Christ either, for Tata Simon has manifested the works of God and Christ. What Tata Simon did he did not do in his own name but in the Name of Christ.' So the life of Kimbangu has constantly been seen as a graphic presentation of biblical history and, above all, of the Gospel. Just as Jesus healed the sick, raised the dead, gave the blind their sight, preached repentance and had to argue with His enemies, so it was with Simon Kimbangu. Just as Jesus suffered innocently, so did Simon Kimbangu. But the great qualitative difference between the atoning suffering of Jesus and Kimbangu's suffering, which testified to the cross of Jesus, is not passed over in silence. Jesus saves from sin and death, but Kimbangu does not. Kimbangu is only Christ's apostle and ambassador, but like Jesus he was permitted to entrust his work to twelve apostles and a few *basandisi* ('assistants'). Jesus was thus graphically portrayed to the Zaïrians, reminding us of what Paul says of the Galatians (Gal. 3:1). Like Paul, Kimbangu bore the marks of Christ in his body (Gal. 6:17) and 'completed in his flesh what is lacking in Christ's afflictions for the sake of His body, that is, the church' (Col. 1:24). Shining through Simon Kimbangu they see Christ. In this there lies a great promise, and also a danger. It is promising because so often in Africa we hear mention of the 'white Christ' whom the missionaries brought (so it is said) as the precursor of colonial rule. When colonial rule ends Christ is rejected too, and there is a turning to traditional African religion—or at least there is an attempt to turn to it! The danger lies in the fact that, in the preaching of simple evangelists, Simon Kimbangu can indeed be made into a kind of messiah. Intensive Bible training of ministers and laiety can alone counter this danger.

6. THE SYMBOLISM OF THE CHURCH AND ITS ATTITUDE TO THE SACRAMENTS

The word 'symbol' has many meanings. Here, we mean images and actions which give expression to a certain spiritual truth. Africa is rich in symbols. It has its own symbols, which in the present great upheaval often get lost, and it has also adopted Christian symbols. Thus we find in the Kimbanguist Church the cross on church buildings and on its coat of arms. As in many Protestant churches it is not used overmuch, as it is, for instance, by the South-African Zionists, for whom it became a new fetish (as in the ancient Kongo and among certain Ngunzists in Luozi), and whose vestments are embroidered with many crosses. All the pulpits as well as the homes of the Kimbanguists have painted on them a vivid white star on a green background. This sign is a pointer to Christ at the right hand of God and reminds us that we are pilgrims on earth and must one day give an account of ourselves before the Judgement Seat of Christ (Rom. 14:10). Green is the colour of hope, whereas white speaks of the purity given in answer to prayer.

The coat of arms of the Kimbanguist Church is to be found on the entrance of the still provisional 'churches' with their palm roofs, and on the flags borne here and there in processions: on a green background there is a red heart, 'crossed through' by a cross; sometimes a serpent is entwined round the cross, and below the heart there are two palm leaves. The heart with the serpent signifies the sinful human heart for which Christ died (represented by the cross). The two palm leaves proclaim the victory of Christ over sin. The red colour of the heart seems to stand for the blood of Christ.

On the arms of N'Kamba there is a dove, below which two palm leaves are seen. The dove represents the Holy Spirit. On official visits to congregations, Joseph Diangienda used always to be handed three doves as a symbol of the Holy Spirit. The number three in this connection signifies the Trinity and also the unity of Kimbangu's three sons.

In Kisangani we noticed that there were fine palm-leaf fibres hanging down from the roof of the provincial church and tied together in knots. Earlier that was a protective spell of certain tribes against evil spirits, and such palm fibres tied together used to surround the villages. In the Kimbanguist Church this symbol has lost its old meaning, or rather it has been transformed. Today these palm fibres knotted together signify that, wherever God's praise is sung and there is prayer and preaching of the word, the powers of darkness are banished. On entering church and when praying, one takes off one's shoes, just as they are taken off in many African royal courts as a sign of respect. The pray-er kneels down and lays aside his jewellery, his watch, his purse, and his papers, to show that we may only approach God in humility and poverty. The taking off of one's shoes is supported by reference to Exodus 3:5 and also goes back, as we have said, to ancient African tradition and not to Islam influence, as Raymaekers assumes.[27]

The most frequently used sign is the water of N'Kamba, which is to be found in every congregation, in distant Rwanda, in the isolated congregations of Djambala and Gamboma remote from Brazzaville, in Lubumbashi and in Kitwe in Zambia. It is taken in great containers from N'Kamba to Kinshasa, and from there the representatives of the remote congregations take it with them when they are gathered for a conference or when the affairs of their districts and congregations bring them to the spiritual head of the church. This water is used when the sick are healed, and particularly when evangelists, ministers and elders pray for the sick. They may not, of course, lay hands on them because this is reserved for Joseph Diangienda and, in his absence, for his brother Charles Kisolokele and the few surviving fellow-workers of Simon Kimbangu.[28] The N'Kamba water is applied to the painful part of the body. The water is also drunk, and when a pilgrimage to N'Kamba can be undertaken the pilgrim dips himself three times in the spring (which has been broadened into a pool) 'in the Name of the Father, and of the Son, and of the Holy Spirit'. The water is used by the head of the church to bless infants in his home, after church services, or on his many travels through the country. Like the holy water in the Catholic Church, the water is sometimes used for the consecration of a new house, a new car, or other objects; and we have seen how, when Joseph Diangienda is visiting a congregation, the women often lay long colourful dress-wraps on the path which leads to the provisional 'church'. He sprinkles drops of holy water on them in order to consecrate the otherwise profane place. Perhaps there is another hidden meaning in the 'consecration' of the wraps.

This frequent use of blessed water is similar to the use of water in many African churches, as well as in the Catholic Church. What does this water mean today? Does it have a purifying, magic power so that it works automatically, *ex opere operato*, in healing and blessing? If that were so (and certainly there are those who believe this) we should have before us a syncretistic element, a vestige of the ancient, pre-Christian religion. For educated Kimbanguists—and in the teaching of the church—the water is a symbol, as in Christian baptism. It is a visible and tangible sign of purification, and an invisible blessing. Without faith and prayer it is useless. It must not, then, be used by or for people who do not believe in Christ. Nor is it indispensable. Consecrations and blessings also occur without the

[27] P. Raymaekers: op. cit., p. 705.
[28] See Ch. 6:5.

water, as a fruit of faith and as God's answer to prayer. Thus, it is prayer that is primary, and there is emphasis on 'Thy will be done'. Perhaps the illness must be borne and God will simply give the strength to bear it. Also blessing, divine favour, need not bring release from suffering but very often manifests itself in the assurance that Christ is at one's side and that one will triumph. The Kimbanguist Church has had to endure suffering too long to promise people cheap release from suffering.

All these ceremonies in which water is used are performed without fuss. Those in N'Kamba who go to the spring do so in silence. One goes on one's own, or in small groups—at certain times the men go, and at other times the women. If they have a special request (it need not necessarily be for release from illness), they speak beforehand with Solomon Dialungana or one of his assistants, who then gather for silent prayer and intercession whilst the person concerned goes to the pool. Before bathing a silent prayer is offered.

Not only is the N'Kamba water used symbolically but soil, too, is taken from N'Kamba as a kind of pledge that the events of N'Kamba, which took place here on earth, will also have their outworking at home in the daily needs of life. There is a biblical parallel to this in the story of Naaman (2 Kings 5:17).

All the healings and blessings are connected not only with prayer but also with the word of God. As with Kimbangu himself, the Bible remains central in all that is done. This is particularly evident in the many requests for healing which are made after the services, that is, when the word has been read and preached. Not infrequently, the one who prays for healing for the sick person first reads a passage of Scripture from the Old and New Testaments. Only then is prayer offered for healing or God's aid and blessing.

What lies at the heart of all these ceremonies connected with the water of N'Kamba? Bazola puts it like this:

> What emerges from all these rites of healing, apart from faith, is the emphasis on the reality of the spiritual world, the fundamental unity of man (there is no dichotomy between body and soul), and the relationship which exists between religion and healing, a relationship which is in keeping with the African view of religion.[29]

What Bazola says with respect to healing is true of the whole spectrum of visible signs and symbols. They express the unity of the psycho-spiritual and physical realms. Greek 'dichotomy' has no

---

[29] E. Bazola: op. cit., p. 320.

place in African thought. That is why missionaries were, and continue to be, accused of only bothering with one side of man, namely the spiritual. The fact that mission hospitals were built and that clinics care for the physical well-being of people is still regarded as 'dichotomous'. You go with your spiritual concerns to the minister or evangelist but you take your physical problems to the doctor in the hospital. The Kimbanguists certainly do not reject medical help and they have their own clinics with trained nurses. But in the first place help is sought from the church elder, who in the villages and towns takes care of a manageable section of the congregation and from whom prayer is first sought in case of illness or other trouble. After that the elder (either a man or a woman) attends to whatever else is necessary. Thus, the church cares for the whole man, and this is also expressed in its symbolism.

What is the position with regard to the sacraments? In the sacraments of the church the visible action with water, bread and wine assists the prayer for forgiveness, renewal, inner strength and blessing, which are promised to the believer through Christ. The Protestant churches limit the sacraments to two: baptism and the Lord's Supper.

These two sacraments are not to be found—or not yet—in the same form in the Kimbanguist Church. Infant baptism is not practised but, as in Baptist circles, there is the ceremony of *presentation of infants*. In the church service the parents bring their children to the front. The minister asks the parents to promise to bring up their children in the fear of God and to raise them as Christians, by word but more particularly by their example. Each child is blessed by the minister and addressed as an adult. The child is already— *in spe* (hope)—taken absolutely seriously as a child of God. When the child is bigger and can decide for himself, he is given instruction and then he receives on his knees the baptism with the Spirit through being shaken by the hand and raised to his feet. Neither at the presentation nor at the baptism with the Spirit is water used, and Mark 1:8 is used to justify this. We may ask whether it is absolutely necessary only to use water in this specific act, or whether it is permissible to use the symbol of water much more frequently to express the prayer for healing and divine assistance and power (a very important concept for Africans), as is in fact the case in the Kimbanguist Church. If the N'Kamba water were used also for baptism proper, there would be justification for speaking of a repetition of baptism. But the Kimbanguists do not intend this. If you have been baptized you cannot be re-baptized. That is why 'converts', i.e. people joining the Kimbanguists from other churches,

Theological Considerations

are *not* given the baptism with the Spirit by being shaken by the hand. They are already baptized and this baptism is recognized. They are merely prayed for.

The introduction of the celebration of the Lord's Supper was being seriously considered, and when I arrived in April 1968 in Kinshasa this was one of the very first questions which I was asked in the ministerial council. It had been hoped to introduce the Lord's Supper in December 1966 on the occasion of the consecration of the large church in Matete-Kinshasa, but people were not yet ready for this. Why? 'The Lord's Supper, the real presence of Christ, means so much to us that we are still seeking the proper form in which to express it,' one of the ministers told me. Prior to 1959 many of the Kimbanguists were given the Communion in the Catholic or one of the Protestant churches, of which they were nominal members. Others (relatively many) were members of the Salvation Army, in which no sacraments are administered, neither baptism nor Communion. Still others became members of the Kimbanguist Church from traditional African religion or—in the towns—from an indefinable religiosity. Hence, an appropriate form of sacrament was difficult to find. Should it be the Catholic rite, some form of Protestant practice, or perhaps the Orthodox rite? (For some years Kimbanguists have had connections with the Greek Orthodox Church.) What are the elements which should be used—manioc or banana bread, or bread made from imported wheat? What should be used to represent the blood of Christ? What meaning does the Lord's Supper convey?

Long and serious considerations had to be made concerning the form appropriate to its content and the African mode of expression. Serious and patient study preceded the introduction of the Last Supper's celebration. The Lord's Supper was celebrated for the first time on the fiftieth anniversary of the Kimbanguist Church, on 6 April 1971.[30]

In the agricultural colony of Lutendele a communal meal is taken in the evenings which in a certain sense seems to approach the early Christian love-feast (*agape*). During the meal passages of Scripture are read and the meal is interrupted with hymns thanksgiving. The joy at the meal which we shared was so great and intense that one of the participants became ecstatic and spoke in tongues.

Marriage is sometimes (e.g. in the Catholic Church) spoken of as a sacrament. The consecration of marriage often takes place on a Sunday before the assembled congregation. The liturgy used on

---

[30] See Appendix, pp. 181–183.

this occasion resembles that of the Protestant churches. The bridal couple are exhorted to fidelity and mutual consideration. When the inevitable difficulties arise in the marriage, the problem should be settled in private and not in front of children and friends. These exhortations are all the more important seeing the Kimbanguist Church hardly sanctions a divorce. When there are conflicts in a marriage, everything possible is done to reconcile the couple, perhaps after a short separation in which the congregation tries, for instance, to make the guilty partner take stock of himself.

Funerals are simple. Outside the house of mourning, people sing and pray for hours until the coffin is taken to the cemetery. Funerals involve the congregation and have a marked anticipation of resurrection and eternal life. This forms a stark contrast to the complicated ceremonies in Africa, where funeral ritual lasts for many days and where, after the minister has left, much traditional non-Christian practice is followed. Death and burial are one of the crisis situations which reveal whether the Christian faith is only a veneer or whether it stands the test. This is the crucial time when a decision is made either to worship and sacrifice to one's ancestors or to trust in Jesus Christ, who is the Resurrection and the Life. It is true that the African non-Christian believes in eternal life, but as a kind of continuation of *this* life in the 'Beyond'. But those who believe in Jesus know of a *new* life. When the believer dies he is with Christ (Phil. 1:23) and awaits the resurrection. Those left behind on earth are, with the dead in Christ, part of the communion of the saints in heaven and on earth. The traditional African 'belief in the Beyond' is thus transformed by the Christian Gospel, where the bonds between the living and the dead are not severed but formed in a new way. The living and the dead no longer belong together in a natural way, through the bonds of blood and kinship, but in and through Jesus Christ.

7. SANCTIFICATION

Unlike Gospel practice, there is in Europe today a tendency to call every fixed code 'legalism'. This may have something to do partly with the 'crisis in authority' and partly with a legitimate concern to repudiate any kind of justification by works.

African life was (and still is to some extent today) marked by rules of life and taboos that must be kept to preserve intact the balance of the community. If this balance is disturbed, the revenge of the ancestors is expected, so they must be reconciled. Witchcraft is seen as concentrated evil. Witches are the anti-social, anomalous elements in the community. They inflict harm on other people without knowing it. They depart at night (perhaps leaving their body behind in their hut); their 'shade' goes out, meets with other shades, and they slay and devour the body of innocent victims. Nothing is feared more than witchcraft (*kindoki* in Kikongo, and *vuloyi, vuroyi* or *boloi* in the dialects of the southern tribes). The 'soothsayer' finds them, and only too frequently those concerned are ready to confess their evil. Protection against *kindoki* is found in the *minkisi*, the fetishes. We have seen how Simon Kimbangu and his church campaigned, and still campaigns, against fetishes. The Kimbanguists do not believe in *kindoki*, but they are aware of the destructive power of evil in the community. Sin must therefore be confessed and brought to light. In almost all of the independent African churches public confession of sin is of importance. But what is sin? How does this socially destructive 'something' manifest itself? Among the Zionists in South Africa—although one cannot generalize—the taking of medicine is *the* sin.

Like traditional African communities, the Kimbanguist Church has also fixed certain bounds which are not to be transgressed and beyond which is evil. We find them in what are known as the *Statuts*, to which we have already referred.[31] Exhortations to obey the commandments are connected with the New Testament injunction to watchfulness, for 'you know neither the day nor the hour in which the Son of Man will come' (which may refer either to the return of Jesus or to death). It is often stressed that it is not easy to be a Kimbanguist: are believers then being placed under a new yoke? Is a person justified before God through works? These are issues which must be considered.

At the same time the sanctifying power of the Spirit of God is pointed to. He alone sanctifies. He alone gives the strength to live a life of holiness. Salvation, healing, and sanctification are three closely interwoven concepts. We know that Kimbangu did not heal without proclaiming salvation in Christ and sanctification through the Spirit. Once more there is here the 'unity' of the African conception of life'. Salvation, sanation, and sanctification cannot be divided up into three different areas. Sanctification is the response of the Christian to the gift of salvation, which includes healing—healing in the widest sense, not necessarily healing of sickness. What impressed us was the joy and willingness of simple and more eminent members of the Kimbanguist Church to obey the com-

---

[31] See Ch. 12:1.

mandments and statutes and thus to be witnesses to a sinful world, groaning under the burden of evil, the Devil, and death. Evil is no longer seen in the *bandoki*, the evil witch-doctors, but in the Devil, against whom all Christians must take up the struggle.

People become *bandoki* by allowing evil to rule them. We must ask again whether all this is legalism. It depends very much on what we mean by 'legalism'. From the point of view of modern situation ethics, the teaching of the Kimbanguist Church would certainly be condemned as legalism. We must admit that there are in fact the beginnings of a new legalism, which indeed is understandable in the light of traditional African ethics with their rules and taboos but which is not necessarily justified in the light of the Gospel, since it can lead to a new bondage against which Paul, for instance, had to contend. The danger of a new legalism is particularly evident when the fulfilment of the commandments of God is described as a 'ticket to heaven' and is bound up with the thought of reward and punishment in the afterlife. There is something legalistic about the distinction which is sometimes made between 'gross' and 'light' sins and about certain regulations, like the taking off of one's shoes in N'Kamba, which is sometimes exaggerated by simple and over-zealous Kimbanguists. The legalism leads here and there to a certain exclusivity, which emerges in the thought that we Kimbanguists are not like 'worldly people' and must therefore suffer. The danger of pharisaism is there.

Nevertheless, in assessing Kimbanguist teaching concerning sanctification we must remember the sociological upheaval in Africa. Traditional values are disappearing in the rapid development and urbanization in Africa. New values must replace the old ones otherwise there will be chaos. Indeed, in many cities in Africa, as well as in the West, we see today this chaos and complete loss of orientation. The 'permissive society' can no longer offer anything for men to cling to. The Kimbanguist Church opposes these disintegrating tendencies, which are particularly noticeable in a country like Zaïre following all its political turmoils and upheavals. The church is not trying to establish a traditional legal system but to give the African in his new situation a framework in which society can live again, and the strength to lead this new life responsibly before God and man. 'Kimbanguism is the only truly constructive force in Zaïre today', a European told us who is himself not part of the church but who, as a humanist in the diplomatic service of a European state, has been able to observe developments in Zaïre for years.

Before we accuse Kimbanguism of 'legalism' we must bear in mind the whole situation and remember that this obedience is gladly shown, as a witness to the reality of Christ. We must, of course, always and everywhere be on our guard against legalism, and this will in future present the Kimbanguist Church with serious theological problems. The church will have to stress above all that sin is not only a transgression of commandments but a turning from God, which disturbs the personal relationship which God in His grace grants man as His covenant partner.

This concern is all the more understandable, seeing it is one of the great aims of the Kimbanguist Church to bring about reconciliation, restoring a sense of brotherhood between people. Because God has reconciled Himself with us in Christ, we must be reconciled with each other. Because of this desire for reconciliation, which was so evident in Simon Kimbangu himself, the Kimbanguist Church works for reconciliation between tribes and nations and repudiates the use of force to settle disputes. It is indeed not by chance that the Kimbanguist Church has not become known in Switzerland so much through missionary publications as through the 'Fellowship of Reconciliation', which 'discovered' this church which repudiates the use of force. In 1966, the Fellowship financed a short 'reconnaissance journey' to Zaïre, undertaken by Rev. J. Lasserre and F. Choffat. It is also not by chance that it is the Moravian Church, with its ecumenical concern for reconciliation, which has sponsored the application of the 'Church of Jesus Christ on Earth through the Prophet Simon Kimbangu' to be admitted into the World Council of Churches and which financed our research journey to Zaïre in 1968.

Reconciliation, however, begins in the smaller sphere. An eloquent testimony of this reconciliation can be seen in the whole work of the reunification of the Kimbanguist congregations, which began in earnest in 1959, though in 1947 Joseph Diangienda had already initiated efforts to unite the scattered congregations. As we have seen, this was a difficult task. Until that time the congregational leaders and 'prophets' had acted fairly independently, and all kinds of tendencies could be observed. We have also seen how Simon Mpadi and others did not want to give up their autonomy and excluded themselves from the Kimbanguist Church. The same was true of Bamba; of the successors of Th. N'Twalani, of the 'vicariate' in Mayumbe, Moïse Kayuwa (who apostasized in 1966 and founded the 'Church of the Light of the Holy Spirit'), and others. In other places, conflicts of a different kind arise. When we visited Lubumbashi, the church there was in danger of a schism because two different tribal groups and their leaders could not agree. In another place there were personal rivalries between church-members and their party leaders. We saw how in both places there was a desire to be reconciled.

Both parties sent their leaders to the head of the church. The disputes and their backgrounds (particularly these!) were eventually unravelled in long hours and days of palavers. When this point was reached, Joseph Diangienda led those responsible for the split, through spiritual advice and exhortation and with his great patience and tact, to confess their faults to each other. Then followed a prayer for reconciliation in the Name of Christ, and those who had hitherto been at enmity with each other shook hands. The evil was put away! The congregation, which was present, thanked God, and a new start was made. The confession of sin in the Kimbanguist Church has become important because of such reconciliation.

CHAPTER 14

CONCLUSION

We have tried to follow the development of the Kimbanguist Church from its beginnings in 1921 to the present, through its long history of suffering, and its organization and spread since the end of 1959, when it was recognized by the state. By looking at the contemporary historical events and at the African world-view we have also tried to understand the Church's theological problems.

Two questions now arise:
1. Is the 'Church of Jesus Christ on Earth through the Prophet Simon Kimbangu' really a church, or is it (as is so often claimed) a sect?
2. Does it run the risk of stressing syncretistic elements, which ultimately lead away from Christ as the one and only Messiah and Saviour? The two questions are internally connected.

From a discussion of these issues we shall draw some conclusions concerning an African theology.

1. CHURCH OR SECT?

The question immediately arises as to what we mean by 'church' and by 'sect'. If we keep to the classical, reformed formulation that the church is present where the Gospel is taught rightly, where the sacraments (baptism and the Lord's Supper) are rightly administered, and where church discipline is exercised, then we run into difficulty on the second point, namely the administration of baptism and the Lord's Supper. Baptism is administered without water (as we have seen), but water ritual is otherwise accorded an important place. The elements of the Lord's Supper are not the traditional ones (see

Appendix). The Gospel is taught, and church discipline is exercised. Whoever sins against God and his fellows and causes offence has to give an account of himself before the church elders, to repent of his sin and confess it, in order to be fully restored to fellowship.

The question is, however, whether this classical definition reflects the character of the church, or whether crucial elements are missing which are perhaps more important than the right administration of the sacraments. Moreover, the 'ecclesiastical' character of our European churches would appear questionable when measured by the classical principle. How often the Gospel is preached incompletely or only one-sidedly! Often ancient and correct formulations have been clung onto which have become irrelevant in the second half of the twentieth century; or the Gospel has been curtailed for the sake of modern, secularized man, who has 'come of age', so that it can now hardly be distinguished from secularized humanism. Thus, we are unable to sit in judgement from a secure vantage-point as the *beati possidentes* (the fortunate possessors) of true churchhood on an African independent church. Along with the Kimbanguists, we must consider the true essence of the church. The church can only come into being in the act of preaching, and of fellowship in the Holy Spirit, but it is never such that one can, as it were, take hold of it and cling to it with human hands.

The Gospel is proclaimed in the Kimbanguist Church on Sundays, in the Scripture classes in the schools, in the catechism classes of candidates preparing for baptism with the Spirit, and in the pastoral care exercised so diligently by the head of the church. Apart from this, the outsanding feature of the Kimbanguist Church is its fellowship, its *communio sanctorum* (communion of the saints), which is not only theoretical but is lived out simply and in the manifestations of which Christ appears as the incarnate Word,[1] as one's Brother.

As a Kimbanguist one belongs to a family, a brotherhood, in which the presence of Christ as our Brother becomes a reality. There is a feeling of responsibility for one another—both materially and spiritually. The Kimbanguist Church is a 'church for others'. Every large 'church congregation' is divided up into small groups, each with a person in charge (either a man or a woman). As soon as neighbour 'A' runs into difficulty (illness, misfortune, death, marriage

[1] John J. Vincent, in 'The Working Christ' (Epworth, London, 1969, p. 11), is surely right in saying, 'The Church does not exist where "the Word is faithfully preached and the Sacraments duly administered". It does not, indeed, exist anywhere where certain human conditions are fulfilled. It exists where Christ becomes incarnate.'

problems, unemployment), neighbour 'B' will tell the person in charge of the group. No one is left alone to bear his worries and troubles. If need be, everyone has access to those 'higher up' in the hierarchy and, as we have seen, people constantly go to Joseph Diangienda, the head of the church, for help and advice. If before we spoke of the 'communion of the saints in heaven and on earth', we are now stressing the reality of the 'communion of the saints' on *earth*. There is a new sense of belonging. In Africa that is of particular importance. The African is not primarily an individual, but he belongs in his natural community to the extended family of his kinship group. That is true also of the educated African, freed as he is from many traditional ties. As soon as a person has a good position, he is obliged to look after so and so many nephews, nieces, aunts and uncles, quite apart from his own immediate family. Nevertheless, old bonds have been severed in the developing industrialization and urbanization of Africa. The person living in the town with his nuclear family, made up of parents and children in a small dwelling, has become 'homeless'. Where the old ties with the wide extended family have become illusory, the moral ties often disappear as well. The individual does not only become homeless but also anchorless and anonymous. In this situation the Kimbanguist Church offers a valuable counterbalance which should not be underestimated. The old community of the extended family is replaced by the 'communion of the saints', in which one brother cares for another, not only spiritually but also materially.

This active fellowship, which exists in reality and not only in theory, is in my opinion one of the principal marks of the church in the New Testament. If we read the Acts of the Apostles or the epistles, we cannot fail to see that all the apostolic exhortations and words of consolation are written against the background of this reality of the communion of the saints. Luke stresses in Acts: 'And all who believed were together and had all things in common; and they sold their possessions and goods and distributed them to all, as any had need' (Acts 2:44–6). 'Now the company of those who believed were of one heart and soul, and no one said that any of the things which he possessed was his own, but they had everything in common' (Acts 4:32). Paul urges: 'As we have opportunity, let us do good to all men, and especially to those who are of the household of faith' (Gal. 6:10).

This mutual caring in a new brotherhood, which is a manifestation of the 'communion of the saints on earth', is present not only among the Kimbanguists but is found in equal measure in the large African independent churches in South Africa and Rhodesia, which (like the Kimbanguists) have set up their 'colonies' where the poor and the unemployed, the widows and young offenders are cared for and where the members know that they are responsible for each other. It is not for nothing, then, that the membership of the independent churches in South Africa has increased by about 75 per cent in the last eight years whereas a number of the 'mission churches' have experienced a slight drop in their membership. And only the missionary living in southern Africa with his eyes open knows how many of his loyal people, in the crises of life, go secretly to the 'prophet', without ceasing to be members of their church. They seem to find there what they have not found in their traditional church.

The 'communion of the saints' living in the Word *and* in mutual help is certainly one of the crucial marks of the 'church'. We in Europe may then well ask whether our churches really are *churches* in the sense of the communion of the saints.

The church is the new People of God which gathers round Jesus Christ, follows Him and is renewed daily through His Spirit. The Kimbanguist Church sees itself as this new People of God, in whose midst Jesus has revealed himself through his messenger Simon Kimbangu. In all afflictions and attacks—a further mark of the church of Christ under the cross—they have followed him faithfully.

They do not regard themselves *alone* as the People of God. The more they hear of other churches and Christians, the more their prominent members, including Joseph Diangienda, have been able to travel to Europe and America, the more they have become aware of the world-wide communion of the saints. Kimbangu himself was able to send a letter to his loved ones in 1945 in which he urged them to join forces with Christians of all denominations for the sake of the love of Jesus.[2]

During the period of persecution, when even the traditional mission churches kept aloof from the Kimbanguists or were even hostile towards them, there was the danger that they would regard themselves as *the* People of God. But this tendency is giving way today to a new understanding of the Kimbanguist Church as being a part of the universal Church. God's People is not bound to be the church founded by Simon Kimbangu in 1921. That is indeed the profoundest reason (along with the desire to be finally recognized as a 'church') why the Kimbanguist Church applied in 1967 and again in 1968 for membership of the World Council of Churches, a wish which was granted in August 1969. I believe that we can call it a *church* in the sense that it is becoming such in its activity, and this also applies to all other churches. 'Church' is not a static but a

[2] Information from Joseph Diangienda.

Conclusion

dynamic concept, dependent on the *dynamis*, the power, of the re-creative Holy Spirit of God.

What is a *sect* as opposed to a church? There are various definitions of a sect. If 'sect' is derived from the Latin *sectari* ('to follow' a certain leader), then most 'churches' can be called 'sects'. The Catholics are obliged to heed what the Pope says—and we are well aware of the tensions within the Roman Catholic Church which have arisen from this since the conclusion of the Second Vatican Council. Many Protestants call themselves 'Lutherans', 'Calvinists', Zwinglians', or 'Wesleyans'. If this were to mean that they follow Luther, Calvin, Zwingli, or Wesley, they would be sects. But if we understand the names aright, we see that they mean (as is equally true of Kimbangu's name) quite simply that through these various messengers of God the Gospel has become relevant and decisive again in a certain historical situation.

We would be dealing with a sect if the messenger of God and his 'new revelation' have become more important in the thinking and life of the church than Jesus Christ, so that he has in practice (if not in theory) taken his place. When this is so, the messenger has become a kind of new messiah, and we would then be dealing with a messianic sect. The danger of such deviation is always there, and certain church members become victims of this—not only among the Kimbanguists, but also in many other, historical churches. However, instead of judging the church by what individual Christians say, we must pay attention to the authoritative leaders and to the tendency revealed in the total life of the church. From this point of view it is certainly wrong to call the Kimbanguist Church a messianic sect, even though we have noticed here and there the danger of messianic tendencies.

This may be true of many a church in southern Africa, but, in the light of what we have observed among the Kimbanguists, the tendencies of the various 'messianic movements' in South Africa would have to be studied afresh every few years. What still appeared yesterday to be a messianic movement may today already be becoming a church of Jesus Christ on the basis of the ever-renewing Spirit of God. None of the 'messianic sects' is excluded from the promise 'Behold, I make all things new.' And none of the 'orthodox' churches is free from the danger of becoming in some way a sect.

A further mark of a sect is not only that a human messenger or a 'new revelation' of some leader intrudes between Jesus Christ and the church, but also that it is absolutely exclusive. Those 'outside' are 'children of the Evil One', they are 'lost'. Salvation is to be found only in such and such denomination, and not outside. By and large the Kimbanguists do not display this mark of exclusivity. They are open, as we see from their wish to be a member of the World Council of Churches. This openness, however, does not mean that every tendency is permitted, any more than would be the case with the historical churches. From the beginning, since the time of Simon Kimbangu himself, they have erected a rampart against 'false prophets' who are no longer concerned with Jesus Christ but with ecstasy, experiences, and the blessings of salvation, instead of with the giver of these blessings.

Here we come to another mark of a sect: a sect may well no longer be concerned with the person of Jesus Christ but with things such as healing of the sick, security, or possession of the Spirit. Again there is no doubt that many Kimbanguists, like members of many and many a Christian church, may be concerned with such matters—with power, bourgeois habit, security, custom—and not with Jesus Christ. But here too it is imperative not to judge the church on the basis of what individual members say and do, but to heed its general tendency and what authoritative voices say. There are in Africa, as elsewhere, sects which are concerned primarily with healing the sick, with ecstasy, and with health and happiness, and Jesus Christ stands only in the second or third place. There are members among the Kimbanguists who give priority to such concerns. But the tendency of the Kimbanguist Church and the concern of its leaders is not to supply this something, but to bear witness to Jesus Christ as the Saviour who makes these blessings available—*ubi et quando visum est Deo* ('where and when it seems right to God').

Thus, the Kimbanguist Church is not a sect in the theological sense. In other languages and outside theology the word often has another meaning. In American English the word is applied to all churches as *sectors* of the one church of Christ. According to this, we would all be sectarians. The French word *secte* refers to a group of people who subscribe to the same doctrine; thus Bazola,[3] perhaps also from the Catholic point of view, calls the Kimbanguist Church a 'Christian sect'. In the theological sense these two concepts are mutually exclusive.

2. SYNCRETISM?

Plutarch speaks of 'syncretism' as a form of political behaviour. The inhabitants of Crete, who usually lived in a state of internal conflict,

[3] E. Bazola: 'Le Kimbanguisme', in Cahiers de religions africaines, July 1968, No. 4, Lovanium–Kinshasa, pp. 332–3.

Conclusion

united to oppose a common enemy. This 'compulsory reconciliation' Plutarch called 'syncretism'. In the post-reformational era the word was erroneously traced back to the Greek *synkerannymi*, which means 'to mix'. It was applied to the first Irenaean ecumenical attempts to unite enemies in the theological realm. What we call today ecumenicism or the ecumenical movement was at that time called 'syncretism'. Were people afraid of ecumenical strivings as threats to the 'pure teaching of the Word'? Unfortunately, there are today still churches—if churches they can be called—which have such fears and stand aloof.

In the history of religion syncretism has meant fusion, the bringing together of various religious doctrines, symbols, religious practices and rites. Thus we see, for instance, extensive syncretism in the late Judaistic period within Hellenism, where the various gods, such as Jupiter of the Romans and Zeus of the Greeks, or the fertility goddesses of oriental cults, were fused together into a single figure. Syncretism is in this case a phenomenon of acculturation (cultural change in consequence of cultural contact).

In present-day theology the word 'syncretism' is used in a somewhat different sense. When we speak of the syncretism of Israel in the Old Testament, we mean the mixture of the belief in Yahweh of the People of God with alien elements, to begin with at the time of the Judges with elements of fertility religion and the rites of the Canaanites and later, at the time of the Kings, with the religions of Assyria and Babylonia. In the theology of missions we speak today of syncretism when the Christian faith is mixed with elements of ancient African religion, or in India with elements of Hinduism or a 'belief in tolerance', like Radhakrishnan's.[4]

In many independent religious movements in Africa we find a great deal of syncretism—hardly any distinction is made in certain Zionist groups between possession with ancestral spirits and with the 'Holy Spirit'; baptism becomes a rite of purification, which is repeated; Christian symbols, like the cross, become amulets and fetishes.[5] Through this process the old, which seemed past, is given a new lease of life. It becomes 'post-Christian paganism', which is asserting itself with great tenacity.

Do we find such syncretism in the Kimbanguist Church? In this question, too, we must not stay with the individual member but must direct our view at the whole. Are the water rites syncretistic? Does

[4] Cf. the publication of W. A. Visser 't Hooft: 'No Other Name', London, 1963, pp. 39 f.

[5] B. Sundkler: 'Bantu Prophets in South Africa', 2nd edn, London, 1961, pp. 201 ff., 228 ff., 238 ff.

bathing in the spring of N'Kamba signify a rite of purification? Hardly. I was assured that in the district of N'Kamba no other purification rites of this kind are known, though we can see these so often among the Zulus in South Africa and among West-African peoples. No magical significance is ascribed to the N'Kamba water, as we have already observed.

The laying on of hands in blessing or healing of the sick plays an important part when Joseph Diangienda is present. Is there here a magic transference of power? The idea of transmitted power, of the *force vitale* (vital strength), is of great importance in Africa. Is there such a transmission? Prayer and faith are central in these rites, the prayer and faith of not only the head of the church but also of the recipient. Without faith it is impossible to receive blessing and healing. This emphasis on faith, which is the gift of God and the operation of the Holy Spirit, precludes a magical transference of power. Again, that does not mean that there are not members who secretly cherish magical notions, but such are to be found everywhere. Often I have found the notion among good church-going Christians in Lesotho (and elsewhere) that, at the ordination of a minister, the fellow-ministers transfer through the laying on of hands supernatural power to the one they are ordaining.

Lastly, there could be a form of syncretism in the reactivation and manifestation through the prophet of the story of the life and sufferings of Christ and the ideas connected with this. Is there here the influence of the ancient cyclical view of the world, which knows no eschatology, nor any progression, but only a cycle? Where one has stopped one begins all over again. In other words, where the ancient Jerusalem stops the new Jerusalem begins again in the same way as the old. The 'realized eschatology' of C. H. Dodd, which is to some extent proclaimed in the concept of the new Jerusalem in N'Kamba, is not to be understood as cyclical thinking, for what follows is not a brand new Jerusalem, but the close of ᵗthe age, the return of Christ, the Day of Judgement, and eternal joy in the presence of God. The future expectation of salvation is indeed still restricted in the Kimbanguist Church to the traditional ideas of the coming Judgement, the return of the Christ, and eternal salvation with God, and what is already and not yet in eschatological expectation plays a small part in its thinking. We are indeed only at the beginning of the theological development of this church. But we must not speak simply of the cyclical world-view of the Kimbanguists and thus of their rootedness in the ancient philosophy of Africa.

Of course, if what is meant by syncretism is quite simply the adoption and transformation of African images, expressions, and forms, then one is on the right track; but this is scarcely an appropriate use for the word 'syncretism', now such a loaded term. A Catholic scholar who eight years ago was still very critical of Kimbanguism, writes, 'Il apparaît en tout cas que le kimbanguisme rejette absolument le passé religieux païen et est à la recherche d'une adaptation de la foi chrétienne à une expression africaine.' ('It is certainly clear that Kimbanguism rejects completely the pagan religion past and is seeking an adaptation of the Christian faith to an African form of expression.')[6]

CONCLUSIONS

Theology in Africa. What we encounter in the African independent churches in general and in the Kimbanguist Church in particular, is that for which missiologists in Europe have been asking for so long—the beginnings of a Christian theology in African garb, related to Africa. Out of these beginnings there could grow that which has long been awaited. It is today still 'experiential theology'; and its written formulation is being developed only gradually.

Hitherto the teaching in many, indeed in most, theological faculties and seminaries in Africa followed quite simply the Eruropean or American pattern. Even the courses were—and still are—in keeping with this pattern. Indeed, the dogmas have been translated into African languages, just as German, French and English hymns have been translated into the languages of the Basotho, the Zulus, the Bavenda, the Bakongo, and of many other peoples, complete with the Western tunes of the Reformation or revival tunes, and even the harmonium! But has this translation brought the Gospel much closer to them? More than such translation is necessary if there is to be a true communication of the Gospel. The Gospel and the church (including the ecclesiastical structure) must no longer appear in Western guise. But such a new interpretation of the Gospel can only emerge from the life of a church tested in suffering and conscious of its mission. I believe that this is what is happening in the Kimbanguist Church, with its forms which differ from those of the Western churches, its existential interpretation of the story of the life and sufferings of Christ, its hierarchy, its symbolism, its rites, its African or Africanized music, and its faith expressed in song and imagery. Here is a promising new beginning. We can only hope that, when

[6] R. P. Decapmaeker: 'Le Kimbanguisme', in 'Devant les sectes non-chrétiennes', Louvain, 1961, p. 61.

the Kimbanguist Church in the forseeable future has its own theologians trained to a higher standard, they will not violate the ideas of their church and translate them into the jargon of Western modes of expression but they will find here too the formulation which is appropriate to Africa. We Western theologians can help in this to a limited extent only by trying to explain the historical background to the biblical record and by pointing out the linguistic and literary forms and the textual transmission, which have so many similarities with African forms and traditions. We can also help where African theologians fall into the temptation of using the customary terminology and where they misunderstand it. We can show them how churches have evolved elsewhere, especially the early church, and the role of the church fathers; and the ancient African churches in Egypt, Nubia and Ethiopia, as far as we are familiar with their development. We can show where possibly harmful developments took place and why certain churches have adopted particular rites and forms. All this will promote ecumenical understanding, and throw the light of biblical theology on the ethical problems of modern Africa, showing them the dangers of a new legalism. Finally, it will be our task to point again and again to the Cross of Christ, the *theologia crucis*, as the vital focal point where judgement is passed on all human activity, all human desires, ideas, symbols and theologies, but where at the same time, running through the judgement, forgiveness, resurrection, and re-creation are promised through the Holy Spirit.

As much as possible must, of course, be left to the Africans themselves: even if the formulations, modes of expression, the forms, the organization and structure, seem to us at first to be imperfect or perhaps even wrong. We must lay aside our fear of possible syncretism, although this does not mean that we should close our eyes to it. But we must trust the Holy Spirit, as Paul did, to lead the African brethren into all truth. If we adopt this attitude then perhaps one day there will emerge from Africa a new formulation of the message of Jesus Christ which could also be meaningful to the West and give the ecumenical dialogue a new dimension.

The Gospel is the message of salvation. It is precisely this that Africa perhaps understands better than the West, since we have limited the word 'salvation' so much to the 'salvation of the soul'. Salvation means in Africa what *shalom* means to the Hebrew: salvation and healing (not only from illness, but redemption in the widest sense), 'a new heaven and, above all, a new earth', social justice, and peace, and, as a consequence no more discrimination, and no destitution alongside abundant wealth; it means brotherhood, order in liberty, development of all one's potentials in life, but in such a way that the community benefits, which to the African, is more important than purely individual development. Salvation includes healing: a new life on the new earth, free from hatred, passion, lying, corruption and oppression; and sanctification as an expression of gratitude and liberty, which God in His love wishes to give to all men. Here we surely have genuine eschatology, the hope of those who know all about the imperfection that still clings to us but who also know that Jesus Christ has come and will come again, and that He promises 'Behold, I make all things new.'

APPENDIX

1. At the end of March 1971, shortly before the jubilee celebrations of the Kimbanguist Movement (and now Church), Simon Kimbangu's courageous fellow-worker John Mayanga (to whom I am indebted for much information) was killed in a car accident in Kinshasa, just as he was about to set off for church to worship. At the funeral services in Kinshasa and N'Kamba I appreciated afresh the great difference between Christian and non-Christian custom in Zaïre. The usual lamentation and weeping, lasting for hours and giving way to wild carousing, was consistently replaced by hymns, music, reading of the Bible and prayer. The death-watch, in which thousands took part for two nights, consisted simply of music, reading the Scriptures, addresses and prayers. The church surrounded his loved ones, who had suddenly been so surprised by the death of their husband, father and grandfather, with brotherly Christian sympathy.

2. In January and February 1971, accompanied by a brass band and a very large team, the spiritual head of the church, Joseph Diangienda, went on what was by all accounts a triumphant journey to the Mayumbe in the west, where, because of threats, he had been unable to go in July 1970. He was received with the highest honours by Kimbanguists, Protestants and Catholics, and even by monks and nuns. The splinter group of the vicariate (pp. 126–7) seems hardly to exist any more, for many have rejoined the Kimbanguist Church. This success was fittingly celebrated after Joseph Diangienda's return to Kinshasa in February with a special service in Matete-Kinshasa in the large church.

3. On this occasion Joseph Diangienda announced that he would bestow a *special blessing*. At the door of the Church the believers knelt, one after the other in quiet meditation, on the cross inlaid in the flagstones and Joseph Diangienda 'sealed' each one with the sign of the cross, which he made on the forehead with N'Kamba water in the Name of the Father, and of the Son, and of the Holy Spirit. This was repeated until 6 April before the first celebration of Communion at the conclusion of each service. This *sealing* could only be done at the meeting place of the church, immediately at the close of the service, and it is evidently based on the eschatological sealing of the believers referred to in Revelation 7:1–4. The word *sceau* ('seal'), which appears in the French Bible, was used for every sealing. Special services were held in the local church of Kinshasa and of Lower Zaïre so that Joseph Diangienda and the former fellow-workers of his father, the *sacrificateurs* and *sacrificatrices* ('priests'), could seal thousands of people. From all over, Kimbanguists, ex-Kimbanguists, members of other churches, and presumably also non-churchgoers, thronged to receive this special blessing. One might ask for how many this sign had the magical meaning of transference of power. I do not mean by this to dispute that it can have its legitimate place within the church as a new symbol, given and received in faith and with prayer, and as a preparation for the Lord's Supper, with its equally eschatological character. The preparation for Communion was indeed taken very seriously, and for weeks it formed the content of sermons, prayers, and meditations.— Only very few religious communities know this sealing, which will continue to be administered before believers outside Lower Zaïre and Kinshasa receive their first Communion in the Kimbanguist Church. The believer can receive this sign only once. We have not as yet been able to find an explanation why this sealing took place. It may well be that Joseph Diangienda was inspired and commissioned to institute this sign by his father in the Name of Christ. It would be premature to make any theological comment on it.

4. From 2 to 7 April 1971, the great jubilee celebrations of the church took place. They began on 2 April in Matadi-Mayo near Kinshasa in remembrance of the day when, in 1960, the coffin with the mortal remains of Simon Kimbangu was taken from Lubumbashi to N'Kamba and was laid there for a night. On 6 April, exactly fifty years after Kimbangu had performed his first healing in answer to prayer, the first celebration of Holy Communion was held. It was at this time that Joseph Diangienda announced that his father had already administered the Communion on one occasion before his

arrest in 1921. 350,000 pilgrims went in the middle of the rainy season to N'Kamba and camped there in the open, despite the rain and the alternating heat and cold, in order to take part in the celebrations. They had reached the 'holy city', in lorries and on foot, on the terrible road going through the bush from Mbanza-Ngungu to N'Kamba. During the special service, Joseph Diangienda announced the nature of the elements to be used in the Communion, namely bread baked from a mixture of potatoes, maize and bananas (in which the latter served as 'yeast') and 'wine' made of honey and water.

L. Luntadila wrote an explanation of this, which was given to the press under the title *Réflexions sur la Sainte-Cène* ('Thoughts on the Lord's Supper'). In it he says that 'The foods used to make the elements are found in Zaïre and the neighbouring countries. In order to be obedient to the spirit of the Gospel our church has chosen African foods, just as Christ in His day used bread and wine, the daily foods of Palestine.' Thus the Kimbanguist Church (in exactly the same way as, for instance, in its attitude towards the place of women in the work of the church) has freed itself from pure dogmatism. 'Honey is praised in the Bible as a noble food.' Luntadila reminds us that the Old Testament manna tasted 'like wafers made with honey' (Ex. 16:31). In Psalm 81:16 Luntadila found a parallel between honey and blood, and quoted, 'I would feed you with the finest of the wheat, and with honey from the rock I would satisfy you.' Behind this, unconsciously, there may possibly be the ancient Catholic doctrine of 'concomitance', according to which in the body of Christ, represented by the bread, the blood is already present as well. He may have also been thinking of the water from the rock, however. A rational explanation followed this biblical explanation: 'Honey is a food which contains the vitamins and minerals which the body needs and which enter the blood directly. That is why honey was the food of John the Baptist (Matt. 3:4), the food which encouraged meditation, prayer, and purity. Hence, honey still continues to be the food of the contemplative monks in Ethiopia.' He referred at this point to parallels between the prayer-life of the Ethiopian Church and that of the Kimbanguists. Then followed a further reference to the Bible, to Luke 24:42, where we read that the risen Christ ate 'a piece of broiled fish' and—according to some ancient textual sources (the author)—'a honeycomb' in order to reveal Himself to the disciples as the living Christ. There then followed a spiritual exhortation: 'Just as pollen is transformed by bees into honey, so we too should be inwardly transformed by the Holy Spirit so that we can be witnesses to the risen Christ.' Finally, it is said that the bee was a symbol in ancient Egypt and therefore in Africa.

After speaking about the honey (there is no mention of the life-giving water!) Luntadila went on to consider the bread.

> Just as the body which was given for us saves us, so maize and potatoes have saved millions in the world. Just as the ingredients maize, potatoes, and bananas are mixed, so the body of Christ is formed of men and women of all races and lands. Just as potatoes were formerly introduced from America and have now spread over almost the whole earth, so it is our task as the light of the world to proclaim to all peoples the Good News from Palestine.

Then there followed a quotation from the Didache prayer (from the post-apostolic period): 'Just as this bread, broken and once scattered on the hills, was gathered and made into a whole, so may Thy church be gathered from the ends of the earth into Thy Kingdom.'— 'The white clothes of those who distribute the Lord's Supper remind us that our sins are washed away and forgiven through the death of Christ. They anticipate the glory and purity of those who will be partakers, as the ransomed, of the Kingdom of Heaven when Christ returns.' This was followed by a reference to Revelation 7:14 and presumably indirectly to the sealing which preceded the Communion. So much for the reflections of Luntadila, which give a picture of the kind of Bible exposition which is found not only in the Kimbanguist Church, but in many churches of Africa.

The elements were consecrated by the sons of Kimbangu in the mausoleum of their father and then borne in solemn procession (after the sermon) to the enormous congregation gathered in the open air. Joseph Diangienda led the way, followed by the *sacrificateurs*, then the highest dignitaries of the church, the members of what is called the *Collège* or *Conseil des Sages* ('Council of the Wise'), which is made up of Kimbangu's fellow-workers from the period of persecution, and which was called into being in 1963 in Mbanza-Ngungu. Behind them came the leaders of the church of the People's Republic of the Congo and Zambia and the regional delegates (the highest church officials in the various regions of Zaïre). All were dressed in white. The elements were borne before the assembled congregation on simple wooden platters, the honey-water already in tiny glasses, by the dignitaries appointed to distribute them. The words of institution were read out, the elements blessed, and then the great moment had come. Joseph Diangienda handed the Lord's Supper first to his two brothers and the aged assistants of his father.

Then Pierre Ndangi handed it to him. The dignitaries of the church came next. Then it was taken to the believers, who were grouped in local congregations, whilst the flute orchestra played quietly in the background. A hundred thousand people knelt on the grass under palm roofs to receive the symbols of the body and blood of Christ. The distribution had to continue on 7 April until all were 'satisfied'. The joy was, despite all the composure and calmness, unmistakable. The Kimbanguists were in the 'new Jerusalem' and living in the 'last times'.

On 11 April the Lord's Supper was celebrated in Kinshasa-Matete for all those who were unable to go to N'Kamba, and a fortnight later in Brazzaville. Since then Joseph Diangienda has undertaken journeys throughout the country, for he wants to be personally present wherever the Lord's Supper is distributed for the first time.

The Communion is to be celebrated three times a year—at Christmas, at Easter, and on the anniversary of the death of the prophet (12 October). 'Why so infrequently?' we asked Joseph Diangienda. 'So that it does not become a mere habit', he replied.

I would like to draw a parallel between the celebration of the Lord's Supper, as I experienced it in N'Kamba, Kinshasa-Matete, and Brazzaville, and the feeding of the Five Thousand in the gospels, which can indeed be seen exegetically as an anticipation of the Communion.—We may ask whether it is theologically admissible to modify the elements used by Christ. I think, however, that passages like John 21:9–13, the feeding of the Five Thousand, and also Luke 24:30 (the meal with the Emmaus disciples) leave this possibility open. Just as the Lord of the church chose a humble and little-educated African as His ambassador, so He is also free to bless African elements through which to be one with believers and to bind them together as the body of Christ.

This first Communion was, contrary to what we had expected, not an open Communion. It was surely not intended as a rebuff to Christians of other churches. It may have been a sign of humility that there was as yet no wish to press this innovation on Christians of other denominations.

5. Since November 1970 there has been in Kinshasa a theological college, *l'Ecole de théologie Kimbanguiste*. Of the thirty candidates, we were able to retain eighteen to the end of the academic year. Three-quarters came from the interior of the country. When they heard that a theological college was to be opened, they gave up their work, income, family, and all their security in life, to follow the call

of God. Since the church was not prepared for this influx of young men, the college began with great financial problems and finally we had to find employment for all the students—so they are part-time students, who attend lectures and theological classes for three hours a day, do their studies, and in addition earn their living in various occupations. About half of them had to work in factories for months with very poor pay in order to maintain themselves. Thus they know from their experience the needs of the ordinary poor man. The fact that many have persevered till now, even in some cases going hungry, is a testimony to their determination. The duration of their training until graduation is to be five years. Already about thirty more new candidates have applied to the head of the church, so that they can receive a solid biblical and theological training. (At the time of this translation, there were fifty-six students organized into three groups and thirty new ones will be added for the academic year 1973/74. Additional staff has been supplied by various Missionary agencies and by the Kimbanguist Church itself.

6. I hope that these students will one day be able to critically assess and influence (in a positive sense) the whole development of the church, as well as its various ordinances, and to look ahead. Understandably, the old warriors now frequently look to the past, but the heritage of Simon Kimbangu is in a good sense 'revolutionary' and must not ossify.—In anticipation of this, I have refrained in this book from commenting from the point of view of the Western theological tradition on food regulations, the use of the water and soil of N'Kamba, and similar things. I have also refrained from examining critically the position of Kimbangu as comforter, mediator, and revealer. Since everything is after all still in flux, I prefer to wait before expressing an opinion until I have been able to note the reaction of the theological students of the Kimbanguist Church. They have for the most part grown up in the Kimbanguist tradition. Our aim is by no means to 'westernize' them, but rather, beginning with their own heritage and tradition, to study the historical, linguistic and religious background and above all the message of the Bible. For this purpose the Greek and Hebrew languages are taught. Future theologians of the Kimbanguist Church should not be dependent on translations of the Bible into western languages, but should be able to assess the meaning of biblical terms by the help of Greek and Hebrew dictionaries and vocabularies. The history of the universal church is studied, with emphasis on African church history as well as history in general. Modern philosophies of life such as Marxism and nationalism, and problems of Christian ethics in modern Africa

and the world are discussed, after a general introduction to African traditional religion and sociology. In this way we hope to be 'contextual' as the modern conception of theological education in Africa demands.

For several years now the Kimbanguist Church, like every movement which is being shaped into an organization, has also been caught up in an inevitable process of institutionalization. Yet it remains the deep desire and longing of the Church that the charismatic element break through again and again. Spiritual retreats have been declared necessary for all church members, particularly for theological students, which last up to five days and include prayer, singing, Bible-meditation, fasting and confessing of sins (called purification). These retreats are held in isolated places, out in the bush, and during them many faithful have become truly 'converted' to Christ: they experience healings, spiritual gifts and visions. New hymns are 'seized' (*captés*) and the spiritual life of the church is being constantly renewed. We are therefore confident that the charismatic element will never be stifled.

Lucerne, August 1973

BIBLIOGRAPHY

I. BOOKS

Andersson, E.: Messianic Popular Movements in the Lower Congo, Uppsala, 1958.

Anene, J. C./Brown, G. (ed.): Africa in the Nineteenth and Twentieth Centuries, Ibadan University, Nigeria, 1966.

Anstey, R.: Britain and the Congo in the Nineteenth Century, Oxford, 1962.

Anstey, R.: King Leopold's Legacy: the Congo under Belgian Rule 1908 to 1960, London, 1966.

Balandier, G.: La vie quotidienne au Royaume du Congo du XVIe au XVIIIe siècles, Paris, 1965.

Balandier, G.: Sociologie actuelle de l'Afrique noire, revised edn, Paris, 1963.

Chomé, J.: La Passion de Simon Kimbangu, Présence Africaine, Paris, 1959.

C.R.I.S.P. 1966 (*Centre de recherche et d'information socio-politique*), in book form, Brussels, 1966.

Decapmaeker: *Le Kimbanguisme*, in Devant les sectes non-chrétiennes, Louvain, 1961.

Dialungana, S. K.: Tanginina Fu Ya Klisto, N'Kamba, 1966.

Doutreloux, A.: *Prophétisme et 'Leadership' dans la société Congo*, in Devant les sectes non-chrétiennes, Louvain, 1961.

Groves, C. P.; The Planting of Christianity in Africa, London, 1948.

Hollenweger, W. J.: Enthusiastisches Christentum, Wuppertal and Zürich, 1969.

Hoskyns, C.: The Congo since Independence, January 1960 to December 1961, Oxford, 1965.

Lanternari, V.: Les mouvements religieux des peuples opprimés, Paris, 1962.

Legum, Colin: Congo Disaster, Penguin, Harmondsworth, 1961.

Lehmann, D./Taylor, V.: Christians in the Copperbelt, London, 1961.

Margull, H. J.: Aufbruch zur Zukunft, Gütersloh, 1962.
Martin, M.-L.: The Biblical Concept of Messianism and Messianism in Southern Africa, Moriah, Lesotho, 1964.
Martin, M.-L.: *Afrikanischer Messianismus und der Messias der biblischen Offenbarung*, in Weltmission heute, ed. P. Beyerhaus, Stuttgart, 1967.
Martin, M.-L.: Prophetic Christianity in the Congo, Johannesburg, 1968.
Massamba-Débat, A.: De la révolution messianique à la révolution politique, Brazzaville, 1968.
Masson, R. P.: *Simples réflexions sur des chants kibanguistes*, in Devant les sectes non-chrétiennes, Louvain, 1961.
Mbiti, J.: *Eschatologie und Jenseitsglaube*, in Theologie und Kirche in Afrika, ed. H. Bürkle, Stuttgart, 1968.
Merlier, M.: Le Congo de la colonisation belge à l'indépendance, Paris, 1962.
Merriam, A. P.: Background of Conflict, Northwestern Univ. Press, U.S.A., 1961.
Nkanda Bisamu bia Tata Simon Kimbangu, Office du prophète Simon Kimbangu, Kinshasa, 1961.
Neill, St.: A History of Christian Missions, Penguin, Harmondsworth, 1964.
Oosthuizen, G. C.: The Theology of a South African Messiah, Leiden, 1967.
Pigafetta, F./Lopes, D.: Description du Royaume du Congo et des contrées environnantes, ed. W. Bal, Editions E. Nauwelaerts, Louvain, 1951.
Poivre, N.: Fils et Filles d'Afrique, Paris and Geneva, 1946.
Rad, G. von: Theologie des Alten Testaments, Munich, 1958.
Raum. O.: *Von Stammespropheten zu Sektenführern*, in Messianische Kirchen, Sekten und Bewegungen im heutigen Afrika, ed. E. Benz, Leiden, 1965.
Rome, J.-F. de: O.F.M. Cap. La fondation de la mission des Capucins au Royaume du Congo, 1648, ed. F. Botinck, Nauwelaerts, Louvain.
Schlosser, K.: Propheten in Afrika, Brunswick, 1948.
Segal, R.: Political Africa, London, 1961.
Shepperson, G.: *Ethiopianism Past and Present*, in Christianity in Tropical Africa, ed. J. C. Baëta, Oxford, 1968.
Shepperson, G./Price, T.: Independent African, Edinburgh, 1958.
Sicard, H. von: Ngoma Lungundu, Uppsala, 1952.
Slade, R.: King Leopold's Congo, Oxford, 1962.
Slade-Reardon, R.: *Catholics and Protestants in the Congo*, in Christianity in Tropical Africa, ed. C. G. Baëta, Oxford, 1968.
Sölle, D.: Phantasie und Gehorsam, Stuttgart, 1968.
Sundkler, B.: Bantu Prophets in South Africa, 2nd edn, London, 1961.
Tempels, P.: Philosophie Bantou, Présence Africaine, Paris, 1949.
Taylor, J. V.: The Primeval Vision, London, 1963.
Turner, H.: African Independent Church, The Church of God (Aladura), Oxford, 1967.

Vincent, J.: The Working Christ, London, 1969.
Visser't Hooft, W. A.: No Other Name, London, 1963.
Westman, K. B./Sicard, H. von: Geschichte der christlichen Mission, Munich, 1962.

II. ARTICLES IN JOURNALS AND MAGAZINES:
STILL UNPUBLISHED MANUSCRIPTS

Andersson, E.: *Le Dieu Nzambi: La notion de Dieu chez quelques tribus congo-camerounaises*, Journal of Religion in Africa, Leiden, 1969.
Annual Report of the B.M.S. (Baptist Missionary Society), London, 1921.
Baptist Herald, London, October 1921.
Baptist Herald, London, January 1922.
Baptist Herald, London, March 1922.
Bazola, E.: *Le Kimbanguisme*, Cahier des Religions Africaines, Vol. 2, Nos. 3 and 4, Lovanium-Kinshasa, 1968.
Bertsche, J. E.: *Kimbanguism a Challenge to Missionary Statesmanship*, Practical Anthropology, Vol. 13, No. 1, 1966, New York.
Beyerhaus, P.: *Kann es eine Zusammenarbeit zwischen den christlichen und den prophetisch-messianischen Bewegungen in Afrika geben?*, Evangelisches Missionsmagazin, 111. Jahrgang, Heft 1, Basle, 1967.
Bulletin de la Ligue pour la Protection et l'Evangélisation des Noirs, No. 2, Brussels, 1924.
Catéchisme 1957, transl. P. Raymaekers in Zaïre, Vol. XIII/7, Brussels, 1959.
C.R.I.S.P. (Centre de recherche et d'information socio-politique), photocopy of the booklet *Le Kimbanguisme*, No. 47, 8 January 1960, Brussels.
Diangienda, Joseph: pamphlet: *L'Eglise du Christ sur la Terre par le prophète Simon Kimbangu face aux problèmes politiques, économiques et sociaux tels qu'ils se posent au Congo, en Afrique et dans le monde*, written in 1962, published in 1970 in Kinshasa.
Diangienda, Joseph: *Eglise et politique*, reprinted in Cahiers de la Réconciliation, May–June 1966, Paris.
Editorial report in the *International Review of Mission*, Vol. LVIII, No. 229, 1969, London and Geneva.
Editorial report in *Kimbanguisme*, N'Kamba, 21 October and 23 December 1961.
Fehderau, H. W.: *Prophetic Christianity*, Practical Anthropology, Vol. 9, No. 4, 1962, New York.
Lanzo del Vasto: *Simon Kimbangu et la non-violence africaine*, Jeune Afrique, No. 385, Paris, 1968.
Lasserre, Jean: *Voyage au Congo*, Cahiers de la Réconciliation, May–June 1966, Paris.
Letter (photocopy, no signature) from a missionary, dated 16 December 1922 and sent from Mariestad, Sweden.

Luntadila, L.: report in Essor, No. 13, 29 September 1966, La Chaux-de-Fonds.
Mabona, A. D.: *Africanisation of the Church*, Pro Veritate, Vol. III, No. 11, 15 March 1970, Johannesburg.
MacGaffey, Wyatt: *The Belovèd City, Commentary on a Kimbanguist Text*, Journal of Religion in Africa, Leiden, 1969.
MacGaffey, Wyatt: A Kimbanguist Diary, still unpublished manuscript.
Martin, M.-L.: Walter Mattita and his Moshoeshoe Church in Lesotho, still unpublished manuscript.
Mise au point, Kinshasa, 1957, mimeographed.
Rapport à la Chambre des Représentants, Session 1958–59, Brussels.
Raymaekers, P.: L'Eglise de Jésus-Christ sur la Terre par le prophète Simon Kimbangu, Zaïre, Vol. XIII/7, 1959, Brussels.
Revue des Missions, Pères de Scheut, Brussels, 1951.
Svensk Missionstidskrift, 1939.
Statuts de l'Eglise Kimbanguiste, 6 March 1960 mimeographed.
Wing, J. van: Le kibanguisme vu par un témoin, Zaïre, No. XII/6, 1958, Louvain.

III. DOCUMENTS

The documents quoted in the second part of the book (*documents secrets belges*) are mimeographed material which were handed out in the 20s to police inspectors, principally in Congo Central (Lower Zaïre), as secret documents. After the independence of the Congo in 1960, a copy of these fell into the hands of the Kimbanguist Church, and there are in any case two microfilms of them in existence. The copy which fell into the hands of the Kimbanguist Church is kept in their archives in Kinshasa, along with a large number of other documents, which have not so far been classified. I was able to look at the church's copy of the *documents secrets belges*, so that I could write as fair a historical account of Kimbangu's movement as possible.

The letters of the British Baptist missionaries and their reports are to be found in the archives of the British Baptist Missionary Society in London. I was given access to them so that the historical account of Kimbangu's movement should also be fair towards the Protestant mission.

Glossary and Indexes

GLOSSARY OF KIKONGO WORDS

Bakongo people 4, 69
Bandoki (witchdoctors) 164
Bangunza (prophets) 42, 54, 56, 145
Bankulu (elders) 144
Bansadisi (assistants) 39, 54, 156
Bantu ba Mpeve ya nlongo (people of the Holy Spirit) 77
Kikongo (language) 4
Kimbangi (witness) 107
Kindoki (witchcraft) 5, 6, 31, 45, 163
Kinlongo (sacred object or temple) 154
Kinsukulu (a bitter fruit) 40
Mbemba a Nzinga (son and heir of King of Kongo) 6
Minkisi (fetishes) 6, 7, 11, 163
Modimo (God or ancestor) 17
Mpanzu a Nzinga (younger son of King of Kongo) 6
Mvwala (staff) 53
Nganza (witchdoctor) 31
Ngunza (prophet) 72
Nsadisi (assistant) 148
Nsinsani (competition) 134, 137
Ntotila (title of ancient kings) 73
Ntumwa (messenger) 146
Nzambi (God) 95
Oye (bravo) 135
Tata mfumu'a nlongo (spiritual head) 150
Zimvwala (bearers of prophetic staff) 149, 154

INDEX OF PLACES

Ambouila 11
America 101
Angola 91, 100–1

Banana 61
Barotseland 25
Boko 51, 94, 96–8, 136, 139
Boma 22, 24, 58, 61, 66, 71, 74, 102–3, 127
Brazzaville 78, 89, 91, 96, 98, 103, 109, 119, 139, 158, 182
Bunkeya 25

Chad, Republic of 96
Congo-Brazzaville 4, 97
Congo Free State 21, 27
Congo, French 78, 79, 90–1, 94, 98, 118
Congo, People's Republic of 77, 99, 136, 181
Crebedji 96

Djambala 98, 158
Dolisie 97

Ekuphakameni 50
Elisabethville (Lubumbashi) 63–4, 75, 92, 101–2, 110, 146, 154, 158, 165, 179

Fort Archambault 96

Gabon 97
Galaboma 92
Gambona 98, 158

Kalahari 98
Kananga (Luluabourg) 63, 102

Kasai Province 24, 37, 89
Kasangulu 92, 101
Katanga (Shaba) Province 25, 63, 100
Kimuanza 32
Kingoyi 94–5
Kinkole 41, 59, 60
Kinshasa (Léopoldville) 4, 24, 41, 44, 63, 74, 78, 82, 92, 98, 100, 102–3, 105–6, 109, 110, 131, 133–4, 137–9, 158, 178–9
Kisangani (Stanleyville) 24, 118, 120, 125, 127
Kitwe 158
Kivu Province 100
Kongo Kingdom 3–4, 7–8, 12–15, 20, 118, 141
Kwamouth 97

Lake Leopold, Province of 89
Lake Malebo (Stanley Pool) 4, 21, 24, 59
Lake Mweru 25
Libreville 97
Luanda 16
Luanga (Luanza) 25
Luebo 25
Luluabourg (see Kananga)
Luozi 59–60, 63, 77, 89, 90, 92, 94, 96, 157

Madimba 82, 91, 92
Maduda 103
Malawi 38, 68
Matadi 24, 61, 89, 106, 127, 136
Matadi Mayo 110, 179
Matete-Kinshasa 136, 148, 161, 178, 182
Mayama 92

Index of Places

Mayumbe 77, 126, 178
Mbanza Kongo (San Salvador) 4, 5, 11, 14, 16, 20, 43
Mbanza Ngungu (Thysville) 50–3, 57–62, 67, 70–1, 74, 77, 81–2, 88, 89, 92, 121, 138, 180, 181
Mbanza Nsanda 59–60
Mpioka river 138
Musana 94–5

Ngafura (Djambala) 98
Ngombe-Kinsuka 45, 65
Ngombe-Lutete 27, 39, 43–4, 50–1, 56, 59, 67, 75
Ngombe-Matadi 27, 66, 87
Ngunzulu 97, 98
Nigeria 145
N'Kamba 27, 40, 42–8, 50, 52, 54–8, 60, 63, 65, 67–8, 74, 76–8, 80, 87–9, 94–95, 101–2, 108, 110, 119, 136, 138–9, 146, 152, 155, 157, 159, 164, 178–80, 182–3; water of, 66–7, 76, 87, 112, 158–60; earth of, 87, 183

Nkamba-Jerusalem 65, 110, 140, 142, 153, 154, 174
Nsona-Bata 39, 101
Nysaland (see Malawi)
Nzundu 61

Portugal 4, 7, 8

Sankuru 37
San Salvador (see Mbanza Kongo)
Shaba (see Katanga)
Stanley Falls 24

Thysville (see Mbanza-Ngungu)
Tombe River 43
Tshela 103, 110
Tumba 70

Upper Congo, French 97

Wathen (see Ngombe-Lutete)

Zambia 38, 158, 181

INDEX OF PERSONS

van Acker 104
Adoula, 103
Afonso, King of Kongo 6–10, 13
Albert, King of Belgium 62
Andersson, E. 9–14, 16, 39, 41, 55, 73, 78, 89–90, 92, 95
Anene, J. C. 20, 25, 49
Angola, Bishop of 16
Anstey, R. 24, 117
Antonio, King 11
Arnot, F. S. 25
Arthington, R. 21, 23–4
St Anthony 14

Baeta, C. G. 32
Balandier, G. 5, 7, 9, 11, 14, 73, 78, 92, 95, 141
Bamba, Emmanuel 101, 110, 126–7, 165
Barrett, D. B. 145
Baudouin, King of Belgium 121
Bazola, E. 41, 119, 128, 146, 148, 155, 159, 172
Beatrice, Donna (Kimpa Vita) 13–19, 23, 37, 57
Becquet, Captain 89–91
Béguin, Rev. W. 39
Bentley, W. H. 11, 24, 69, 108
Bertsche, J. E. 39
Beyerhaus, P. 74, 76, 126, 142
Bismarck 21
Blumhardt, Johann Christoph 29, 133
Bontinck, F. 10
Bowskill, J. S. 67
De Brazza, P. S. 21
Brown, G. 20, 25, 49
Braekman, Fr 62
Buana-Kibongi, D. 47, 147

Cameron, Rev. G. R. R. 43
Cão, Diogo 3, 4
Casebow, Rev. H. J. 42, 75, 108
Choffat, F. 165
Chomé, J. 41, 60, 62
Clark, Joseph 62
van Cleemput, Fr 57
Comber, Thomas 24, 42
Crawford, Dan 25
Crudgington, H. 24
Cuvelier, J. 9

Decapmaeker, R. P. 111, 175
Dialungana, Salomon Kiangani 61, 65–6, 103, 110, 126, 140, 144, 149, 151–154, 157, 159, 181
Diangienda, Kuntima (Joseph) 41–2, 44, 48–9, 61, 63–6, 68, 75, 98, 100–2, 104–6, 109–12, 117, 121–7, 130, 132–133, 135–6, 145–7, 149–52, 155, 157–158, 165–6, 169–70, 174, 178–82
Diasiwa, Stephen 105
Diata, Norbert 108
Diogo, King 10
Diomi, G. 121
Dodd, C. H. 174

van Eetvelde 26
Ekstam 95
Epikilipikili 37

Fadouma, Antoine 97
Fehderau, H. W. 39
Forfeitt, Lawson 60
St Francis 14
Fumaria 13

Index of Persons

de Gallo, Fr Bernardo 14
Garvey, Marcus 68
de Gaulle 97, 118
Gisenga 117
Graham, Rev. R. H. C. 43, 51
Grattan Guinness, H. and F. 24
Grenfell, George 20, 23
Groves, C. P. 5, 11
Gungu, Chief 70

Harris, W. 145
van Henecxthoven, Fr 30
Henrique, son of Afonso 8–9
Hillard, Rev. A. W. 39, 50–1, 57, 67, 108
Hollenweger, W. J. 149
Hoskyns, C. 119–21

Ileo 103

Jadin 9
Jennings, Rev. R. L. 50–1, 57, 59, 80, 108
Joan of Arc 16
João, King of Kongo 5, 8

Kaku, Mrs 139
Kasa-Vubu, J. 117–18, 120–1
Kaunda, K. 38
Kayuwa, Moise 165
Kiabelwa, Alphonse 46
Kiamusi (N'Twalani's son) 58
Kimbangu, Simon 18, 32, 39–48, 51–71, 73–6, 78–82, 86, 88–98, 100–5, 107–8, 110–11, 117–19, 121–2, 126, 128, 141–9, 151–6, 163, 165, 170, 172, 179, 181, 183; arrest, 60–1, 73–4, 80; conversion, 18, 63–4, 103; death, 64, 75; faith-healing, 18, 31, 45–7, 50–2, 163; false prophets, 54, 73–4, 76; followers, 58, 69, 79, 81, 86, 89, 91; imprisonment, 63; legends, 73; life, 38, 42, 44; persecution, 27; prayer, 49; preaching, 31, 48, 50; teaching, 49, 57; trial, 61–2
Kimpa Vita (see Beatrice)
Kimu, Rev. Alexandre 39, 91, 101
Kina, Rev. Paul 39, 105
Kinzembo 40, 42–3, 61, 143
Kisolokele, Lukelo (Charles) 41, 59, 61, 63, 66, 101–2, 104, 109–10, 121, 126–127, 149, 151, 157–8, 181
Kitoko 69
Kufinu, Philippe (Mavonda Ntangu) 91–92
Kuyela 143

Lanternari, V. 100
Lapsley, S. 24
Lasserre, J. 126, 165
Lavigerie, Cardinal 26
Legum, C. 117
Lehmann, D. 19
Lekganyane, Edward 141, 149
Lenshina, Alice 19, 38
Leo XIII, Pope 26
Leopold II, King of Belgium 21, 26
Limba, James 149
Livingstone, David 23
Lopes, D. 4–5, 7
Lubaki, Pierre 78
Lumumba, Patrice 103, 117–18, 120–1
Luntadila, Lucien 39, 103, 105–6, 108, 180–1
Lutunu, Chief 87
Lwezi 42, 143

MacGaffey, Wyatt 53, 75, 140
Mabona, A. D. 111
Mafuta 45
Mandombe, Mikala 39, 43, 46, 54, 58–60, 108, 134
Manikongo (King of Kongo) 4, 5
Mantsopa Makheta, 17–19
Mantuidi, Jean 105
Manuel, Prince 6
Margull, H. J. 73–4
Martin, M.-L. 12, 16, 38, 47, 74, 126, 142, 149
Massamba-Débat, A. 11, 14, 16–17, 92, 118
Masson, R. P. 86
Matswa, André 77–8, 92
Matuba, Samuel 39, 94, 96, 98, 147
Matubuka 46
Mayanga, John and Clementine 76, 130, 178
Mayunga, André 98
Mbaki, André 57
Mbiti, John 15
Mbonga, Telezi (Thérèse) 54, 108
Mbumba, Philip 89
Merlier, M. 26, 32, 37, 91
Merriam, A. P. 119, 121
Mhlakaza 37
Mobutu, President Sese Seko (J. D.) 30, 117, 121, 127–8
Monika, Paul 57
Morel, L. 38, 52–9, 74
Moshoeshoe, King 17
Mpadi, Simon 41, 91–3, 96, 132, 135, 165
Mpanzu (Pango) 6, 13
Musiri, Chief 25

Index of Persons

Mvubi, Yoani 77–8, 96
M'Vuendy, F. M. 95, 109
Mwilu Marie, 40, 43, 61, 65–6, 74, 103, 107, 134, 139, 143, 146–7

Ndangi, Pierre 39, 46, 53–4, 182
Neill, S. 24–5, 27
Nfinangani 38, 40, 45, 58, 61
Nganga, E. 92
Nganga, Pierre 78, 92
Ngoma 46
Ngoma, Thomas 91
Nkaya, Romain 41, 60
Nkiantondo 45
Nlemvo 69, 108
Noirot 71–2, 79, 81
Nongqause 37
Nsomi, David 97–8
Ntotila, King of Kongo 75
N'Twalani, Thomas 58, 61, 126, 165
Nzundu, Chief of 65
Nzungu 38, 40

Obambi, P. 17, 98
Oosthuizen, G. C. 73, 142
Ouatoula, Matthieu 109

Pango (Mpanzu) 6
Pedro IV, King 16
Pétillon, Governor-General 104–6, 119
Phillips, Rev. H. Ross 60, 62
Pigafetta, F. 4–5, 7
de Pittens 27
Poivre, N. 60
Pollé, Fr 60
Portugal, King of 4
Price, T. 68

von Rad, G. 150
Raum, O. 17
Raymaekers, P. 119, 140, 158
Rodrigo, Dom 7

de Rome, J.-F. 10
de Rossi 61

Schlosser, K. 39, 41
Segal, R. 117
Sekoto, Fr F. 64
Senkatana of Lesotho 12
Shembe, Isaiah 142, 149
Sheppard, W. H. 24
Shepperson, G. 68
von Sicard, H. 12, 21
Simpson, Albert 24
Slade, R. 22–3, 26–7, 29–30, 118
Slade-Reardon, R. 32
Snoek 60
Sölle, D. 50
Sonyo, Governor of 5, 7
Stanley, H. M. 21, 23
Sundkler, B. 50, 142, 173
Sungudilwa, Pierre 61

Taylor, J. V. 19, 143, 150
Tempels, P. 8, 16, 150
Thomas, Rev. George 44, 51, 55, 61
Thomas of Lombo 46
Tilsley 29
Toko, Simão 100–1
Tshombe, M. 120
Tumansangu, Chief 70
Turner, H. W. 145

del Vasto, Lanzo 124
Vincent, John J. 168
Visser 't Hooft, W. A. 173
Voisin 62, 79–81

Westman, K. B. 21
Wikisi, Raymond 108
van Wing, J. 41, 108

Yowani, Albert 108

SUBJECT INDEX

ABAKO (Alliance des Bakongo) 102, 118, 120–1
African Independent Churches 28, 31, 48, 73, 76–7, 110, 126, 145, 163, 168–169, 175
American Baptist Foreign Mission Society 24, 62, 91
American (Southern) Presbyterian Congo Mission 24
Amicale Balali 92
Amicalism 77, 92
Antonian Sect 16, 32, 37
L'Avenir Colonial Belge 62

Bakongo 102, 118, 120, 123, 140, 150, 155, 175
Baluba 25, 155
Baptist Missionary Society 21, 23–4, 27, 38, 43, 57, 59, 62, 108
Baptist Missionary Society (BMS) Missionaries 63, 67, 80–1
Belgian Government 104, 107, 118
Berlin Conference 21, 26
Black Christ 15
Bolenge Conference 67
Brethren, Plymouth 25, 29
Brussels Round Table Conference 120

Capuchin missionaries 10, 11, 13, 16
Chilembwe Rising 68
Christian Brothers 61, 66, 102
Christian and Missionary Alliance Mission 126
Church of the Light of the Holy Spirit 165

Church of the Salvation of Jesus Christ through the Witness Simon Kimbangu 102, 126
Church of the Two Witnesses 58
Conféderation des Associations de Katanga (CONAKAT) 120
Congo Balolo Mission 24
Conseil Protestant du Congo 33

Ecumenical Movement 173
Eglise de Jésus-Christ sur la Terre par le Prophète Simon Kimbangu (see Kimbanguist Church)

Fellowship of Reconciliation 165
Ferme-Chappelle 30, 32
Féticheurs (sorcerers) 37, 76
Franciscans 5, 10

Galaboma Church 92
Garenganze Evangelical Mission 25
Greek Orthodox Church 161

Jehovah's Witnesses 38, 100
Jesuits 10, 13, 27
Jeunesse du Mouvement Populaire de la Révolution 139

Kholumolumo, (a dragon) 12
Kimbanguism 3, 72, 75, 77, 81–3, 86, 89, 91–2, 95, 101, 103–4, 108, 112, 131–2, 164, 175
Kimbanguist Church (Eglise de Jésus-Christ sur la Terre par le Prophète Simon Kimbangu) 28, 42, 56–7, 60, 69, 73, 75–6, 81, 93, 97–9, 101–2, 104, 107–9, 111–12, 117–18, 121–4, 126–31,

133–4, 136–42, 148, 151–3, 156–7, 161–3, 165–72, 174–6, 178–80, 183–4
Kimbanguist Church: Communion, 161, 179, 180–1; constitution, 131; divorce, 162; funerals, 162, 178; guiding principles, 123–5; healing, 75–6, 135, 174, 177; hymns, 69, 82–6, 98, 105, 130, 133, 146; *Institutions*: (schools, 109; School of Theology, 109, 131, 182–3; training institutions, 139); marriage, 161–2; ministers, 41; non-violence, 124–5; prayers, 157; sacraments, 142, 156, 160, 167; Sacrificateurs, 179, 181; schisms, 126–7, sermons, 128, 134; symbols, 156–61, 173; teaching, 112, 164, 177; women, 19, 134, 139; worship, 104, 133–5
Kimbanguist Church Documents and Texts: 66, 141, 143, 147; Hymns, 41; Prayers, 41, 148; Psalms 41, The Beloved City (Zolanga Yelusalemi dia Mpa), 53, 140, 145, 153–4; Catéchisme du Kintwadi, 140, 143–4; The Church and Politics, 117, 121–5; Mise au Point, 49, 107–8; Nkanda Bisamu Bia Tata Simon Kimbangu (Office du Prophète Simon Kimbangu), 40; Réflexions sur la Sainte-Cène, 180–1; Statutes, 113, 131–2, 163; Tanginina Fu Ya Klisto, 144, 148, 156
Kimbanguist Movement, 64, 69, 72–4, 79–81, 86, 88, 94, 96–7, 101, 104, 117, 178
Kimbanguists, 15, 32, 40–1, 66–7, 70, 72, 74, 76, 79, 80, 88, 92–3, 95–6, 98–99, 106–8, 110–13, 117, 120, 126–8, 130, 133, 145, 148, 155, 158, 160–1, 163–4, 168, 170–2, 174, 179, 181
Kimbanguists: deportations, 63, 82, 88, 104; exile, 69, 89, 98, 104, 109
Kinshasa Rising, 76, 78, 120
Kitawala Movement, 38, 77, 100
Knights of St John 5

Lekganyane Church 48, 141
Livingstone Inland Mission 24
Le Kimbanguisme 104
London Missionary Society 23
Lovanium University 118
Lumpa Church 38
Lutendele Farm 137–8, 161

Matadi Rising 76, 107, 120
Matswaists 97
Mayumbe Vicariat 126, 165, 178
Messianism 50, 142, 171
Methodist Missionaries 101

Mission des Noirs (Mission of the Blacks, Khakism, Mpadism) 91–3, 132
Mission N'Twalaniste 58
Monogamy 48
Moravian Church 139, 165
Mouvement National Congolais (MNC) 120
Mpadism 91

Nazarite Church of Isaiah Shembe 48, 50, 141–2
Ngounzism 82, 90–1, 130
Ngounzist Movement 18, 63, 72, 74–7, 91–2
Ngounzists 27, 32, 40–1, 66, 68–9, 73–8, 82, 88–90, 92, 94–7, 100, 101, 104, 106–7, 117, 120, 132, 141, 157

Pan-Africanism 57, 120
Pentecostalists 33
Polygamy 11, 30, 48, 93, 132
Procos (Pro-Congo) 126
Prophet Movement 67
Pygmies 98–9

Redemptorist Fathers 59
Red Star Movement 101
Revival Movement 95

Saint Esprit, Pères de 26
Salvation Army 77, 89–91, 108, 112, 131, 161
Sankuru Rising 37, 52, 78
Scheut Fathers 26–7, 41
Secret Societies 37
Shembe Church (see Nazarite Church)
Simba Rebellion 125–6
South African Zionists 77
State University, Lubumbashi 118
Swedish Missionary Society 24, 94, 96
Syncretism 173–5

Trappists 27
Trembleurs (Quakers) 76–7

United Nations Organization 104

Vatican Council, Second 33

Watchtower Movement (see Kitawala)
White Fathers 26
World Council of Churches 33, 165, 170, 172

Yaga people 10–11, 20

Zion Christian Church 141